Marketing Marianne

Marketing Marianne

FRENCH PROPAGANDA IN AMERICA, 1900–1940

⚜

ROBERT J. YOUNG

Rutgers University Press

New Brunswick, New Jersey, and London

Library of Congress Cataloging-in-Publication Data

Young, Robert J., 1942–
   Marketing Marianne : French propaganda in America, 1900–1940 /
Robert J. Young
     p. cm.
Includes bibliographical references and index.
   ISBN 0-8135-3377-5 (alk. paper)
  1. United States—Relations—France. 2. France—Relations—United States.
3. Propaganda, French—United States—History—20th century. 4. Marianne (French
emblem). 5. Marketing—Political aspects—United States—History—20th century.
6. Marketing—Political aspects—France—History—20th century. 7. France—Foreign
relations—1870–1940. 8. France—Foreign public opinion, American. 9. Public
opinion—United States—History—20th century. I. Title.
   E183.8.F8Y68 2004
   327.1'4' 09440973—dc21

2003005739

British Cataloging-in-Publication information is available from the British Library.

The publication program of Rutgers University Press is supported by the Board of
Governors of Rutgers, The State University of New Jersey.

Manufactured in the United States of America

For Nathalie, Corinne, and Christian

CONTENTS

INTRODUCTION

It has been more than a half century since the end of the Third French Republic. Launched in 1870 on a sea of uncertainty, it foundered in 1940 and sank swiftly to the bottom. On balance, the historical attempts to refloat its reputation have been outnumbered by critical appraisals.[1] Its earliest attempts to reestablish order quickly offended the Left and bestowed upon it a lifelong reputation for being callous toward the interests of the working class. The common-enough moniker, "bourgeois" republic, was intended to convey a sense of diminishment if not disdain. It was capitalist, imperialist, and middle class in inspiration. And male: this regime was no pioneer in women's rights, and not particularly attentive to women's voices. But the strongest conservatives were not happy with it either. At the dawn, the traditional Right hated it for being a republic and, at dusk, first for flirting with the communists and then for succumbing to the Nazis. Arguably, its finest moment came in the autumn of 1918 when, with the indispensable assistance of allies, it had barely managed to survive the destructive best efforts of the German army. Incontestably, its darkest was when, twenty-odd years later, it withered before a new German assault. Not, it would seem, a very creditable record and not, therefore, a regime much worthy of redemption.

Naturally, the very lucidity of such a reading gives rise to flickers of apprehension. There seems to be so much conviction in these acerbic judgments, and so much consensus, that some inner instinct is put on alert. Not since the eighteenth century has so much harmony been detected in nature. Could it be that this, still the longest-lived French regime since the French Revolution, was not quite as benighted, backward, illiberal, and inept as is often alleged?

Admittedly, my own eye may have a mote, for I seem stuck in another tradition. Irrespective of subject and database, over the years I have uncovered as much competence as incompetence in the world of French performance. That was true, or so it appeared, of France's interwar military doctrine and strategic planning, of its diplomacy in the 1930s, even of its often devalued civilian leadership.[2] This was never to suggest that the republic and its decision makers were beyond criticism—an argument that would have been astonishing for a regime attacked far more frequently since 1940 than during it—but rather that there is a need to review its record and to drop whatever charges seem inconsistent with the evidence.

Such might imply an ambition greater than what has inspired the present volume, for the following pages do not represent a broad assessment of the republic's record. Rather they derive from just one more of its alleged shortcomings, which is to say its failure to master the arts of modern propaganda. The origins of that criticism roughly coincide with the starting point of this book, namely the advent of the twentieth century. It was then that the French government realized it was being outstripped internationally by the publicity machines of the German government. Such admissions quickly led to reforms and adjustments that, predictably, drew another round of fire. What was needed, domestic critics charged, was more improvement, and more quickly, complaints that intensified with the transition from peace to war in 1914. Thereafter, the circumstances changed dramatically, although the pattern remained familiar. France had to invest more funds and more energy, be more imaginative in its delivery system, if it were ever to win the war of public opinion at home and abroad. Peace in 1918 brought no end to such criticism. A handful of parliamentarians kept the issue alive by periodically upbraiding the incumbent government for its failure to develop an effective foreign propaganda machine. Thus by 1940, with Hitler already in power for seven years, the tradition of well-intentioned, domestic criticism of French propaganda abroad was deeply entrenched.

So come together two characteristically critical appraisals of the republic, one general, one specific. In keeping with its overall reputation for being a low-energy regime, slow off the mark, the republic was seen to be at the end of the pack even when it came to public relations. Contemporary critics said as much, and the government for its part seemed loath to contradict them. Even when the criticism seemed exaggerated, there were obvious limits on how often a minister could rise in the Chamber of Deputies and boast about French propaganda abroad. Given foreign sensitivity to such propaganda, indeed given the sensitivity to foreign propaganda in France, this was not a subject that lent itself to the most open and candid of discussions. For those reasons, critics of and spokesmen for the government combined to leave a common impression. The republic was just not very good at propaganda.

Perhaps it is that—the power of uncontradicted belief—which explains the gap in the historical literature. Although historians have been attracted to the pre–1870 propaganda apparatus of Napoleon III's Second Empire, as well as to that of the post–1940 apparatus of Pétain's short-lived Vichy regime— both of which focused on their own populations—little in the way of books has been written on the Third Republic's propaganda efforts.[3] Perhaps it is because what little we knew was confused with a belief that nothing much had been done. In any event, this neglected subject soon seemed to me worthy of inquiry. Conceptually speaking, here was one more gap in the republic's history that had proved too deep to be filled by wispy innuendo and frail assumption. But how to pack it with substance, and to do so within one author's life span, became a question of another order and a problem of another magnitude. It was precisely here, however, that the interaction between concept and method became more lively.

An intensive exploration of the regime's entire experience with propaganda was out of the question. Seventy years of history, multiplied by the records of every ministry with some kind of propaganda function, equaled a formula for futility if not disaster. Forty years, from turn of the century to the collapse, seemed more prudent, but even then. . . . That still left the prospect of several thousands of document-choked archival cartons—indeed, far more than that if one were to survey all ministerial activity in France, as well as around the world. Again the voice of prudence called. Thus, and in part, it is her councils that have framed the following investigation of the Third Republic's propaganda experience.

This volume focuses on the period between 1900 and 1940, and on the archival resources of the French foreign ministry in Paris and in Nantes. While I have consulted other repositories as well as the newspaper press, and certainly do invoke some of the propaganda activity of ministries, such as commerce, education, and fine arts, my emphasis on the foreign ministry accords with its undisputed prominence in French propaganda work abroad. That prominence takes us to the third device that has been employed to render this work more manageable—namely, the decision to use America as a case study for the republic's approach to propaganda. That decision, it must be made clear at the outset, means that little attention is paid here to propaganda aimed at French citizens, at enemy or presumed enemy countries, at allied or presumed allied countries, or at neutral states other than the United States of America.[4]

To be sure, behind that choice were considerations beyond that of a simple if important narrowing of scope. For me, as for the French, America was full of potential. For one, in the period under review there was a gradual growth—in some respects remarkably gradual—in French appreciation of the United States as world power. While hardly unaware of competitors such as the British, the Italians, the Russians, and the Japanese, the Third Republic never denied the primacy of its "German problem." It was Germany that represented the greatest threat to the security of metropolitan France. Given the presence of the other powers, congregations of potential enemies and potential friends, French diplomats became increasingly more attentive to the disruptive effect that American resources would have once committed to one side or the other of the global balance. Those resources, raw or manufactured, fiscal or military, had become a factor by the turn of the century, a factor that also preoccupied policy makers in the German foreign office. So the pursuit of an American bride, common enough in society circles where European suitors often pursued heiresses from New York or Chicago, had its equivalent on the international stage.

A second reason for the selection of America is evoked by the reference to "society circles" and by the related, elitist-driven nature of the foreign ministry's propaganda. Here, on the one hand, was a French meritocratic elite charged with transmitting positive images of France to receptive audiences in the United States. Here, on the other, were select audiences of an American elite who had been nurtured on money, new and old, and fine schooling. Senders and receivers both, understood that ladies and gentlemen, wealth notwithstanding, were people of culture. Both understood that art, literature, music, architecture, and similarly aesthetically inspired pursuits were the rightful preoccupations of people of refinement. And both understood, albeit not in identical measure, that art, literature, and the rest had a particularly French resonance, that French had a special cachet as international language, and that Paris was a place to be and to be seen. What better, French diplomats stressed again and again, than to capture such people in this mystical net and then release them as willing volunteers for the propagation of French culture.

Yet a third consideration contributed to the choice of America as case study, namely, the potential it bore for an understanding of propaganda in an age of mass politics and mass marketing. Increasingly, after World War I, the French foreign ministry came to appreciate that its voice had to be heard outside the lecture halls provided by chapters of the Alliance Française, or the reception rooms booked in connection with traveling exhibitions of art collections from the Louvre. Positive images of France, graphic or textual, had to find their way into the regional press, some of them placed by professional press agencies and public relations firms. Popular magazines became of greater interest to France's would-be opinion molders, as did radio broadcasts and cinema releases. Eventually, more energy was expended on trying to change the mood in the Midwest, a region of agricultural communities where suspicions of France, as well as of eastern elites, traditionally ran high, and where Main Street was more likely to have some kind of German association than French. Certainly by the 1920s, promoters of Marianne, female symbol of the French republic, were starting to lean more on the experience of the public relations and mass marketing industries.

From this it might be inferred, correctly, that it was more than some scholarly lacuna that attracted me to the Third Republic's essay in propaganda. It was also the siren call of twentieth-century propaganda itself. The impulsion behind French propaganda efforts is not solely explained by the presence of a particular German problem or by the particular promise of an American solution. Economics, the global competition for markets, was a vitally important spur in the propaganda efforts of all great powers. Just as wartime propagandists were to borrow from prewar commercial advertisers, what they learned about the arts of manipulating public opinion after 1914 was quickly adapted to the rough-and-tumble world of postwar economic competition. Consumers needed to be educated to the ways of smart and sensible buying, just as they, as citizens, needed to be instructed in the rightness of their country's cause.[5] Similarly, governments had to rethink their approach to the conduct of foreign policy so as to ensure that the nation's economic interests were served as diligently as were its traditionally conceived diplomatic and strategic interests. That meant, in the case of the French foreign ministry, not only elevating the division of Affaires commerciales to approximate equality with Affaires politiques, but also incorporating commercial objectives within its propaganda services.[6]

Besides the motive represented by mass markets, there was that summoned by mass politics. The greater the global momentum toward representative and responsible government, the greater the number of citizens who could read and vote, the more incentive there was for governors to listen to the governed—and in an instant, for governors to start shaping the messages that they deemed appropriate for the governed to send. The first front, to be sure, was domestic, for it was there that the fate of all governments was determined. But increasingly as the nineteenth century gave way to the twentieth, it became clear that crucial issues, even those of peace and war, could be heated up or cooled down by propaganda addressed to foreign governments and, particularly, to the citizens of foreign countries. Equally pertinent was the issue of Empire, an issue that invoked the concept of large, European-managed colonial domains in Africa and Asia in which, typically, the indigenous majority remained voiceless. Barring a complete turnaround of a system that had worked so well for Europeans, governments had to spend more time mollifying those indigenes—and their anti-imperialist allies—by promoting the advantages of belonging to enlightened empires. Western education, Western law, Western science, as well as Western dress, were part of elaborate propaganda campaigns to keep the lid on imperial-style mass politics.[7]

Yet the incentives of money, and those of social control, still leave the issue of propaganda insufficiently invested. Another force that helped summon the need for propagandists was that of political centralization. As governments became more modern in the course of the nineteenth century, they became bigger. And they became bigger, in very large part, because they were expected to assume more and more responsibilities. By the end of that century, no one thought it was enough for the state to confine itself to relations with other states, to determine the big issues of war and peace, and to maintain some sense of public order. By then it was drafting school curricula and labor codes, financing urban sewage systems and national railways, and preparing new laws on divorce, pension plans, and strikes in the public service. More and more obligations fell to it, more and more services were required of it, and more and more people expected to be employed by it. In other words, the bureaucracy was expanding, fed not by some sinister intent but rather by growing consensus on where and how governments should fulfil their responsibilities to the people who had elected them. The need to be seen as being accountable to these people and, before that, the need to educate the people as to their needs, were among the great forges for modern propaganda.

Finally, the various needs we have identified happened to coincide with a force of a very different nature. Modern propaganda would never have assumed its twentieth-century character had it not been for modern technology. Railways, steamships, automobiles, and, by the 1920s, aircraft, had done much to shrink the globe and multiply the physical contacts between peoples of different nations. Telegraphic, telephonic, photographic, and radiophonic services, many of them transoceanic, further facilitated the exchange of ideas, especially through their subsequent application in more familiar media such as newspapers and magazines. And by the 1920s the technology of the motion picture industry was commanding more and more interest from people paid to market ideas and shape perceptions in both the private and public sectors. Again, by way of example, the interwar French foreign ministry had to assume a role in the distribution of films both French and foreign, a partisan role that sometimes offended the Hollywood-based American industry.

Still, detecting the varied inspirations of propaganda, and tracing its many faces, are not at the heart of the intrigue. What is, is definition. And from the beginning, the word was trouble. Perhaps not coined but widely circulated for the first time in the seventeenth century, the word *propaganda* stood for the process by which the Roman Catholic Church delivered spiritual truth to those of insufficient faith. The aim was to inform, and ultimately to convince, through campaigns of honest but relentless exposition. From the beginning, therefore, even in the eyes of believers, it was education by repetition—earnest, humorless, dogmatic. For the doubtful and the rebellious, it was idea that could not tolerate thought.

Nonetheless, over the intervening four hundred years the idea itself has sustained much thought, none more secular, concentrated, or anguished than in the twentieth century. By the 1920s, in the wake of World War I, one contemporary observed that propaganda was the work of an invisible government, which is to say a trifling fraction of the entire population that claims to "understand the mental processes . . . of the masses." By the 1940s, in the wake of the World War II, another was able to confirm this manipulation by a few, and was amazed that Americans saw no connection between the advertising that they loved and the propaganda they had learned to detest.[8] The 1960s were no less bewitched by propaganda, by which time more of its elements were emerging from the shadows: the necessity of playing upon the subconscious sentiments of the masses; the willingness of those masses to conform to views that they believed to be widely held; the potential role of famous writers, artists, and sports figures in crystallizing public thought. And early in the twenty-first century there is a sense that propaganda is less a phenomenon and more an ever present condition of life. It has become "a synonym for all kinds of mass persuasion," and as a result, "just about every institution and organization could be counted a vehicle, as well as a source, of propaganda."[9]

That is why we still wrestle with the text and subtext of the word. Adolf Hitler believed that lies were indispensable to propaganda, the bigger the lie the better. Since little people tell many little lies, they are apt to detect them. Tell them big lies, he reasoned, and they confuse the improbable with the truth.[10] Conversely, only too well aware of how the word had been corrupted in modern parlance, the French *dirigeants* confined use of the word to themselves and to nonpublic discourse. But when they used it, they consis-

tently used it as a "propagande de la vérité," selected but truthful information. So does propaganda mean falsehood, or truth? The answer is yes. Or,
as Harold Lasswell put it more colorfully: "Propaganda as a mere tool is no
more moral or immoral than a pump handle."[11]

That is why two other criteria seem more useful for our purposes. First,
propaganda promotes a point of view that, its practitioners hope, will be useful
to their cause, whether that usage is measured by action or merely by sentiment. Second, unlike educators who teach both a body of knowledge *and* the
critical methods to evaluate that data, propagandists use data to direct us to
their own conclusions, offering "ready-made judgments for the unthinking."[12]
Their goal is sympathetic accord, not thoughtful analysis, at least not analysis that disrupts the accord. In short, propaganda can be true, false, or a mix-
ture of both. It can encourage thought along certain lines, or discourage
thought all together. It is not the resort of dictators alone, or of regimes in
wartime, or even of governments large or small. It is not confined to either
text or graphics, or to a one-medium delivery system. It is not necessarily
the preserve of paid agents, nor even necessarily a conscious act. The problem with the word *propaganda,* as Alfred Cobban once said of the French
Revolution, is its singularity. It has so many faces, is detected in so many
places and forms, and is read so differently even by its students, that one has
little choice but to stop chasing the elusive abstract and start concentrating
on its manifestations in a given time and place. In our case, that would be
the sundry ways in which France was packaged and sold in the United States
of America.

At this juncture, the reader might find useful three sets of signals to
the ensuing text. The first is a forecast of narrative pattern, the second a forecast of narrative structure, the third a forecast of potentially troubled waters.

As for the first, one can affirm that, prior to 1914, the Third Republic's
experience with *propagande* was limited. Although the word was used commonly enough in private communication, and although there was a slowly
escalating pattern of expenditure on educational promotion abroad, the Quai
d'Orsay's administrative structure included no formal office for propaganda;
and no extraordinary resources, human or financial, were allocated to propaganda abroad. Modest word, modest objectives.

Among the many things the war changed, this was one. So deadly did
the struggle with Germany and its allies become between 1914 and 1918,
and so close did France come to losing that struggle in the first and last years
of the war, that the efforts of her propagandists could only have been expected
to intensify. Within a year of the war's outbreak the foreign ministry had laid

the foundations for a new propaganda agency, discreetly called the Maison de la Presse; and about a year before that war's conclusion, it had mounted a larger and more complex service that it called, again discreetly, an Information Commissariat. But between them, whatever their names, both agencies became more and more adept at portraying Germany as barbaric and Germans as barbarians. Pressed by the intense demands of a prolonged war, in which public opinion at home and in the Allied countries was critical to a sustained effort, the propagandists sharpened their pencils and got busy demarcating barbarism from civilization.

The end of the war marked the beginning of a slow diminuendo in the intensity of French propaganda. For approximately the following two years the Commissariat for Information continued its wartime efforts to associate Germany with aggression and mass destruction, an association that helped justify the stiff conditions that had been imposed on that country by the armistice of November 1918 and by the Versailles Treaty of June 1919. Thereafter, the commissariat and its successors sought to defend the peace settlement against calls for treaty revision, principally by combining their much voiced commitment to international reconciliation, with reminders of Germany's wartime perfidy. Eventually, by the mid–1920s, when reconciliation was indeed in the air, and when foreigners had tired of France's constant evocation of the war, the propagandists shifted back to their quieter, more subtle, more positive prewar strategy. Intent on not further alienating an America that fidgeted over French delays in paying war loans, propagandists at the Quai d'Orsay now concentrated on the many and varied virtues of France and French civilization. And so they continued, to the end in 1940, convinced that persistent but gentle promotion campaigns built around democratic values and freedom of expression were the most effective ways of appealing to an American public already on edge over the more combative propaganda tactics adopted by the Nazi regime in Germany.

The preceding, encapsulated narrative finds its full self in the following structural outline. Chapter 1 covers the period to 1914 and offers materials on the crucial administrative evolution of the foreign ministry after 1907, including the bureaucratic support structures that were installed for propaganda abroad. That surveyed, it introduces some of the ministry's key propaganda agents and explores their perceptions and their efforts within the context of prewar Franco-American relations.

Chapter 2 represents a change of pace. Not so much about policy as attitudes, it could be called social history if one is not too disturbed by the inclusion of elites under the rubric *social*. In any event, it amounts to two group portraits. The first, that of the senders, has as its subject the French political and diplomatic elite, a portrait that should take form naturally enough from remarks in chapter 1 on some of the prewar propaganda agents. The other, that of the American receivers, tries to characterize the male and female elite on which the French cultural propagandists trained their cupid arrows. It is here, too, that the reader will find some consideration of the complex relationships that exist among various sectors of opinion: official, elite, and mass.

Chapter 3 is addressed to the war years and to the first year of nominal peace. It monitors not only the administrative growth of the French propaganda services, but also the shift in their intensity. Increasingly better funded, and more imaginative in their choice of delivery systems, these services also become less subtle in form and message. The larger and more popular their audience became, the more sharply drawn their confrontation between good and evil, between the civilized world and that of the barbarian enemies of France.

Chapter 4 treats the period from 1920 to 1929, the years in which the European world slowly executed a transition from nonviolent belligerency to a qualified conviction that peace might be possible as well as desirable. Paralleling that shift was one within the field of propaganda. That is why the chapter contains early evidence of bitter French frustration with German postwar propaganda, and later evidence of a less combative strategy. Indeed, mindful of the effectiveness of Weimar Germany's cultural promotions in America, the French responded in kind. The struggle for the affections of America would be waged politely in the libraries, the galleries, the theaters, and the concert halls.

Chapter 5 covers the period from the onset of the Depression, and all the torment that unleashed, to 1935, the year Hitler started talking openly about rearmament. It was during these years that the bloom withered on Europe's hard-won optimism, that the doubts deepened, and that continued attempts to preserve the peace were inspired more by desperation than by confidence in the Führer's capacity to be satisfied, appeased. By then, Franklin Delano Roosevelt had been in the White House for two years. Sympathetic to the plight of France, and apprehensive of Hitler's intentions, he was president of a people who wanted nothing to do with another war in Europe. Isolationist to their core, and suspicious of foreign wiles, Americans offered limited opportunity to the propagandists of the Quai d'Orsay.

Chapters 6 and 7 cover the years from 1936 to 1940. Increasingly, as Hitler's actions became more disruptive in Europe, the words of his sympathizers abroad became less subtle and less discreet. One effect, certainly, was that Americans became more agitated. Long alert to the lies of all foreign propagandists, they slowly came to the conclusion that the real problem of recalcitrance was German, not French. It was a ponderous evolution of views, but one that never hatched into a determination to intervene in Europe. Not, at least, until after the Third Republic had been crushed. Still, the change of mood was unmistakable, and with it came a strengthened admiration of France. Doubtless Hitler had been indispensable to that shift, without whose center stage excess French prudence would have seemed less worthy. But behind the scenes, patient, subtle, immodestly modest, were France's self-effacing propagandists.

Finally, or, on reflection, penultimately, there is the matter of that third forecast—one of potentially troubled waters. As usual, there are things that a reader has a right to know from the outset: certain decisions that had to be made in advance of his or her appearance.

This is not a history of Franco-American relations, if by that one means a record of the foreign policies pursued by the respective governments. There is a little on State Department policies toward France, a little more on the Quai d'Orsay's policies toward America, and obviously much more on that ministry's propaganda efforts on American soil in times of peace and in times of war. Despite important gaps in the archival record, it is possible to appraise those efforts—partly by employing the still-voluminous resources that have survived the last great European war, and partly by monitoring the international perceptions of some of America's principal newspapers. In an age when successive American administrations were resolved not to get ahead of an isolationist electorate, there is something to be said for concentrating on the public mind and on the various agencies—domestic and foreign—that can influence it. Similarly, it is possible to explore the motives and rationale behind French efforts to cultivate American opinion. Relatively speaking, these are the easy parts, reassembling the French propaganda machine, rediscovering the activities of its agents, outlining the principal themes of the messages conveyed, exploring the range of media that they employed, all with a view to currying opinion in the United States.

Measuring their effectiveness, quantifying the results—those are often the insurmountable problems, as every student of propaganda discovers sooner or later. Much has been written on the complex and ultimately elusive relationships among official opinion, elite opinion, and public opinion—including the abbreviated reflections in Chapter 2.[13] But the old question of whether the press reflects or shapes public opinion remains unresolved, in any absolute sense, except perhaps in case studies of a particular press in a particular time setting. Even here, however, an intensive monitoring of several of America's principal newspapers, and their representation of France between 1900 and 1940, can yield but limited results. We can establish what editorials and stories appeared, courtesy of an elite that followed foreign affairs, what photographs and cartoons, what book reviews and letters from readers. But we do not know with certainty how many readers—not necessarily subscribers— read how many pages of any given issue. More to the point, we cannot be sure how they reacted. Therefore, there is no use mincing words, or delaying the truth until the Conclusion. I will disappoint those who expect proof of collective perceptions in the first half of the twentieth century, and proof of the propagandist's impact on either policy or perception. Certainly, in the absence of public opinion polls for all but the final years of the period under review, there is no reliable way of proving what the average American thought of France or of French-related issues, or proving how that thought limited or inspired American policy toward Europe. Infer and suggest, one most certainly can do. Prove, no.

There is a related warning. Earlier, I affirmed the voluminous nature of the French documentation but confessed that it was sometimes flawed. The story, in a sentence, is that substantial quantities of France's propaganda archives went missing during World War II—some of it lost through French design, some through German, some through accident. Half a century later the blemishes remain. Despite archival remnants that still number in several hundreds of cartons, the researcher is frequently reminded of what is not there. This is true of the archives generated by the Maison de la Presse, more true of that pivotal interwar agency known as the Service des Oeuvres françaises à l'étranger, and truer still of the Information Commissariat of 1939–1940.[14]

What that means is this. The documentary base, though substantial and revealing, is frankly uneven—a condition, again frankly, that is common enough in historical research. And that means that one has to stick with what is known, and resist the temptation to speculate across the gaps. That limitation, if such it is, compels me to say through reason what I would be inclined to say through temperament. This book is far from being the last word on the subject. Although representing better than a decade's work, in too many places it barely scratches the surface of an exceedingly complex subject. That said, what has been uncovered seems both reliable and significant enough to advance our understanding of the republic's propaganda machine and more broadly, as I see it, our appreciation of the regime itself.

Since candor is running high, there is something else that might be said about my approach to the extant documentation. Pockets full of data beside pockets nearly empty means finding a plane that has the promise of some evenness. In this case, that means two things. First, it means getting to an elevation from which we can discern patterns more clearly than detail. Second, it means a concordance not only between the documentary base and my sense of what most satisfies a reader, but also between those two and my publisher's even stronger sense of readership. Rutgers did not want an eight-hundred-page tome on French propaganda in America. Nor did I.

And that takes me to a few specific methodological problems, and their would-be resolution. I have been cautiously imprecise about French expenditures on propaganda, partly because these particular records are so incomplete, and partly because it is difficult to translate into today's monetary values and purchasing power a currency that in forty years underwent several revaluations and attendant adjustments in exchange rates. Next, because of alternating, in-text use of English and French for the names of many organizations and associations, I have had to cross-reference the index accordingly.[15] Finally, how does one demonstrate the number and nature of any country's propaganda agents over forty years without identifying them by either individual or organizational name? One cannot. But how does one identify names in the thousands, without turning text into inventory? Again, one cannot. So compromise remains the order of the day and, as usual, runs the risk of pleasing no one. I have come nowhere near to naming every French and American citizen who did something positive for France's image in America. I have, however, identified enough of them, often in representative samples, to convey the sense of sustained commitment from the French republic's citizens, and the sense of sustained Francophilia from leading citizens of the American Republic. Some will prefer more, some less. But the choice, like the responsibility, remains mine. Credit, however, can be more evenly distributed.

The support of the Social Sciences and Humanities Research Council of Canada has been indispensable. Two of its grants permitted several extended research trips to France and funded a succession of research assistants. To the latter, whose work on American and French press materials was invaluable, I express my thanks: Kristine Alexander, Elizabeth Beazley, Dan Davies, Valerie Deacon, Jennifer Dueck, Maureen Justiniano, Ciara Shattuck, and Christopher Young. Thanks are also owing to my "Americanist" friend and colleague, Garin Burbank, from whose counsel I greatly profited.

In France, I owe a special word of gratitude to the archival services of the French foreign ministry in Paris and in Nantes. In particular, I wish to acknowledge the sustained support of Mme Monique Constant, Director of the Archival Services at the Quai d'Orsay. Closer to home, I am indebted to the various support services provided through the University of Winnipeg.

At home itself, the debt has multiplied for years, sometimes, I regret to say, undetected and unacknowledged. Only recently, and since her death, have I discovered that in 1932 my mother was a member of Le Cercle Français at Central Collegiate, Moose Jaw, Saskatchewan—a circle, I surmise, of limited radius. Might some genetic residue account in part for an offspring's interest in French flavors, or was it simply her interest in words of any tongue? More surely, the debt to my own family got out of hand long ago. Not even the interest will be paid. To my children, I owe much. To my wife, Kathryn, everything that remains.

Marketing Marianne

CHAPTER 1

From Peace to War, 1900–1914

❧

$\mathcal{P}$aris, 14 April 1900. This day was not going to disappoint. Departing the grounds of the Elysée Palace, the procession of five landaus moved slowly toward the river, from the Champs Elysées, to the Invalides bridge, and across the Seine to the Avenue of La Motte Piquet. Escorted by a detachment of mounted *cuirassiers*, the horse-drawn open carriages solemnly bore President Emile Loubet and Prime Minister René Waldeck-Rousseau toward the heart of the World Exhibition. It was the day of the official opening, and they and those behind them were about to preside over the formal ceremonies. Arriving at the hastily constructed Festival Hall, across the road from the Ecole Militaire, the president's party ascended the dais, and took their seats before the invited assembly.

> The spectacle that met President Loubet's eyes when, amid the resounding strains of "La Marseillaise" he stepped to the front . . . was probably never seen before within the walls of any building. The vast circus was filled with a sea of human beings, who overflowed the balconies. . . . The decoration of the interior was certainly a triumph of artistic skill, with a handsome stained glass dome, through which the rays of sunlight filtered down upon the concourse below. . . . The galleries and balconies were draped with red plush, and the hall was profusely adorned with trophies of tri-color flags, opening fan-like from shields bearing the letters 'R[épublique]. F'[rançaise].
> . . . The group among the great assembly which was the most attractive was the body of foreign representatives. . . . In a mass together were turbaned chiefs, Arab Sheiks in flowing white robes, and with faces muffled in linen cloths; Hungarian magnates in magnificent

velvet dolmans trimmed with valuable furs, with green breeches and top boots, and wearing fur toques surmounted by waving aigrettes; Chinese and other Oriental Embassy officials in characteristic silk garments; tall Cossacks in sumptuous cloaks with bandoliers slung across their chests.[1]

Prominent among the platform party was Alfred Picard, the commissioner general for the entire exhibition, and destined for promotion to the highest order within the Legion of Honor. The presidents of the Senate and Chamber of Deputies were also there, as were all but one cabinet minister, including the savvy foreign minister, Théophile Delcassé, and the ex-socialist minister of commerce, Alexandre Millerand. On Loubet's invitation, it was the latter who rose. Invoking the language of miracle, he boasted that visitors to Paris could now travel the world without ever leaving the French capital. Architecture, interior design, fashion, food, technology, art, music, theater, and dance, from all corners of the world, were laid out in Paris like a formidable international banquet. The variety of offerings was stunning.

But, the minister observed, more stunning was the recognition that everything came from the same family, a family of diverse nationalities whose science and technology had slowly disciplined, even subdued, the "forces of nature." Machinery, he proclaimed, had become "the queen of the world." And this new dominion promised unlimited progress, not only in productive capacity, but also in efforts toward international peace. In this new century, work remained a virtue, and through it ignorance and suffering would be vanquished.

Not to be outdone, Loubet, too, glided on the wings of optimism. The exhibition, he acknowledged, was not free from French patriotism, French pride, or French self-interest. But its ultimate goal was the promotion of "concord between peoples." Although most of the fair's edifices were to be demolished before the end of the year, what would not be destroyed was a strengthened commitment to "less misery of all kinds" and to a patient evolution of "man towards humanity."

Having declared the exhibition officially open, the president, to the strains of Saint-Saens's "Hymn to Victor Hugo," left the platform and led the official party through the concourse of the great Salle des Fêtes and eventually out to the open air of the Champs-de-Mars and the splendid vista afforded by the Eiffel Tower, the river, and the Trocadéro Palace. Slowly, the party made its way toward the Iéna Bridge, past pavilions designed for the mechanical, chemical, textile, and metallurgical industries, past pavilions for fashion and modern optics, to the river and an awaiting naval tug. It was that conveyance that took them back upstream to the river frontage of the great Invalides Esplanade, past the Left Bank exhibition halls of many nations: the Greeks, Romanians, Germans, British, Americans, Turks, and Italians. There, Loubet officially opened the new bridge bearing the name of Czar Alexander III, led his party down Avenue Nicholas II, between the new Grand and Petit Palais des Beaux-Arts, before returning to the Champs Elysées and the Presidential Palace.[2] The Third French Republic had reaffirmed its position in the world, but more loudly and on an even vaster scale than it had done in 1889 or 1878, more vast still than through the Paris exhibitions of 1867 and 1855, when France had been ruled by a monarch, and a Bonaparte.

Included among those who had been stunned by this international showcase were the Americans, whose total number of exhibitors was second only to that of the host country. They had come in such numbers, more than sixty-five hundred of them, for reasons that went far beyond a desire to visit the City of Light. Speaking publicly, Ambassador Horace Porter acknowledged his nation's hopes that such occasions would promote the "goodwill which is so necessary among nations for securing an era of harmony and peace." But before speaking of peace, he had spoken of profits. He was sure that an increase in commerce would come from this display of American products, and that the returns on America's promotional campaign would far exceed the monetary investment.[3]

That said, there was evidence within the large American contingent, and within the corps of journalists who covered the exhibition for the American press, of interests that exceeded fiscal advantage. There was, for example, a genuine rush of admiration for what many referred to as French genius. The fashion pavilion on the Champs-de-Mars was a French hostage, wherein foreign designers competed for attention with Barroise, Bonnaire, Félix, Margaine Lacroix, Morjeange, and Worth. They competed with difficulty, judging by the stream of fashion articles that Juliette Domaine directed to midwestern readers of Chicago's *Tribune*.[4] James B. Townsend, writing through the Paris heat wave of July 1900, was similarly transfixed by what he called "the Mecca of the architects, sculptors, and artists of every land." Here, he told New York readers, was "the place where the most satisfactory and comprehensive manifestation of the world's progress in the allied arts could be made." And if one visited the Grand Palais and saw the number and quality of work by Claude Monet, Edgar Degas, and Pierre-Auguste Renoir, there was no mistaking the fact that their combined force was "too strong . . . not to influence the art of other lands."[5]

Happily, or so Rowland Strong adjudged, the same was true of French cuisine. This Paris-based writer could not say enough of French wines and food, in that order. Having sampled his way from Saumur to Savoie, he concluded that the French were a race "endowed with the most delicate taste in all matters appertaining to the beautiful conduct of life." Once through the armagnacs and cognacs, the rosés of Angevin, the whites of Lorraine, the reds of the Gironde, he was convinced that "the Frenchman's sensitiveness in all artistic matters, his wit and his fluent eloquence, his high courage and chivalry toward women, [had] been fostered by exquisite viands and unrivaled wines." And lest anyone miss the point, about the French and possibly about foreign correspondents, Strong concluded with this grave counsel: "To produce a beautiful flower you must feed the plant well and richly."[6]

On a very different plane, Americans in Paris felt good about themselves and about the French for another reason. The exhibition provided unlimited opportunity for public expressions of amity between the two sister republics. One of the first came on 14 April, the day of the official opening, when Loubet's vessel had passed the American pavilion. At that precise moment, to the president's great pleasure, two uniformed marines had waved tricolor flags while an assembly of Americans had cheered his passage from the bank of the Seine. Three months later, on 3 and 4 July, two statues were unveiled in the heart of Paris, one to America's first president, George Washington, the other to America's early French ally, the marquis de Lafayette. The former, a gift to France from an association of American women, was installed in the place d'Iéna; the second, a gift in the name of America's children, was unveiled in the place du Carrousel.

Both occasioned outpourings of unwavering friendship between France and the United States. In the place d'Iéna, following a spirited rendition of "La marseillaise" and the "Star-Spangled Banner," Ambassador Porter expressed the conviction that the "good will of the soldiers of '76 [would] never wither, nor the stars cease to shine on the friendship of the two republics." In the place du Carrousel, Ferdinand Peck, commissioner general of the American exhibitions, reminded the assembled audience of the courage, sacrifice, and friendship that had inspired Lafayette to stand with Washington. France's support, he said, "when a nation was in the throes of its birth, . . . will live in grateful memory so long as our institutions shall endure." For their part, the editors at Chicago's *Tribune* suggested that the two American commissioned statues were a fitting recompense for the famous Bartholdi statue, *Liberty Enlightening the World*, that now graced New York's harbor. Concluding their thoughts, the writers were pleased to remark on the popularity "of all things American in Paris."[7]

There was some substance to this mood of self-congratulation, although for reasons not confined to matters American. While the Germans were in Paris in numbers far greater than had been the case for the exhibition of 1889, they were at no risk of being embraced too vigorously by the French. Memories of France's military defeat in 1870, and the German appropriation of Alsace and Lorraine, were enough to constrain French enthusiasm for German exhibitors forty years later. But for the moment, it was England and the English who occupied pride of place when it came to French disdain. Long-standing conflicts over imperial interests in Africa and Asia, currently inflamed by Britain's heavy-handed treatment of the Boers in Southern Africa, ensured a palpable dislike of English visitors in the summer of 1900. Indeed, so strong was the bias that many Americans—conscious of the resemblance between their language and English—took to wearing in their lapels or on their dresses enamel pins that bore, unmistakably, the Stars and Stripes.[8]

But American popularity was more than a matter of forfeit. Making up by far the largest foreign delegation, the Americans seemed ubiquitous. Not only was there the principal pavilion, modeled after the Capitol in Washington and complete with dome and eagle, but there was also an annex dedicated to agriculture on the Champs-de-Mars, one to forestry on the Seine's Left Bank, and one to the merchant marines on the Quai d'Orsay. Furthermore, if American art were prominently displayed in the Grand Palais, and America's machine tool industry on the spacious exhibition grounds of the Vincennes park, America's bartenders made their own splash at the long bar—a facility thus described in one breathless, apparently alcohol-induced, non-sentence:

> And when behind it you catch a glimpse of a round, rubicund, earnest face surmounted by neatly clipped black hair, shining and impeccably parted in the middle, of a splash of white, which is the short linen coat of the bartender; of long yellow streaks like pre-Raphaelite sunbeams imprisoned in a glass, which are the straws; of rapid noiseless movements, which are the mixing and the absorption, you rush forward, your mind conjuring up visions of cocktails and cobblers and fizzes prepared as they never were before in Paris, and perhaps never will be again.[9]

More remarkable, perhaps, was French enthusiasm for American wines and brandies, beefsteaks and lobsters, all of which they consumed in great quantities at the restaurant below the American pavilion.[10]

For their part, the French were especially interested in American consumption. Quoting at length from a recent article in a French magazine, Grace Corneau titillated her readers in distant Chicago. Americans, she said, are seen as the one nation of tourists with serious money to spend, millionaires, many of them, who subsidize the grand hotels on the Champs Elysées and the place Vendôme. The Italians and the Russians are poor, the Germans are cheap, the Mexicans and Brazilians an undefined "plague," but America's elite go to the theaters, the restaurants, the cabarets, and the department stores. Not for them the common fare of the English trippers, and the common vans of Thomas Cook. "Informed as to our tastes," Corneau's source proclaimed, "our habits, our literature, our pleasures, they are at home among us—at their ease."[11]

Not all were, of course. Not the lady contemplating hats in a shop on the Rue de la Paix, whose pride and determination regrettably were much in advance of her French—according to one onlooker, "the very worst French that I have ever heard." Unhappy with the selection thus far appraised, and unmollified by the attendant's willingness to speak English, the lady in question insisted on carrying out her mission in a rough approximation of the language of the country—leaving her compatriot, the unnamed journalist, both vexed and embarrassed by this incident in international diplomacy. Her editors in Washington, however, were only partially sympathetic. Never mind the shoppers, they thought, how is it that America could have sent to this World Fair a total of eighteen commissioners, not one of whom spoke the French language? And in a deliciously ironic note, they added that French officials "have utterly failed to appreciate" this disability. No more seemly, the same paper reported, was the torrent of applications from American commission members for appointments to the French Legion of Honor. It was one thing for Commissioner General Peck to be so honored, but doubtful whether ninety other applications should meet with success.[12]

But apprehensions such as these about perceived American peccadilloes were nothing compared to what Americans detected among the French. Yes, the French knew how to put on a show, even if they had refined the ideas first practiced in Chicago at the time of the World Fair in 1893. But in American eyes there was an endemic disorder in Paris that disturbed, or at least irritated, many a visitor from the New World. It did not seem to matter where one looked. Only months before the fair opened, the papers had been full of news on the latest parliamentary fireworks, rhetorical showers in which "liar," "bandit," and "scoundrel" lit up the daily press coverage. And in May, the same paper had given some prominence to a new report on increasing alcoholism in Paris.[13] With the Chamber adjourned for the exhibition, other signs of ill-discipline were even more easily detected. There were complaints about price gouging on the part of the hotels and the taxis.[14] Bus service was judged by some to be totally inadequate, evidence of which were the hours-long lines at the bus stations. Too much heat had brought on a water shortage, and too many automobiles a gasoline shortage—although it was said that the latter was a blessing in disguise, given the hair-raising practices of the city's inexperienced but foolhardy drivers.[15]

Other shortages were brought about by strikers anxious to pressure management when the demand for their services was optimal. First it was the washerwomen, then the coal stokers on the liners, then the taxi drivers. Conversely, some things were in abundance: too many rabid dogs, too many impolite taxi drivers, too much sewage pollution in the Seine, and too many panhandlers in the streets. Even in the autumn, Grace Corneau considered the streets to be "uninhabitable," rendered so by a surfeit of *camelots* intent on selling everything from newspapers to kitchen utensils—and more besides: pictures "that dare not be shown" and "items" that "would mean immediate imprisonment in any city in the United States."[16] It was smut, and it was everywhere, including in the cheap cabarets where "scantily clad women" sang songs lewd enough to make even Frenchmen "redden." Indeed, despite its extensive facilities, the exhibition offered "no place where a respectable woman could go alone and take a cup of tea."[17]

Broadly speaking, Americans nursed two kinds of complaints, those that pertained to the exhibition, and those that pertained to the French. As for the former, while recognizing many a merit in the host country's promotional campaign, American observers were anything but uncritical. They derided the fact that by the time of the official opening in April, many of the pavilions were transparently unfinished, the American pavilion among them. They liked less the "careless workmanship," to which they attributed the accidental deaths of nine persons shortly after the fair opened.[18] They grumbled about the official insistence that American track-and-field competitors compete on a Sunday, or risk disqualification. They scorned the sometimes inflated costs of admission, and the exaggerated claims of some exhibitors whose ingenious devices seemed better suited to a carnival midway. And they particularly disliked the fair's "melancholy financial failure," despite a record-breaking admissions gate by November of 50 million visitors. Not to put too fine a point on it, editors in Chicago suggested that most of the problem derived simply from "mercenary practices and mismanagement" on the part of French officials.[19]

That reading fit rather snugly with a broader, and not entirely flattering, appreciation of the French as a people. Once again, it was Grace Corneau who captured the sometimes mocking, sometimes resentful, mood of many Parisians. Those who attended the fair, many of them, complained about everything. "They all seem to have gotten out of bed on the wrong side." Many others, it seems, left Paris or stayed at home, convinced from a distance that the fair simply was too much. Too big, too expensive, too noisy, too popular, too foreign. Indeed, while one writer only gently referred to the "temperamental insulation of the French people" and to their limited knowledge of the "outside world," another, less gently, concluded that the mere presence of foreigners "seems to fill the Parisian with fury."[20] There were reasons for their reaction, some writers speculated. Already, the French were feeling linguistically threatened with the increasing international prominence of German and English; and readers in the Midwest were assured that, while the "vogue" for dropping French words into English conversation had long since passed, the French now faced an invasion of English nouns and verbs.[21] In other words, their sometimes exasperating smugness was a cover for mounting twentieth-century insecurities.

All this public and popular speculation about the strengths and foibles of the French on one side, the Americans on the other, might have been of small account had it not been for calculations on another level. However remote the connection may first appear, there were indeed substantial links between the French government's desire to impress American exhibitors and tourists and its desire to promote closer ties with the American government. The foreign ministry, in particular, demonstrated a clear interest not only in attenuating foreign visitors' varied complaints about Parisian practices but also in extending the mood of goodwill that had accompanied the celebrations connected to 4 July, America's national holiday. With its blessing, countless French newspapers carried enthusiastic stories about America's latest gifts to France—the Washington and Lafayette statues—and expressed confidence in the healthy future of Franco-American relations. Indeed, one deputy from Guadeloupe published an article calling for an alliance along the lines of that which France had established with czarist Russia in the 1890s. To accomplish that task, he wrote, what was needed was a propaganda effort waged by true believers in both countries.[22]

Foreign ministry officials on the Quai d'Orsay certainly approved of the goal and endorsed the sentiments behind it. While it would be quite mistaken to suggest that in 1900 they ranked the question of relations with America above, or even on a par with, that of problems in Europe, Africa, the Near East, or Asia, so too would it be mistaken to suggest an indifference on their part to the gathering might of America. Whatever their differences in cultural perspective, in economic interest, and in international politics, French and Americans were said, nonetheless, to share a vast community of interest. And the Exhibition of 1900 was heralded as both a testament to, and a new departure point for, the long friendship between sister republics.

That there were obstacles in the way was apparent to all, not the least of these being the sometimes unflattering reading of the other's national character. If Americans were seen as characteristically bumptious, materialistic, and straitlaced, the French were regarded as overly refined, impractical, and prurient. Economically, and like most countries, the two experienced the tension generated by the realities of competition and of symbiosis. Protectionism in both countries had long restricted the markets of foreign competitors, thus offending would-be exporters whose products were assured of a competitive disadvantage, as well as would-be importers whose profit margins were reduced by their own government's tariffs. When it came to international politics in 1900, the differences were also there, if less intrusive. Americans were commonly critical of French imperialism in Africa and Asia, on the grounds that its "obnoxious system . . . ruthlessly destroyed native life, character, and energy";[23] and for a while they suspected that the French government had responded to what it regarded as American imperialism by actually abetting Spain in the recently concluded Spanish-American War.[24] Furthermore, if Catholic communities within the United States were deeply offended by what they considered the Third Republic's ham-handed and shameful anticlerical legislation, German American immigrant communities held France responsible for the testy relations between the republic and their mother country.

At the same time, however, obstacles such as these were not without compensatory assets. For one, French politics, domestic or international, were not very central to the concerns of most Americans. Or so Jules Jusserand concluded early in his tenure as ambassador in Washington.[25] At least in some respects, public ignorance and indifference were useful allies. On the economic front, the news was far from being all bad. In the period between 1890 and 1914, France was behind only Britain and Germany in dollar value of exports to the United States and usually enjoyed a favorable balance of trade with her American partner. The issue of that balance, and the attendant question of tariffs, would continue to preoccupy trade negotiators, but mutual interest was as evident to both sides as competition.[26] Finally, while there was certainly a negative side to the clumsy but ubiquitous attempts at national stereotyping, there also was a potential upside. Americans were seen as physically robust, industrious to a fault, and technologically inventive; the French, as intellectually subtle and artistically creative; and each other, as partners in the ideals of republican freedom and equality. In other words, there was as much room, more in fact, for concord as for conflict.

That was just as well, given French readings of the international situation current around 1900. If the reality of America's great power status had not fully registered in the minds of most Europeans, the true picture of France's already threatened position was no more obvious. The Third Republic still retained most of its prestige as an international kingpin, still had colonial possessions around the world, and still had one of the largest armies and navies in Europe. Indeed, and ironically, it was precisely because of its lingering great-power status that it felt threatened by its always acquisitive and resentful European rivals. Except for Russia, now a partner in a defensive alliance, the others were deemed unreliable at best. Leading the way was Germany, author of the punitive Treaty of Frankfurt in 1871, and architect of the Dual and Triple Alliances which had enlisted Austrians and Italians in anticipated anti-French and anti-Russian combinations. And as for Britain, one could never be sure. Although there were signs by 1900 of Anglo-French imperial accommodations in Africa and the Far East, tensions over the Boer War together with memories of recent colonial clashes in Africa and Asia and of recent English overtures to Berlin conspired mightily against English visitors to the Paris exhibition.

All of which is to say that the French government was increasingly mindful of the burgeoning power and potential of the American republic. Junior that republic might be in tradition and experience, but its economic, fiscal, and demographic resources assured it of an ascending role in world politics. More to the point, in the European cockpit it had the potential to be either a powerful ally or a mighty enemy. And if further evidence were needed that it had come of age, filled out, made itself desirable, there were unmistakable signs of German courtship. Indeed, the truth was that the turn of the century marked a heating up of an old Franco-German rivalry, this time not only on land and sea, but also in the minds of America's educated elite. Here, there was a prize to be won, by whichever foreign ministry managed most successfully to insinuate its way into America's affections.

Significantly, it was an earlier German conquest, that of France in 1870, that inspired France's new interest in America—not simply out of a quest for friends in a hostile world, but also out of a widespread, post–1870 emulation of German methods.[27] In the American context, it was the steady promotion of German language and culture in the United States in the 1870s and 1880s that prompted a French counteroffensive on the same linguistic and cultural terrain. By the end of that first postwar decade the newly founded Ecole Libre des Sciences Politiques was offering courses in contemporary America; and by the end of the second, the education ministry was injecting much more American content into the instruction of students in the senior secondary and university levels. This added subject matter included, it should be noted, American literature. By the early 1890s doctoral work was being done at the University of Paris on subjects pertaining to American law, economy, and politics, as well as literature; and a limited system of subsidized exchanges was bringing American scholars to the Sorbonne, as visiting fellows, and French academics such as Charles Cestre and André Siegfried to the United States.[28] By the nineties, too, the distinctive style of the Ecole des Beaux-Arts had won many American adherents in the fields of architecture, painting, and sculpture, enough at least to make a deep impression at the 1893 Columbian Exhibition in Chicago.[29]

Slowly, in the decade before the Paris fair, and in the decade that followed, the French ministries of foreign affairs and education made important inroads in America, ones that sought to scorch German propagandists with their own fire. Not only did the university exchanges accelerate, at Harvard, Princeton, Columbia, and Johns Hopkins, but new strategies were applied. The Alliance Française was introduced to America in 1895, with the express purpose of promoting French language and culture. Late in the following decade came that key propaganda agency, the Comité France-Amérique, an organization with offices on both sides of the Atlantic, and with a membership of high-profile public figures from the worlds of finance, arts, and politics.[30] Two years later, in 1911, another milestone was reached by American Francophiles in New York, which is to say the creation of a French Institute with a mandate to promote more awareness and appreciation of France's special cultural genius. As one Boston editor observed, with France more self-confident "as to what she has to give," German influence in America was certain to be challenged in the twentieth century.[31]

Of course, it was not as easy as all that. The gains, though real, were modest and always qualified. The Germans struck back in 1910 with a two-volume work by Professor A. Bernhardt Faust, which, boiled down, claimed that the American people were really a German nation; and their ambassador,

Count Bernstorff, was an assiduous masseur of the East Coast press.[32] Conversely, Ambassador Jusserand of France was frustrated by how much better the German press agency Wolff covered American affairs than did its French equivalent, Agence Havas.[33] What is more, many in France still had difficulty accepting the notion of a distinctive American culture. To the extent that the latter was a culture at all, it was identified as European, understandably imitative. But the lower university admission standards, the reduced emphasis on classical languages, and the increased emphasis on applied learning made it suspect. Indeed, it was said that no other civilized nation had as many trained, and as few learned, men as the United States.[34] Yet further proof that old ideas die hard came from a reverse stereotype, this time of France's special status in the arts. It was fine to acknowledge this, Jusserand complained to the Quai d'Orsay, but it had a downside, especially in the Germanophilic hands of a man like Andrew Carnegie. When the latter acclaimed French art, he was only trying to pigeonhole France, celebrating its plastic and performing arts but willfully underplaying the art it produced as warrior and peacemaker, as agriculturalist, commercial agent, colonial developer.[35]

This reminder of the republic's principal diplomatic agent in Washington occasions another turn of direction, this time toward the foreign ministry itself. It was from here that the major initiatives had to be taken once the exhibition grounds closed in November 1900 and the last of the temporary pavilions was demolished. New efforts would have to be taken to constrain the too positive impressions left by Germany's modern designers, from fashion to machine tools—lest their reputations rise disproportionately to those of France. New efforts were required to assuage the feelings of English visitors who had not appreciated the palpable Anglophobia of the streets—lest such unhappy experiences impede the path to rapprochement with England. And new initiatives were needed with the Americans, a people who thirsted for approval and whose government insisted on a respect worthy of the resources it could bring to world politics.

It was no coincidence that the French foreign ministry undertook a major reorganization within the decade following the exhibition, although the inspiration for doing so was more complex than America's ascending star. Broadly put, the Quai d'Orsay was rushing to catch up to the twentieth century, or rather to get abreast of the myriad developments that had come so furiously at the end of the nineteenth. Included among these was the steady democratization of western Europe, by which was meant the growing influence of public opinion and the attendant phenomena of universal manhood suffrage and universal education—phenomena that underlined the importance of a better-informed electorate. Included, too, was the related phenomenon of more and more centralized states assuming more and more responsibilities for the welfare of their citizens, among them responsibilities that required intervention in the economy, even in the business practices of the private sector. Finally, governments at the outset of the twentieth century were having to adapt to the quickening pace of technology. In the communications field alone, there was a flood of new devices: the faster steam locomotives and vessels on land and sea, the automobile, the undersea telegraphic cables, the infant airplane and the infant radio. Together, they multiplied the pace of information gathering, abbreviated the time for decision making, and made requisite the expansion of specialized services within every ministry. Bureaucratization seemed the only answer for governments expected to better inform their public; to regulate everything from railway gauges and urban speed limits, to pension plans and school curriculum; and to modernize its infrastructure with electric lights and telephones.

Nevertheless, within this mix of forces promoting changes in practices and perceptions, there were also motivations of a geopolitical nature. For a few decades at the end of the nineteenth century the world seemed to have become Europe's oyster. Africa, the Near East, Central Asia, and the Far East offered up visions of endless resources and bottomless markets for men who had mastered the steam and combustion engines, the repeating rifle and field howitzer, as well as the rulebook on how to civilize and Christianize the backward of the earth. For the frontrunners, the British and French in particular, this had meant the expansion of their already substantial empires, and with it, the attendant problems of administering far-flung lands and defending them against avaricious competitors. And that had meant more and more officers, civilian as well as military, to engage in the enterprise—people who were experts in international law, commercial conventions, and currency exchange; people with cartographic, cryptographic, and linguistic skills. Indeed, language was essential, whether in the interests of cultural expansion in Indochina or North Africa, of military conventions with Russia, or of commercial advantage with a fast-maturing Japan in the Far East or a rapidly developing America in the West.

With little more than a hundred Paris-based employees at the turn of the century, and a budget too small to provoke much interest in the legislature, the Quai d'Orsay was not well situated to begin a serious courtship of America. Most grave was the fact that it still ran its two operational *directions* as if political affairs were a different species from commercial affairs— the latter, according to tradition, being the strict preserve of the consular service, the former that of the diplomatic service. That said, and on a brighter note, the 1880s had seen the advent of a designated *sous-section* for North America within the Direction for Political Affairs, and the addition to the minister's personal office of a new *service* for relations with the French and foreign press.[36] Which is to say that ministerial reformers had not waited for the Exhibition of 1900 before starting to address the mounting presence of the United States, and the related need to monitor American newspapers—among others—and to work with their journalists.

It was the combination of all these forces—domestic and geopolitical, bureaucratic and technological—that inspired a new round of reforms in 1907. One of these came with the creation of a single Direction des affaires politiques et commerciales, an administrative restructuring that gave formal expression to the linkage between matters political and economic and that brought diplomatic and consular reports from abroad into the same office. Moreover, each geographical *sous-section* was to be equipped with its own commercial, financial, and legal advisers—an allocation of specialists that guaranteed new administrative divisions, like that of America, a greater voice and prominence than had existed hitherto. Developments such as these, together with the creation of two new departments, the Translation Service and the Geographical Service, further increased the Quai's chances of addressing the diplomatic and commercial challenges presented by the country that had sent the largest delegation of foreign exhibitors to the World Fair.[37]

More striking still were the new provisions for affirmative action. These included the 1907 reform of detaching the press service from the minister's own personal *cabinet*, modestly enlarging it, and attributing the functions of this new Bureau des communications to the ministry as a whole. Officers here were to increase, first, their vigil of the domestic and foreign press—which is to say, to determine what was being said—and, second, their efforts to publicize the government's point of view in that same press. More significant still, for the purposes of this study, was the 1909 addition of a companion agency to the Communications Bureau. This was called the Service des écoles et des Oeuvres françaises à l'étranger, an office charged with the mission of promoting French language and culture around the world. Working in the fields of education, medicine, religious faith, charitable enterprise, and the creative arts, this was the agency that would take charge of the counteroffensive against German propaganda in America and that would work in concert with such bodies as the Alliance Française and the Comité France-Amérique.[38] It was this office, for instance, that recruited teachers for schools abroad, provided suitable examiners for schools anxious to earn the cachet associated with rigorous French academic standards, did what it could to encourage foreign students to study in France, and cooperated with French cultural organizations abroad. And while it did so, the ministry made modest financial contributions to the work of more than one hundred charitable associations worldwide. In all, through learning and generosity, it prided itself on furthering the influence of France and fulfilling "la tâche patriotique."[39]

There were, then, some grounds for optimism on the part of those committed to the expansion of French ties with the American republic, including a decree of August 1910 that saw the *service* status of Schools and French Work Abroad elevated to that of an actual *bureau*. Here was one small measure of the ministry's growing appreciation of its propaganda services. Another, equally significant, was the provision in 1909 of a separate line for Amérique within the Schools' budget, and the allocation of a modest financial subvention to support the recently founded (1908) France-Louisiana Alliance, an organization dedicated to the promotion of the French language in New Orleans public schools.[40]

Developments such as these, between 1907 and 1909, explained the cautious optimism that slowly developed in the Washington embassy of Jules Jusserand. Never inclined to underestimate the skill of German propagandists in America, expertise that he deemed "remarquable," Jusserand took encouragement wherever he could find it. American public opinion seemed to have sided with France in the latter's celebrated clash with Germany over Morocco in 1911, and appeared to have understood that it was German rearmament that had provoked the French government's decision to increase the length of military service in 1913. Happily, too, although Americans were fascinated by the pomp and circumstance of the kaiser's imperial court, they also detected the showmanship of a P. T. Barnum. If the king's rhetorical extravagance widened their eyes, it also provoked a certain shrugging of shoulders.[41]

And as important as German mistakes were to the improved atmosphere in Franco-American relations, there was more to it than that. Not unnaturally, Jusserand was convinced that he understood the best way to strengthen American affections for France. In part, it was English method, for he admired the way the British government played upon traditional Anglo-American ties, stressing their community of views and their shared concept of civilized behavior. That course he recommended to his own government. Not that France could boast Britain's ethnic ties to America, or even those which large numbers of German immigrants subsequently had forged between America and Germany, but it could play upon American memories of France's service to North America, both before, and especially during, the American Revolution.

Well before the European war that threatened from time to time, Jusserand had concluded that France had but one road to follow in America, the high one, and but one message to send, the truth.[42]

Such conviction, however, did not for a moment suggest that Jusserand thought everything was well between France and America. On the contrary, he believed that Germany's persistent efforts were certain to bear new fruit unless a collection of problems was addressed and resolved. One was the need to recognize once and for all the importance of the growing American giant. Far too often, he said, even good newspapers such as the government-linked *Le Temps*, and such entities as the similarly affiliated Havas Agency, minimized or ignored American news and treated this nation of nearly 100 million people as a "negligible factor." And conversely, on those few occasions when they did allocate coverage, they somehow managed to offend. Take for example, he reported, the mocking reports by the French press on German plans to build a new, lavish embassy in Washington. Even the sympathetic *New York Times* judged French press reaction to be churlish, the product of a badly disguised case of jealousy.[43]

Another problem was underfunding. In 1910 the budget of the Bureau for Schools and French Works Abroad was still according a trifling amount to the Americas, a small fraction of the funds dedicated to Europe, the Near East, and Africa. Three years later, when reporting on the opening of a Maison Française for the France-America Society in New York, Jusserand conveyed American disappointment over the fact that the French government had provided no material assistance whatever.[44] Furthermore, these manifestations of an underappreciation of America were sometimes magnified by French faults of another kind. Stupidity was not far from the ambassador's mind when, in November 1910, he reported on the results of a recent aerial tournament in Belmont Park, on Long Island. The winner had been an English pilot flying a French-built Blériot. The big loser had been a French rival lucky enough to survive a collision between his plane and a telephone post. The reason? He had run out of gas. No matter how skilled our flyers, Jusserand muttered, no matter how technically advanced our planes, we look silly when the problem proves to be "so banal, so impossible to imagine."[45] Clearly, more would have to be done, more money and sense invested, if France were to remake her image in America and, by so doing, to lay the foundation for closer diplomatic relations.

So it was that on the eve of war in August 1914 Franco-American relations might have been described as broadly cordial, although intimate they were not. While on the one hand, trade between the two continued to flour-

ish, with a substantial increase being recorded for each other's imports between 1900 and 1914, on the other, irritations over tariff policy—particularly
American policy—continued undiminished. And certainly American enforcement of the Pure Food Act of 1906 was seen by French exporters as a badly
disguised tactic for protecting American producers.[46] At the same time, Americans could not help but notice that while record amounts of French monies
were being invested abroad by 1914, very little of those funds were finding
their way to the United States. Thus, even from this particular and important
quarter, there was reason to doubt that the French had as yet fully acknowledged the power and potential of America.[47]

A similar temperature reading might come from the field of international politics. The two nations were neither close nor hostile, partly because
there were no seriously contentious issues between them either in the European theater or in the Americas. Residual Franco-German abrasions did not
much impress the American government, and the latter's interests in China
made it chary of the Far Eastern ambitions of Russia, France's principal Continental ally. Similarly, by 1914 American diplomats could now associate
France with Britain and, indirectly, with Japan, Britain's recent ally and a rising
power with ambitions in China. Nevertheless, neither the American government—under Theodore Roosevelt or William Howard Taft—nor the American public showed any interest in risking money or labor in theaters that were
not vital to national security—including one square foot along the Franco-
German border. Any idea of capitalizing upon the sometime euphoria of 1900,
and translating it into a formal Franco-American alliance, remained no more
than a pipe dream.

Only in the theater of ideas and the arts was there appreciable progress
in the decade after 1900. And there, the gains appear to have been substantial enough for observers to conclude that France had regained, from the 1890s
on, the ground that it had lost to Germany in the previous two decades. Such
at least was the gist of a lead article in *Le Temps* of July 1913, in which the
writer judged that France had regained its once prominent position in American university life—a position temporarily forfeited during Germany's post–
1870 cultural offensive. Drawing upon the personal example of President
Lawrence Lowell of Harvard, a prominent political scientist whose boyhood
in France had inspired his promotion of regular scholarly exchanges between
Harvard and the Sorbonne, the paper looked optimistically on the future of
France's intellectual relations with the American republic.[48] Such optimism
was fueled in part by the progress that had been made in French-language
instruction in America. Although German retained its foreign-language pride

of place right up to 1914, the Bureau des écoles did make significant progress between 1900 and the conclusion of the war in 1918. By then most colleges and universities had French-language programs; more and more faculty exchanges were taking place between France and the United States; and more student scholarships were available on both sides of the Atlantic. Furthermore, in less than ten years the Alliance Française had increased its chapters from zero to one hundred, while the membership of the National Society for Teachers of French in America had gone from zero in 1900, the year of its formation, to 233 in 1906.[49]

Still, even in the more benign world of education and culture there were apprehensions as real as those that were surfacing anew in the world of Franco-German relations. And it is as fitting to end our passage up to 1914 on this note as on one that is more harmonious. The fact is that, in the period since the Paris Exhibition, the foreign ministry had failed to attenuate the ambivalence with which the educated elites in both countries regarded each other. For their part, if the French by 1914 had finally abandoned the enduring image of America's rustic frontiersmen and women and acknowledged the presence of a cultivated, urban, European-like class, they still struggled with what they considered the preposterousness of claims to cultural superiority on the part of Americans, articulated in the latter's inimitable, "best-in-the-world" vocabulary. Quite possibly, deep down, the French understood that France's grip on ideas and self-expression was more firm than was its grip on the productive resources that would be required of a twentieth-century great power. For their part, Americans had the same problem, but in reverse. They resented the condescension, the air of superiority, the eagerness with which the French elite posed as tutors to country cousins. Again quite possibly, deep down, they had not quite rid themselves of doubts about their own cultural finesse and level of maturity.[50] Whatever the explanation, the elites of both countries had been as successful in preserving the psychological divide between their two nations as in narrowing it—which is at least part of the reason why they responded so differently to the coming of war in 1914.

CHAPTER 2

Senders and Receivers, 1900–1940

❖

Communications within the transatlantic, elitist world were as problematic, and as promising, as those that now depended on the new technologies inspired by electricity and radio waves. On some subjects, as on some days, connections were clear and instant. On others, periodic static interrupted or confounded communications. What was said was not always heard, what heard not always understood, what understood not always appreciated. Doubtless, respective self-appraisals were part of the problem. For their part, and more than once, the French have been diagnosed as a people afflicted by a "superiority complex writ large." As one wit observed, they were God's compensation to other nations for having endowed France with disproportionate natural beauty and resources.[1] Whatever the cause, it comes as no surprise that Americans sometimes struggled to contain both their envy and their resentment of France and the French. And because those two very human emotions often arise from the same bed, the reader should be alert to their coexistence in American perceptions of French society and of the history from which that society emerged.

Superficially, if enduringly, there was a sense of old versus young, beneath which was a world of subtexts where old meant civilized and young callow, or where old meant decrepit and young vital. Even stripped of such judgments, however, it was clear to everyone in 1900 that France was old, with a history running back to the Romans, if not earlier, and that America—in many respects aboriginally unaware—was a young descendant of Europeans. For the United States, there was no Vercingetorix, Charlemagne, or Joan of Arc; no "Chanson de Roland"; no "Roman de la Rose"; no Sainte-Chapelle or Bayeux Tapestry; no Rabelais; no Ronsard. Culturally, making any comparison between France and America was like measuring a newborn against an adult in his or her prime. And it was that sort of simile, precisely because it seemed self-evident, that could inspire smugness in the adult and a resentful awe within the child. Unless one used another measure.

That famous Franco-American specialist André Siegfried once observed that Caesar and Napoleon had traveled at the same speed, mutually ignorant of internal combustion engines, winged flight, air waves, or electricity.[2] Reframed for our purposes, when it came to modern, mid-nineteenth-century technology, France's illustrious history was suddenly irrelevant. Nations young and old were starting from the same line, an imposition of *égalité* that encouraged the former and caused apprehensions among the latter. More precisely, well before 1900, French observers had remarked on the growing productive, and thus competitive, powers of a United States that had become the world leader in coal, iron, steel, and steam production, and that now produced more wheat than France and Russia combined. Another product by 1900, as sure as the wheat and the steel, was the seductive specter of "Americanization," an expression that alluded to vast physical resources, new methods of production, and what some regarded as an underlying cult of materialism.[3]

French interests in the subject of modernization—which some equated positively, others negatively, with Americanization—were not, however, all transatlantic inspired. Indeed, whatever degree of promise and peril they discerned in America's arrival on the world scene, the French were more preoccupied by the threat of modernism from another quarter—namely, Germany. The latter's stunning victory over French armies in 1870 had led to an intensive, decades-long soul-searching in France during which both the reasons for the defeat and the solutions for redressment had been thoroughly canvassed. Tersely put, the answer was to reposition France as a modern world power, which is to say modern militarily, industrially, technologically, educationally, and politically. Rephrased in reverse, the state needed to create in its schools a united, patriotic, literate citizenry and working force that would ensure the prosperous, technologically proficient economy upon which great nations depend in peace and war. Thus Germany, as both mentor and menace, provided both the model and the provocation for this strategy through the 1880s and 1890s, just as it was behind the French foreign ministry reforms of 1907 and the underlying determination to compete with Germany for international prestige and respect.[4]

So in ways reminiscent of post–Civil War America, France, too, reembarked on the path of modern nation-building first mapped out by Revolutionary regimes in the 1790s. A nation-state for centuries, in the 1870s this was still a country of culturally distinct regions in which a significant majority of peasants received little or no formal education. Less than a century before, half the population had spoken no French at all, relying, as they always had, on German, Italian, Spanish, Basque, Béarnais, or Breton; and at the same time, less than two decades distant from the American Revolution, only 12 percent spoke French well. In 1872, more than 20 percent of army conscripts were still illiterate in any language, and the still-powerful combination of regional languages and attachments meant that the French citizenry's knowledge of France was both minimal and flawed.[5] By 1900 the situation had improved from the point of view of politicians, soldiers, and educators alike. The majority of children, boys and girls, were receiving primary-level education, all in the national language. Accordingly, the level of illiteracy among French conscripts continued to drop, while the level of patriotic commitment to the republic—so consciously instilled by waves of newly graduated republican schoolteachers—continued to accelerate up to and beyond the great national celebration that was the Paris Exhibition of 1900.[6]

By then, primary education had become the mainstay of the republic's instructional program, which is to say that most French children were learning to read, write, and calculate at a basic level. But the republic's agenda was more ambitious than that. Included among its educational objectives was a determination to solder together the disparate regions of France with one national language. That meant a heavy emphasis upon the correct use of French, a vehicle that also served as the principal medium for acquainting students with unfamiliar regions of France and inculcating patriotic commitment to the republic. But there was more still, as was evidenced in the most famous textbook of the period, Mme Fouillé's *Tour de la France par deux enfants*, which first appeared in 1877 under the pseudonym G. Bruno. Here, and in countless subsequent editions, French children found an encyclopedia of conduct. Not even a child could miss the state-accorded importance of family, country, education, personal responsibility, personal hygiene, and even moderation when it came to the consumption of tobacco and alcohol. And if religion were to decrease in prominence over the years, the importance of a humanist-based morality would not. Indeed, classroom instruction continued to honor Jules Ferry's credo from the 1880s: "We believe in the natural uprightness of the human spirit, and in the ultimate triumph of good over evil." And what went with that was a commitment to what was beautiful—the sword and buckler for what was true, and for what was good.[7] Finally, in the minds of generations of French schoolchildren, all these elements were associated with France, an entity larger than the republic itself. In its humanism and related internationalism, in its endorsement of unity and progress, in its rehearsed paean to Goodness, Truth, and Beauty, France was said to occupy a very special place in the world of nations.

Such was the foundation upon which the republic built itself, a formally instructed citizenry of urban and rural workers whose productivity would sustain France in the twentieth century. But it was the foundation of a pyramid, a foundation well and truly separated from the small penthouse where decisions of state would be made. Between bottom and top the republic carefully constructed or renovated a series of floors, each with successively fewer tenants.[8] Secondary education, not publicly funded until the late 1920s, was the preserve of a wealthy minority, to which were added small numbers of scholarship-winning students. By the first decade of the twentieth century, out of a population of perhaps 30 million there were fewer than 170,000 boys and 35,000 girls enrolled in state lycées and religious-run secondary institutions.[9] There, and for the few who would advance still further to *l'enseignement supérieur*, the emphasis was on French history, geography, and literature; on philosophy and mathematics; and, above all, on language: that of France, first; of the Ancients—the Greeks and Romans—second; of modern languages, third. Increasingly, as the twentieth century was ushered in, more schools were doing more with instruction in the natural sciences, while at the same time the marked emphasis on French culture—history, literature, philosophy, art, and music—continued unabated.

The few who received such advanced instruction at this secondary level became many fewer still in the postsecondary institutions, where more specialized work would be conducted from this solid cultural foundation. Such, at least, was what the republic expected of its provincial universities or the Paris-based, new Sorbonne, and of the prestigious *grandes écoles,* such as the institutions that the republic had newly consecrated for studies in political science and commerce, physics, and chemistry. Of particular remark was the Ecole Normale Supérieure, a prestige-laden institution that Napoleon had created in 1808 for the purposes of teacher-training, and from whose graduates the Third Republic recruited large numbers of its most competent public servants. Extrapolating from the findings of one recent work, it would seem that there were fewer than thirty thousand students enrolled in these *grandes écoles* by 1900, and a comparable number in French universities.[10] Philosophically a democracy inspired by the rhetoric of equality and of popular progress, the republican regime betrayed a remarkable patience when it came to the academic education of most of its citizens.

Truthfully, the well-to-do and the well educated who already ran the republican regime—almost all of whom were men—saw merit in such a patient, long-haul, elitist, and masculine approach. Ernest Renan, for example, one of the key influences in the creation of the Ecole Libre des Sciences Politiques in 1872 regarded the school as a birthing ground for a new republican elite of "haute culture," just as successive directors of the Ecole Normale regarded their task as one of fashioning an elite worthy of a democracy.[11] That the goal was an elite of ability, is unmistakable, but no more so than the fact that most of this elite had its roots in at least moderate amounts of money, as attendance at secondary school has already made clear. If less than 5 percent of age-eligible students attended secondary school, whether in 1920 or 1870, it was because such education was unaffordable by most. This was unsurprising in a society where nearly 40 percent of the population left no estate at the time of their death, and 70 percent of inherited wealth was claimed by 3 percent of the population. And it was unsurprising that so few attended university when tuition costs were three thousand francs a year in a land where, in the 1890s, fewer than two hundred thousand people had incomes in excess of ten thousand francs. Nor was it astonishing that three-quarters of France's senior civil servants were recruited from strata above that of the lower middle class, and less than 10 percent from the families of workers and farmers. Predictably, too, this was an overwhelmingly urban elite, in a society where the rural population was in a slight majority until about 1930.[12]

The backgrounds of those who directed the affairs of state were predictably similar. Take, for example, the elected members of parliament's lower house, the approximately six hundred men who represented the population of approximately 30 million. If less than 5 percent of the latter had some form of secondary education, fully 70 percent of the six hundred had some form of postsecondary credentials. Some had entered politics with professional backgrounds in medicine, education, journalism, engineering, and architecture, but no field was more heavily represented than law. Indeed, nearly a third of the deputies elected in 1889 had been trained as lawyers or notaries public. Furthermore, although the majority of these deputies came from families of lower-middle-class incomes—still substantially above the national average— as many as 40 percent were beneficiaries of upper-middle-class or aristocratic affluence.[13]

A similar if even more pronounced profile applied to those who were elevated to ministerial status, either from the ranks of the six hundred deputies or from the three hundred senators. No more than a fifth of them came from the nonaffluent majority. Indeed, three-quarters came from the top 7 percent of France's affluent population—and virtually none from the working class. By the time of their death, an even larger percentage of them departed this world from the country's wealthiest 2 percent. Furthermore, more than 90 percent of them had postsecondary education; of these individuals, more than half were from faculties of law, more than a quarter from the *grandes écoles*, and more than a tenth from professions such as medicine, pharmacy, and science. This, again, in a society that sent fewer than 5 percent to secondary school. Finally, given our interest in methods of public persuasion, it is worth noting that most of these prewar cabinet ministers combined some measure of public writing with their political careers—in their capacity either as press writers, editors, or owners, or as authors of books covering the gamut from archaeology to theater.[14] Elite by virtue of achievement and political power, almost all also fit into the precursor elites of wealth and education.

Their diplomatic agents at home and abroad betrayed very similar profiles early in the twentieth century. Virtually all were beneficiaries of a postsecondary education, giving them a status that once again confirmed their typical ascent from urban, moderately affluent, middle-class families that had not only financed a son's education but had also first fostered an appropriate mix of industry, ambition, and self-confidence. Some had demonstrated such a combination during their student years at a university, principally in faculties of law. Most had chosen the more applied routes available to the Brahmin caste, namely the old, prestigious institutions such as the Ecole Normale Supérieure and the Ecole Polytechnique—the former characteristically for teachers, the latter for engineers—or the new and already prestigious Ecole Libre des Sciences Politiques. Certainly as the century matured, it was the latter that became the customary portal for candidates aspiring to diplomatic or consular service, candidates who knew they would receive classroom instruction from experienced and senior ministerial officials.

Already exceptional by virtue of their advanced education, those accepted for careers with the foreign ministry became more exceptional still. At the turn of the century, half the candidates who wrote the very stiff entrance examinations regularly failed, a condition that still applied to the forty men who attempted this *grand concours* in the 1920s. Those who were successful were accepted for a three-month probationary period, at the end of which came another round of examinations in international law, geography, economics, history, and foreign languages. Only after this second round of written examinations and oral interviews was the aspirant accepted into one of the two related services and given a junior posting abroad or within the ministerial offices in Paris. Eventually, of course, such first steps might lead to the position of ambassador or that of consul general, to a senior niche as *directeur* or *chef de section* at the Quai d'Orsay itself, or to various secondment postings in the ministries of commerce, finance, education, or national defense.[15]

Because significant numbers of French politicians maintained business associations with the press, and because a striking number of French diplomats were writers whose contributions either appeared in, or were covered by, the press, a word about French journalists is in order—especially considering the role that politicians and diplomats expected them to play in the propagation of France's image abroad. Typically lower-middle-class and therefore urban in origin, typically well educated by the standards of the day, and again, typically male, here was yet another instance of elite formation. By the time of the Paris Exhibition, there were roughly three thousand French journalists working in Paris alone, a number that had tripled in less than two decades thanks to improved literacy rates and print technology and to the growth of commercial advertising. And if their increased numbers did something to explain a slight drop in their social origins—broadly speaking from upper- to lower-middle class—the numbers alone did not explain their more elevated levels of education. The fact was that more and more were entering the profession with some form of postsecondary education, a trend reflected in the opening of the state-supported Ecole Supérieure du Journalisme in 1899, a school directed by the eminent philosopher Emile Boutroux. Still further evidence of the associations that were operative within these coexisting elites is to be found in the connections between the French government and that formidable news agency the Agence Havas, a private company that sold news and advertising within and beyond France but that by the 1880s had a virtual monopoly on government-sourced information on international affairs.[16]

Such affairs obviously included those of the United States of America, a subject on which this political-diplomatic-journalistic elite was slowly becoming familiar in the course of the nineteenth century. The 1840s had seen the introduction of American subject matter into the baccalaureate, that crowning achievement of French secondary education. In the decades that followed, more and more American materials—history, geography, literature—were introduced at the secondary level. At the postsecondary level the same phenomenon was even more pronounced as courses in American studies were introduced, and as more and more dissertations on American subjects were written. In 1895 the Franklin Library opened in Paris. Two years later the French education ministry created the *doctorat de l'université* to mark a level of academic achievement consistent with the American doctorate of philosophy. By then, Emile Boutroux, André Siegfried, and Charles Cestre were among the French academics doing lecture tours in the United States—Cestre being the first Frenchman to complete graduate work in the United States; and within a decade, Americans such as Bliss Perry and George Santayana were lecturing at the Sorbonne.[17]

Outside the strictly academic world, this Paris-based elite clearly participated in the growing fascination with America and its culture. Only among the educated affluent was there a strong market for Tocqueville's classic *Democracy in America*, or for the many translated editions of Benjamin Franklin's *Way to Wealth*. Even the translated novels of James Fenimore Cooper, Harriet Beecher Stowe, or Henry James, popular as they were in France, remained heavy going for a readership of only elementary reading ability. But among the truly literate, works by French authors on America, or works by American authors on sundry subjects, sold well in book or magazine form. And they sold well because the French elite was exquisitely divided on the meaning of America, some writing and reading of the benefits to be drawn from the New World, others writing and reading of the American menace. And of course the promise and the threat of America were manifest in a great many other quarters: in the opening of an American Express office in 1895; the related growth of American tourism in France; the lucrative commercial interest in French art, antiques, and fashion; and the publicized philanthropic efforts of Americans such as Edward Tuck and John D. Rockefeller to restore to the French nation Napoleon's residence at Malmaison and Louis Pasteur's home at Dôle. It was no surprise then, by 1914, that there existed "a whole body of French literature fascinated by American women, crowds, cities, trusts and businessmen."[18] Fascinated, but ambivalent.

The foregoing, France-focused remarks should be substantial enough to support a summary. In the three decades prior to World War I, the elite-directed French republican regime undertook a plethora of measures designed to return France to the ranks of the world's modern great powers. Germany was the principal, if negative, inspiration, a young nation, newly united, demographically larger and industrially more powerful than France. For the latter to compete in the future, whether on the fields of economy, culture, or battle, there had to be a truly national revival; and the wellspring of that revival had to be education, that state-driven strategy by which an essentially middle-class elite could nurture a better-trained, work-respecting, republican, and patriotic labor force. Consistent with that strategy was a determination to advertise the greatness of France at home and abroad. Such, surely, was at least a part of the renewed emphasis, beginning in the 1880s, upon the wondrous human and material resources of the French empire.[19] Such, too, was central to a related renewal of focus upon France as the world's greatest cultural bene-factor. By the first decade of the twentieth century that latter resolve was being expressed in the new cultural offensive launched by the ministry of foreign affairs, in truth a worldwide offensive, but one with special significance when it came to the wooing of America. To capture the sympathies of Americans, within whose ranks there were very few French-born immigrants, seemed to be a challenge of major proportions. To whom should responsibility for this campaign of persuasion fall, to whom should it be addressed, of what should it consist?

The answer to the first question should be transparent. The representa-tion of France in twentieth-century America, as elsewhere, would be deter-mined by its *dirigeants*, the same governing elite whose social profile we have sketched earlier. More specifically, for the purposes of this inquiry, our at-tention must focus on the principal agency for the conduct of propaganda abroad—namely the foreign ministry located on the Quai d'Orsay. But it might be useful at this point to be more specific still, more illustrative, by turning to a few concrete examples of individuals who would play some part in the marketing of France abroad. These examples, like the years I have cho-sen for the purposes of illustration, may be taken as loosely representative of the elite that we have been discussing in rather more abstract terms.[20]

In 1900, Emile Loubet was president of France, a position that he ac-quired in the wake of a law degree, seats in the Chamber of Deputies and the Senate, and extensive ministerial experience, including in the office of prime minister. The president in 1910 was Armand Fallières. Born in 1841, the son of a clerk of the court, he was trained as a lawyer and had served as mayor, parliamentary deputy, cabinet minister, and even briefly prime min-ister before being elected president in 1906. In 1924, the president was Alexandre Millerand. Son of a middle-class Parisian family, Millerand was a lawyer and active journalist early in his career, a deputy as of 1885, a several-times cabinet minister, and once prime minister before being elected head of state in 1920. In 1936 the president was Albert Lebrun, a brilliant engineer-ing graduate of the Ecole des Mines, a deputy, a cabinet minister, and a senator before being elected president of the republic in 1934.

In 1900 the prime minister was René Waldeck-Rousseau, the scion of a prosperous family in Nantes and a highly paid commercial lawyer before entering politics. His foreign minister was Théophile Delcassé, another law-yer, and a successful journalist before his first parliamentary election in 1889.

In 1922, Raymond Poincaré was both prime minister and foreign minister of France. Son of a state-employed engineer, he was a graduate of the Paris Law Faculty and a man of considerable ministerial experience, following his first cabinet portfolio in 1893. By then, the most senior civil servant at the Quai d'Orsay was Philippe Berthelot, the son of a former foreign minister, a career diplomat via the rigors of the *grand concours*, and a confidante of such poets as Stéphane Mallarmé, Jean Moréas, and José-Maria de Héredia. For much of 1932 the premiership and foreign ministership were held by Edouard Herriot, a man of less elevated social origins but a scholarship student, a graduate of the Ecole Normale, and a distinguished teacher at a lycée in Lyon, before being elected to the Senate in 1912. By 1933, Camille Chautemps was premier. Son and brother of parliamentary deputies, and trained himself in law, Chautemps took as his foreign minister Joseph Paul-Boncour, another child of middle class parents, and another recipient of a doctorate in law from the University of Paris.

By 1933 the Chautemps-Paul-Boncour administration had at its service a new secretary-general at the Quai d'Orsay. His name was Alexis Saint-Léger Léger. Son of a lawyer, a graduate of the University of Bordeaux, and a successful candidate in the *grand concours*, Léger not only served the foreign ministry for some three decades but also was to distinguish himself as a Nobel Prize–winning poet under the pseudonym Saint-John Perse. Distinguished, too, were a number of his diplomatic colleagues, from whose ranks I have selected only a few with some Franco-American significance. Among them was Jules Cambon, in 1900 ambassador of France in Washington. The son and grandson of judges, a graduate of that famous lycée Louis-le-Grand in Paris, a lawyer by training, and for long an administrative officer of the interior ministry, Cambon became the first secretary-general of the foreign ministry in 1915 and, three years later, a member of that select body, the Académie Française. Jules Jusserand, ten years younger than Cambon and a generation older than Léger, was ambassador to Washington between 1902 and 1924. Born of a middle-class family in Lyon, where he completed a doctorate on theater in medieval England before attaining a law degree in Paris, Jusserand entered the consular service in 1878. By the time of his retirement in 1924 he had won the first Pulitzer Prize in history; and just before his death in 1932 he was elected to the Institut de France as a member of the Académie des Sciences Morales et Politiques. By then, his most prominent successor at the Washington embassy, Paul Claudel, was coming to the end of a posting that had begun in 1926. Claudel, then, like Léger later, was already a figure of immense literary reputation, one that owed something to his exceptional *formation*. He, too, had been at Louis-le-Grand, then at the Ecole Libre des Sciences Politiques, and then the School for Oriental Languages, from which he entered the consular-diplomatic service, in which he spent forty years. Author of plays, poems, biographies, and travel literature, Claudel, like Cambon, was elected to the Académie Française in 1946.

Truly exceptional as each of these individuals was in his own right, it takes few powers of discernment to see that each was a member of a certain caste, an affluent, urban, educated, cosmopolitan caste that was far removed from that of the man who drove an omnibus in Paris or a locomotive between Lyon and Marseilles, that of the miner in the Pas-de-Calais or of the women and children who toiled in the fields and vineyards of France. In these few individuals, in their social and professional profiles, one finds illustrations of the French elite, mainly men, sometimes women, who would try with their own tools to sow the seeds and to harvest the crop of American affections for France.

The task was less arduous than might be imagined by someone inclined to exaggerate the cleavage between refined France and rustic America. The fact is that at the end of the nineteenth century both were preponderantly rustic. The whole point of French reform legislation of the 1880s and 1890s was to modernize, effectively civilize, a citizenry unsure of its language and still largely unaware of indoor bathrooms and electricity. Across the eastern reaches of the United States and into the Midwest, the affluent citizenry of the larger cities were intent on a similar mission to civilize and, simultaneously, to impose order. And their vision of the future was based on a new-wave industrial economy combined with an old-wave, Europe-derived culture—this last a term that embraced everything from Judeo-Christian morality to what Europeans now regarded as "classics" in art, literature, and music. However much some like Theodore Roosevelt grumbled about American dependence on European models, the momentum in Boston, or New York, or Philadelphia, was with "high-brow" circles intent on raising up and edifying the masses. No question but that they agreed with Henry James's remark that, deprived of literature, museums, art, and architecture, America had the makings of a modern civilization "with *culture* quite left out." Hence the resolve to redress, to import from abroad what could be imported, and to replicate what could not.[21]

It would have been surprising had such a French elite, distanced by affluence, education, and power from their own citizenry, chosen to fix their attention on the miners of Pennsylvania or the farmers of Nebraska. Rather one would have expected, and been right, that their campaign of persuasion would be directed at people like themselves: affluent, educated, and influential Americans who not only conducted official policy but who also were best suited to shape public opinion in ways most conducive to the execution of such policy. Before turning to that elite directly, and along the lines of our previous exploration of their French counterparts, attention must be drawn to the base of the American pyramid.[22]

The population of the United States in 1900 and 1920 was approximately 75 million and 105 million, respectively—or something like 2.5 times greater than that of France. But by 1940, the very end of the period under study, when the population was more than 130 million, fully 60 percent of Americans over the age of 25 still had no measure of secondary education. Fourteen percent had completed four years of high school, 4 percent had up to three years of college experience, and 1 percent held a college diploma— figures that would have been roughly comparable in France in 1940, following the advent of free secondary education at the end of the 1920s. Given this educational profile, it was not surprising that a good three-quarters of the American electorate ranged between ignorant and uninformed on matters of foreign affairs.[23] Neither was it surprising that press surveys conducted in the 1920s concluded that only 5 percent of American news coverage was awarded to foreign subject matter.[24] Whether public ignorance inspired the press, or the press public ignorance, the result was the same. Except for moments of crisis, with their attention reawakened by the leadership, the American public was not going to be much of a player—either in the shaping of American foreign policy or in conditioning the thinking of its officers.

Although ethnic, religious, and regional considerations could color the ways in which recent American immigrants might perceive events in other parts of the world—very often the parts from which they or their antecedents had come—the principal factor seems to have been education and its associate, wealth. Extrapolating from the data for 1940, it seems reasonable to suggest that forty years earlier, at the time of the Paris Exhibition, at least three-quarters of the American population had no familiarity with secondary schooling. The few who did, however, and the fewer still who graduated at the end of four years, were likely to have had significant exposure to European history and culture. In 1890, for example, upward of thirty thousand students were studying German or French at the secondary level, although the fact that a million were studying Latin, Greek, or both, in 1908 suggests an enduring, European-like bias in favor of ancient over modern languages. By 1925, however, in the wake of a war that had ended with a Franco-American alliance, French had become number one in foreign-language instruction, with half a million studying it in the private and public schools. Rephrased, while only 11 percent of the national student body were studying a modern language, two-thirds of those who were, were studying French. This, in comparison to the collapse of German-language instruction to a paltry 2 percent.[25]

A similarly upward trend was apparent at the college level, although there, the interest in *langues vivantes* had always been more pronounced among the tiny minority affluent enough to afford postsecondary education. Indeed that interest was suggested by the fact that in 1888 some 60 percent of American colleges actually required a course in a modern, foreign language. By that time, some sixteen thousand postsecondary students were studying French, or nearly 17 percent of the ninety-five thousand then enrolled. And for the following two decades the picture and the proportion improved, with French slowly gaining ground on German; with the creation of the National Society for Teachers of French in 1900; with the growth of the Alliance Française to one hundred chapters by 1913; and with the steady expansion of Franco-American exchange programs for students and for professors. By 1925 nearly a third of the enrollments in foreign languages were in French, or some seventy-four thousand students, compared with a meager 10 percent for German.[26] Moreover, by the 1920s the United States government had evinced a more pronounced interest in postsecondary education, one consequence of which was the advent of many college-level courses aimed at explaining the background to the Great War through which Americans had lived, and during which some had died. War inspired, such courses quickly expanded into variations of Western Civilization surveys, which quickly in turn became mandatory.[27]

To be sure, American responses to France and the French language varied considerably. Not only was there a difference between those who had only a primary school experience and those with secondary or postsecondary experience, but there is reason to think that many of the private schools attributed a much stronger cachet to the study of French and French culture than did schools in the public system.[28] Doubtless there was a much greater chance that those wealthy enough to afford private school for their children would also be able to support travel and future study abroad. This familiar coincidence of education and money was also manifested in another way, that of regional responses to the study of French. Certainly the concentration in New England of prestigious private schools for males and females was part of the reason why enrollments in French were higher there than anywhere else in the country.[29] But only part of the reason, for the fact is that such interest was also much more obvious in the public schools of New England and the state of New York than it was in the public schools of the Midwest or of Arizona or Texas. And that raises the issue of culture, beside that of money. In particular it is suggestive of two influences. One was the preponderance enjoyed by the Roman Catholic Church in the parochial school sector, a church long nourished by and nourishing French cultural traditions. The other was the presence of francophone communities in New England—a million strong in 1935—which continued to grow in that decade with the annual arrival of three hundred thousand job-seeking Canadiens from Quebec and New Brunswick. At the other extreme from the patrician class of New England, with its acquired Francophilia, here were people who simply wished their children to be brought up in the linguistic traditions of their parents.[30]

As we begin the transition from the broad features of this educated and characteristically well-to-do elite, to the particular features of certain individuals, it would be well to rehearse our intent to this point. As in France, so too in America was there a small intellectual elite whose family money, typically, assured them of an exceptional education, and whose education acquainted them with an international world and with international languages. This, of course, was no guarantee that recipients of such a benefice would end up with a bottomless reservoir of affection for the foreign cultures they had savored, even if one suspects that the possibilities for genuine affinity would be greater among the informed than the ignorant. That certainly seems to have been the case for Americans schooled in the history of France and in the marvels of its cultural present. The cuisine and the fashion, the architecture and the interior design, the art and the literature—all beckoned to those with money, time, inclination, and taste.[31] Still, if familiarity can provide comfort, it can also inspire contempt. Not everything Americans saw in France, or discerned from a distance, was appealing. Especially the French themselves, a people who seem to have managed to blend excessive formalism with excessive frivolousness, elegance with prurience, orderliness with impulsiveness.[32] And speaking their language, like following their politics, or purchasing their art, was no assurance that you would come to like the French, or they you. This uncertainty, this ambivalence, that Americans and French frequently expressed about each other, must be kept in mind as we intensify our inquiry into the American elite.

American heads of state, like those of the French republic, were not of the common mill.[33] In 1900 Emile Loubet's counterpart was William McKinley, a successful lawyer—though the only head of state to 1940 who did not complete a college degree—and a former congressman from and governor of the state of Ohio. In 1910, Armand Fallières's opposite number was William H. Taft, a graduate of Yale and, like Fallières, a lawyer; Taft subsequently became a judge, American solicitor-general, and secretary of state for war. In 1924, Alexandre Millerand's presidency was complemented by that of Calvin Coolidge—two more lawyers—the American a graduate of Amherst College, a former governor of Massachusetts, and once president of the Nanotuck Savings Bank. Finally, Albert Lebrun's homologue in 1936 was Franklin Roosevelt. Born to wealth and a Harvard graduate and lawyer, prior to his successful presidential campaign in 1932 Roosevelt had been a New York legislator, state governor, and assistant secretary of the navy under Taft.

McKinley's secretary of state in 1900 was John Hay, a graduate of Brown University, a former ambassador to Britain, and a longtime member of the board of directors of Western Union Telegraph. His ambassador in Paris was Horace Porter, a graduate of the United States Military Academy, a former vice president of Pullman's Palace Car Company, and board member of several railroad and insurance companies. Ten years later, Porter's embassy was occupied by Robert Bacon, a graduate of Harvard and a partner in J. P. Morgan and Company. His boss at the State Department was Philander C. Knox, a graduate of Mount Union College in Pennsylvania, a Pittsburgh lawyer, and general counsel for Carnegie Steel Corporation. Calvin Coolidge's secretary of state in 1924 was Charles Evans Hughes, a Brown graduate, a partner in a New York City law firm, a former governor of New York and an associate justice on the United States Supreme Court. By then, the ambassador to France was Myron T. Herrick, a man of extensive banking, industrial, and diplomatic experience, as well as college experience at Ohio Wesleyan University. Finally, in the autumn of 1936, Roosevelt's secretary of state was Cordell Hull, his ambassador in Paris, William C. Bullitt. Hull had graduated from Cumberland University Law School and had served terms as a state legislator, judge, congressman, and senator, all in the state of Tennessee. Bullitt, a man of independent wealth, was a graduate of Yale University and a former ambassador to the Soviet Union.

By way of a collective summary, and retreating for a moment from individuals back to mass, certain data emerge from any statistical survey ranging from the McKinley administration to that of Franklin Roosevelt. At the outset, two-thirds of McKinley's cabinet and senior diplomatic officers had college degrees. By Roosevelt's day the figure had risen to 80 percent for the same cohort, 87 percent for senators, 88 percent for representatives, and 93 percent for high-level civil servants—at a time when only 1 percent of

Americans were university graduates. In both cases, that of McKinley and of Franklin Roosevelt, a quarter of those degrees had been obtained from Harvard, Yale, or Princeton. Disproportionate in other ways was the voice of New England, New Jersey, New York State, and Pennsylvania—regions in which the interest in France and French culture was most elevated. In the forty years between McKinley in 1900 and Franklin Roosevelt in 1940, their lowest representation in the cabinet and among senior diplomatic officers was under Woodrow Wilson, at 32 percent; their highest, under Theodore Roosevelt, at almost 55 percent. A similar phenomenon was in effect when it came to the regional origins of nonelected, senior federal officials. From the 1860s to the 1930s, nearly a quarter of this cadre came from the state of New York, and the vast majority of them from New York City—at a time when the city accounted for something like 5 percent of the national population.[34]

Given this geographical bias, and given that this geography had a cultural history that included ethnic French-speaking communities, a higher incidence of French-language instruction in the secondary schools, and a disproportionate share of prestigious private schools and universities where French language and literature had a special cachet, one might well infer the presence of a latent Francophilia among the highest members of successive administrations. That is not to suggest, even for a moment, that such suspected sentiment was comparable to the force of Anglophilia. Historically, linguistically, and culturally, the region owed far more to England than to France. At the same time, however, nineteenth-century Anglo-American commercial and strategic competition in North America and the Caribbean suggested a rivalry that by 1900 had long since surpassed any between France and America. Thus the constrained quality of this prevailing attachment to an English heritage afforded a resident and largely elite-associated Francophilia some room to grow. How it did so is a highly complex tale to tell, probably far too complex for it to be told well, anywhere. But central to its telling would certainly be the interrelationships between and among America's power elite and elites of other orders.

One of the latter, and one that has a particular significance in opinion formation, is the newspaper press. It has the potential not only to express its own views, but also to articulate the discerned views of the public and the discerned views of governments, one to another. While the problems inherent in this multiple role await further discussion, it seems clear enough that publishers, editors, and reporters are capable of creating, confirming, and occasionally even erasing the biases of decision makers. In short, there are likely to be connections of a sort between the perspectives adopted by the power elite and the views expressed by an elite of professional writers. Recalling the latter, in particular those in the 1920s and 1930s who spent much of their career abroad, one recent author has attributed to them "enormous" power in influencing government and public opinion alike.[35] It is to this latter group that we now turn, or rather to a few examples. In this first instance, I identify a collection of men and women who had extended experience with France, and whose generally sympathetic reports on that country appeared frequently and, for a time, in many American newspapers. Whatever their brevity, the profiles below testify to exceptionality—in their family background, education, and international experience.[36]

A few had studied in France. Among these was Harold Callender, a student at the University of Kansas as well as of the Sorbonne, a Paris-based reporter for the *New York Times* between 1926 and 1929, and a London-based European correspondent until 1940. Edgar Mowrer, long of the *Chicago Daily News*, was another, a man with university experience in Michigan, Chicago, and the Sorbonne. So, too, was Herbert Peyser, longtime music critic for the *Times*, whose career was predicated by studies in Berlin and Paris and at Columbia University. William Shirer was one more. Born in Chicago, the son of an assistant district attorney, Shirer graduated from Coe College before moving to Paris in 1925 for courses at the Collège de France, and before beginning a Paris-and-European-based career as press and radio correspondent. One of Shirer's colleagues in the Paris edition offices of the *Chicago Tribune* in 1925 was Alex Small, a graduate of Harvard, a graduate of the American Expeditionary Force in 1918, and since the war, a graduate student at Paris, Grenoble, Lyon, and Strasbourg.

As suggested, that war had produced a range of graduates, including the men and sometimes women who began long journalistic careers as war correspondents in France following the outbreak of hostilities in 1914. Two of them were James O. Bennett, employed by a succession of Chicago papers after studies at the University of Michigan, and Richard Harding Davis, son of a newspaper editor and student at Lehigh and Johns Hopkins. Two more were Wilbur S. Forrest, son of a doctor, graduate of Bradley Polytechnic Institute in Illinois, and wartime manager of the United Press in Paris; and Charles H. Grasty, with some academic experience at the University of Missouri before wartime work for the *Kansas City Star*, the Associated Press, and the *New York Times*. There was Edwin L. James, graduate of Randolph Macon College, *Times* correspondent in Paris from 1918 through most of the 1920s, and senior editorialist within a decade. Joseph Pierson was another. Once a student at Illinois Wesleyan University, Pierson's wartime creation was the Paris edition of the *Chicago Tribune*, the paper with which Bernard Ragner began his career following graduation from Ohio Northern University and, in 1918, from the Eightieth Infantry Division in France. George H. Seldes had a similar career: studies at Harvard, press debut with the United States Army Press Corps in France, postwar career as European correspondent for the *Tribune* and the *New York Post*. Paul Scott Mowrer was yet one more. Older brother of Edgar, and a student for two years at the University of Michigan, Scott Mowrer was to have a remarkable career as foreign correspondent for the *Chicago Daily News*, reporting on European affairs, mainly from Paris, before, during, and well after World War I. And none, perhaps, was more famous as a journalist than Wythe Williams, a man whom the *Times* sent to Europe before the war had begun and who subsequently spent most of the 1920s and 1930s reporting on European affairs for a variety of American and British newspapers.

This talented group of France-familiar correspondents included others no less remarkable; and not all were men.[37] Betina Bedwell, once a student at the Chicago Art Institute, in 1922 went to Paris, from which city she pursued a twenty-five-year career as fashion critic with the Chicago Tribune–New York News Syndicate. May Birkhead's career as fashion and society reporter for various American newspapers was even longer, twenty-nine years before she fled Paris in 1940. Kathleen Cannell left the same year, after a ten-year stay in Paris as fashion columnist for the *New York Times*—a job partly facilitated by her previous studies at the Sorbonne. On more cerebral lines, there was Anne O'Hare McCormick, as of 1922 a regular European correspondent for the *Times*. Armed with a bachelor of arts degree from a Catholic academy in Columbus, Ohio, McCormick became an itinerant reporter, moving from one European capital to another through the interwar period and acquiring a reputation for her penetrating interviews with European statesmen. Dorothy Thompson was no less remarkable. Daughter of a Methodist minister, she graduated from Syracuse University in 1914 and began a long career as a European correspondent six years later. There she stayed, in Vienna, Berlin, and Paris, writing evocative, discerning, and especially antifascist articles for the *Philadelphia Public Ledger,* and for such magazines as the *Saturday Evening Post* and *Cosmopolitan*. Evocative, too, was Carolyn A. Wilson. A talented, Paris-based correspondent for the *Chicago Tribune*, her eyewitness reports on French civilian life during World War I could not but have inspired much sympathy for France among her American readers.

Women also figured prominently among another category of elite members—those who combined journalism with prominent careers in other fields. The prolific novelist Edith Wharton was one such example. Having moved to Paris in 1912, where she stayed until her death in 1937, Wharton, during World War I, published a series of newspaper articles and books, all of which were obviously designed to evoke great sympathy for France among American readers. The novelist Robert Herrick, son of a Cambridge lawyer and graduate of Harvard, betrayed similar loyalties during the period of his wartime correspondence in France. The same was true of some educator-journalists. Dr. William Crawford, an ordained Methodist minister and president of Allegheny College, saw wartime service as a secretary of the Young Men's Christian Association in France—a country that had earned his public sympathies. More committed still was Dr. John Finley, a graduate of Knox College, a prewar exchange lecturer at the Sorbonne, a prewar president of New York's City College, and a man whose postwar career included further academic distinction as well as a senior editorial position with the *New York Times*.

The same paper employed the services of music critic James G. Huneker. Progeny of an old Philadelphia family, trained in law and in music—including instruction at the Paris Conservatoire—Huneker combined a journalistic career with that of a piano teacher in New York's then newly founded National Conservatory. Brigadier General Henry J. Reilly combined the life of a soldier with that of a France-experienced military correspondent. Son of an officer, and a graduate of West Point, Reilly wrote for the *Chicago Tribune* prior to and after his active military service in France in 1917–1918. More occasional as a journalist, but more overt as a member of the American Francophilic elite, was the New York architect Whitney Warren. Privately educated, Warren studied briefly at Columbia, and then for the better part of a decade in Paris at the Ecole des Beaux-Arts, from whence he found lifelong inspiration.

It is at this point that some stocktaking is in order, lest in the foregoing data on these American elites arguments are discerned that I do not intend to make. First, these sketchy representations of American political and press circles are but that, representations; and, severely incomplete in themselves, they only occasionally raise the veil on relations between such elites and those of truly exceptional commercial and industrial wealth. Doubtless, however, the latter will figure in the ensuing text—the Morgans, Vanderbilts, and Rockefellers, or the moneyed press lords such as Hearst of California, Meyer of Washington, Ochs and Munsey of New York, the McCormicks of Chicago. In short, the foregoing has been nothing like a census of America's elite in the first half of the twentieth century.

Second, while it has been my intention to highlight the exceptional credentials of this higher caste—astronomically above average, in wealth, education, and opportunity—I have not taken such benefices as assurances of Francophilia. France-familiar William Randolph Hearst and Robert McCormick would be cases in point, publishers of papers seldom well disposed to the Third Republic. What I have implied, however, is that from the turn of the century this elite, characteristically, evinced a cultural predisposition toward things French—a predisposition fed by college-level courses in French literature and language, by impulses from France in art and architecture, cuisine, fashion, and music, and by frequent, sometimes extended, travel abroad.[38] Unlike the onetime, weeklong tourist who is distressed to discover that Paris is not Providence or Pittsburgh, those whom we have canvassed often studied and stayed in France. They vacationed there, honeymooned there, worked there, invested there, returned there, and in some cases died there. And not a few were embarrassed by the conduct of the momentary tourist, "vulgar, inane, and insensitive to the French."[39] This did not make them less American, any more than it made them enemies of France's international competitors. But more so than the farmer in the Midwest, the rancher in the Southwest, the steelworker in Pittsburgh—the writers and educators, the artists and musicians, the affluent tourists and consumers, saw Paris as a beacon to an exotic but familiar cultural terrain.

Third, these responses were acquired through a process more complex and covert than that of simple osmosis. That process, of course, is at the heart of the present study, for it involves a state strategy by which desired images and impressions of France could be distributed abroad. And those who determined what was desirable, and those who distributed the impressions, were precisely those members of the French elite whose profiles have been sketched in advance of their American counterparts. That process began in the decade before 1900 and escalated thereafter, spearheaded by the foreign ministry, but supported by specialized services in other ministries. Gifts to school libraries, prizes for high performance in French, visiting French lecturers, attractive tourist brochures, subsidized travel to France, exchange scholarships, recipes for French cooking, sketches of the latest Parisian fashion, appointments to various ranks of the Legion of Honor—these were but some of the ways in which positive images were to be developed in receptive American minds. And words accompanied images, as sundry press and information services in Paris packaged text, statistics, and even analysis, to be used by members of a resident or itinerant press corps for convenient dispatch abroad. It was not entirely left to chance, therefore, that a James or a Shirer, a Thompson or a Wilson, a Mowrer or a Williams, should transmit copy homeward, parts of which had been inspired by French information officers.

Fourth, if it is difficult to know precisely which parts—that is, to what extent American elite opinions were designed in France—it is equally difficult to ascertain the impact of elite opinion on America's "public opinion." The latter, an expression that made its first appearance in *Webster's Dictionary* in 1920, is a subject on which experts in opinion formation write books rather than paragraphs.[40] Two questions will sharpen the point for our context. In a society that practices universal suffrage, how significant are the views of a few percentage points of the population, their wealth and education notwithstanding? Or, approached from the opposite direction, to what extent can that elite get the majority to conform? The consensus seems to be, for America as elsewhere, that the closer to home the issue, the tougher the time the elite has in budging the electorate's critical mass. Conversely, the more geographically distant the issue, the less familiar is the electorate; and that limited familiarity—a condition that is in the news media's powers to mute or amplify—makes the lesser educated and the less cosmopolitan more vulnerable to elite-acquired skills and elite-controlled media. In short, the public is more malleable on foreign issues than on domestic issues. Offered in advance of much argument, this conclusion warrants further inquiry.

In the 1940s, one opinion expert offered an estimate of public interest in foreign affairs. Thirty percent of the American public, he ventured, were "unaware of almost every event in American foreign affairs," leaving only 25 percent who were "reasonably well informed," and that despite "large areas of ignorance." Thirty years later another expert estimated that 80 percent of American voters, what he called the "mass public," read few editorials, spent more time on the sports and comic sections, and paid "little or no attention to foreign affairs." This included, incidentally, those with high school certificates. The remainder, optimistically up to 20 percent, were principally college graduates and those with college experience, who read foreign news coverage in one of the metropolitan dailies. I say "optimistically" because, on further reflection, he reckons that only 15 percent constitute the "attentive" public. The other 85 percent, reflecting "general public indifference to most foreign policy issues," are content to leave such matters "to the President, Congress, and the bureaucracy."[41]

The initiative, therefore, lies with no more than a quarter of the electorate, and probably substantially less than that. Apart from very specific issues, of the sort that have special resonance for groups formed around ethnicity, religion, or region, the "attentive" public are people who are no more than reasonably well versed in world issues. And they are so because of education, a condition often enough preceded by modest or immodest wealth, and because they attend to foreign as well as domestic news.[42] How they do so varies, but not by much. Even in the 1970s it was judged that Americans who followed foreign news did so principally through newspapers and periodicals—radio and television coverage having been found to be too brief and too lacking in analysis.[43] For the pre–1940 period, despite the inroads made by radio broadcasts and newsreel footage in cinemas, the question is largely moot, given the heavy reliance on printed text. Such a finding, in turn, must have the effect of elevating the significance of the print medium and of those members of the fourth estate whose profiles have been sketched earlier. Elevated higher still, when one contemplates Walter Lippmann's estimate that around the time of World War I there were fewer than two hundred daily newspapers being published in cities of more than one hundred thousand inhabitants, most of them dependent for foreign news on a handful of press associations, on the foreign news services operated by a small number of mass-circulation dailies, and on the swelling numbers of contracted publicity agents.[44] And higher still, if there is anything to the observation that State Department officials sometimes find it convenient to equate press opinion with public opinion—which is why, because they "read a mountain of newspapers," they think they know what the public thinks.[45]

Some would disallow even this contrivance, and with even more arresting estimates of public ignorance. Working from data generated in the 1950s and 1960s, William Domhoff perceived three categories of adult Americans. Like Lippmann before him, he concluded that the "overwhelming majority" were unaware of foreign policy issues. But by that, Domhoff meant not 75 percent but more than 95 percent. A second category, comprising the better educated, more well-to-do, and more news attentive, represented "at best a few percent" of the population. Generally people of the business and professional communities, it was this constituency that provided the "sounding board" for the remaining 1 percent who either shaped opinion in the media or made decisions in light of that opinion. "Public" opinion, in other words, was reduced to the views of a tiny, informed minority, from which a comparative handful took their cue.[46]

Statistically, based on a population of 105 million in 1920, and attributing, like Domhoff, as much as 5 percent to the really informed and "attentive" public, we would be looking at something in the order of 5 million Americans who inform, shape, and implement the nation's foreign policy between the two wars. Drawing data from entirely different sources, compiled for completely different reasons, we may be able to make some useful if un-deniably loose correlations between this defined public and the readership of some of the nation's leading newspapers. At the beginning of the 1930s, combined circulation figures for New York's *Times*, Boston's *Christian Science Monitor*, and Washington's *Post*, three eastern papers that demonstrated an exceptional interest in foreign affairs, totaled something in the order of one million.[47] Combined further with the Midwest subscriptions of Chicago's *Tribune*, a paper large enough to operate its own foreign news service, one arrives at a figure of 2 million—or the equivalent of roughly half the genu-inely "attentive" and knowledgeable public.[48] To this, in turn, may be added the 5-million circulation figure for the entire Hearst chain, a press empire that extended from San Francisco's *Examiner* to New York's *American*, and that, in the International News Service, had its very own supplier of foreign news. Add to these very raw numbers the five thousand subscribers of the specialist journal *Foreign Affairs*, founded in 1922, and the much smaller memberships of the Council on Foreign Relations and of the Foreign Policy Association, both founded in 1918, and one has a clearer sense of the rough contours of Domhoff's opinion leaders and decision makers.[49]

In summary, while it is true that the "public," in the generally accepted sense of the word, does play a critical role in the election of its political elite, it would be rare for that determination to be based on foreign policy consid-erations. Thus, once elected on the basis of local or national platforms, this elite seems to enjoy considerable and sustained latitude when it comes to the conduct of foreign affairs. And when for the alleged purposes of "consul-tation" and "dialogue" it turns for "public" advice, the consensus seems to be that it will knowingly mistake the views of a tiny, informed minority for those of the majority. There is, to be sure, an undeniable logic in this decep-tion, one more compelling than that of advising leadership to listen to the ignorant. But logical or not, the fact is that this is how the system works, or rather has worked in the United States, according to those with expertise in opinion formation and policy making. For better or worse, it is a system that accorded well with the social and political views of the contemporary French elite, and with the strategy that they devised in the 1890s for strengthening France's international position in both real and perceived terms. A meritocratic elite nourished on substantial family money and on superior education, they detected in the United States, amid all the differences, a similar elite, simi-larly nourished, similarly disposed to the textures of European culture, and similarly mindful of what was to be won or lost on the international stage.

CHAPTER 3

Words as Weapons, 1914–1919

❖

The outbreak of war in the summer of 1914 shook the Franco-American world of elites and non-elites to its core, and more so in France, of course, where conscripts and volunteers of every station were thrown into hastily built defensive positions to meet a stunningly successful German army. But Americans, too, were early involved, despite their own government's officially proclaimed, scrupulously honored policy of neutrality. Some of those efforts were ostensibly consistent with the official line: for example, the organization of hospital and ambulance services in France, or assistance with the mushrooming *ouvroirs,* where working-class women could exchange labor for the cash needed to support families currently deprived of husbands and fathers. But some Americans made no bones about where their sympathies resided. That included their ambassador to Paris, Myron Herrick, who in December 1914 received the exceptionally prestigious *grande croix* of the Legion of Honor. It also included the celebrated novelist Gertrude Atherton, who reported favorably on American civilian activity in war-torn France and on the voluntary enlistment of young Americans for active service in British or French field units—educated men, whose family culture had long nurtured associations with elite circles in Britain and France.[1]

For the French themselves, the suddenness of the German military offensive, and the speed with which it surged toward Paris, demanded an equally swift sociological and psychological response. Whatever internal divisions had caught the eye of journalists in prewar July now had to be subsumed by the desperate calls for unity in postpeace August. Whether one believed that the republic had been too harsh or too lenient on Catholic clericalism, too harsh or lenient on socialists or royalists, the time had come to shelve the differences and unite in what came to be called the "union sacrée." Now, so it was said in virtually all the national media, there was but one enemy, the German invader, and but one cause, to drive that enemy from every square inch of French soil.

Clearly, the latter mission was a job for soldiers—for infantry, artillery, and cavalry—men and weapons that would take back Germany's gains and, at the very least, expel that country from French soil. And the shorter the campaign, the less matériel would be required, the fewer the men, and the more modest the financial expenditure. The longer that campaign, however, the greater the mobilization effort would have to be, to sustain not only armies, but civilians as well—children, women of all ages, men judged unfit for military service or indispensable to the national economy. It was they whose morale would have to be reinforced as they waited for the soldiers to finish—waited and worked in cottage, field, and factory; in offices, schools, and hospitals; on the roads, railways, and canals. The longer the war lasted, the more critical the civilian became to the entire national effort. If he or she flagged in productivity, if doubts were allowed to settle in his or her mind about the rightness of the cause or the certainty of victory, the consequences could be severe for all. Which is why the issue of controlling information grew in proportion to the elongation of the war.

Or rather it is one of the reasons why, for however important the morale of French civilians, the information issue was not confined to them. Just as an ever elongating war increased the material and psychological demands imposed on all French citizens, so it raised the question of extranational sources of assistance. Evidently, the morale of countries like Britain, allied with France in the war effort against Germany and the Hapsburg Empire, was of no small account in a war of long duration. Similarly, the responsiveness of countries like the United States, currently neutral but rich in material resources and rich in potential sympathy, was an important consideration for those who intended to use words as weapons. Finally, the latter phrase was especially appropriate for those concentrating on enemy soldiers and civilians. The longer the war went on, the more French officials addressed the issue of their own public's morale, the more they were sensitized to the public morale of the enemy. Once again, the control of information—its shutting off, its turning on, its direction, and its delivery—all became part of the experience of World War I. And there was much learning to be done.

At the war's outbreak, no one had spent much time anticipating a rapid expansion of the existing news services, or their use as propaganda instrument. Few expected even a yearlong war and, accordingly, no greater effort had been made to create a wartime propaganda office than to have stockpiled thousands of 75-mm artillery shells. And for awhile, as Paris was nearly overrun in the first two months of the war, such expectations of sudden victory or sudden loss seemed the more credible. But with the settling down of the front by late 1914, and the gradual extension of its flanks into a long line of entrenched fortifications, the tenacious character of this dug-in, stationary war became monthly more obvious. War on the western front, principally on German-occupied French soil, became one of attrition. Eventually, it was said, when one side had amassed enough soldiers and shells, there would be a breakthrough and an end to the misery. Until then, the final push would have to await the buildup of giant fuel depots and huge inventories of bayonets, binoculars, and ball bearings, as well as of machine guns and trench mortars.

That was not, however, anyone's perspective in August 1914. Given the expectation of a short campaign, waged mainly by men in uniform, the French war ministry was more interested in curtailing information than supplying it. War's outbreak did see the ministry create a Bureau de presse, but chiefly with a view to minimizing what appeared in that press. In short, its function was primarily one of censorship, of both military and diplomatic information, and to the cause of which the foreign ministry contributed a senior representative. For the first months of the war, this office received no war correspondents and allowed no visits by civilian journalists to the military front. In any event, the censorship law of 5 August had forbidden reporting on just about anything pertaining to the army and navy—from troop movements, casualties, and prisoners taken, to armament production, health provision, and command changes. Indeed, anything construed as remotely useful to the enemy or harmful to France was deemed unfit to print.[2]

The ironically named press bureau continued to operate throughout the war, from offices near the Invalides on the rue de Grenelle. From there, it supervised the work of numerous provincial censorship agencies, agencies originally staffed with personnel appointed by the interior ministry and war ministry, and after 1917 solely by the latter. Its bible was Circular 100 of September 1915, a document that alerted censors to every instrument of published propaganda then available—from newspapers, books, magazines, and pamphlets, to postcards, photographs, and posters. However considerable their charge, in most press offices the censors in major cities found plenty of compliant patriots and pragmatists, editors and journalists, willing to delete offending items, not only to serve the national cause, but also to avoid a shutdown of their presses. Certainly none could risk indifference to the hundreds of censors who worked the country under the auspices and direction of nearly two hundred such officers in Paris alone.[3]

But the war ministry was not long in extending its reach over information control, from one of ensuring silence to one of calculated provision. By November 1914 French commander in chief General Joseph Joffre had seen the merits of having at his headquarters a Section d'information, the headship of which he awarded to the prominent journalist and deputy André Tardieu. Staffed with a small team of writers and publicists, the section was to provide carefully selected information on military operations to a carefully screened cohort of journalists. Not long afterward, in February 1915, the ministry created a second organization for the dissemination of military information, this being the Bureau d'informations militaires—which meant there were now two such bodies under the same minister. Predictably, cooperation gave way to competition, and competition to friction. In May 1917, the then minister, Alexandre Ribot, replaced them both with a new Service des informations militaires, under the presidency of the novelist Lieutenant Colonel Marcel Prévost—a service still charged with supplying the media with ostensibly accurate, if transparently incomplete, information about the course of the military campaigns.[4]

Already the astute reader will have detected an early sign of the war's legacy. As the war grew, so did government, and with it, its coral-like accretion of bureaucracies. The war ministry was no exception. By spring 1917 it not only had the *service* under Marcel Prévost, but indeed another, this one called the Service des missions de presse aux armées. It was under the umbrella of this office that there operated several specific press missions, including one expressly for the servicing of the French domestic press, and another for the Anglo-American press. The latter appeared in September 1916, in response to a perceived need for reassuring British public opinion about France's determination to carry on to victory, and for maximizing American public sympathy for the Anglo-French war effort. In the interests of both causes, the war ministry would enable select journalists to visit the military front and provide them with some measure of logistical support—in particular, easy access to army information officers. Although this small press contingent was expected to pay for their own accommodation and food—an expectation consistent with the journalists' sense of independence and the ministry's sense of economy—it was clear that the French government had more covert ambitions. Of the Americans, it was hoped that they might prepare their reading public for the United States to enter the war on the Allied side. Certainly, the French army reckoned that the war correspondent should be its "collaborateur constant."[5]

The foreign ministry had similar hopes but fewer illusions about the press's malleability. At the end of August 1914, following the lead of the war ministry, the Quai d'Orsay created its own Bureau de presse; this one, however, had more of an informational than a censorship role. Headed by Henri Ponsot, a senior functionary, the bureau monitored reports in the foreign press, controlled Agence Havas dispatches to newspapers abroad, and distributed officially sanctioned information to Paris-based foreign journalists.[6] Thus it was that the Bureau Ponsot, as it was called informally, did its best to control the kinds of information destined for readers in England and America.

But still more was needed, at least by the lights of some. Within six months of war's outbreak, the foreign ministry had become complicit in an ostensibly private propaganda initiative by a former deputy named Etienne Fournol. It was he who opened his own Office de propagande on the rue Edouard VII, and whose friendship with the then foreign minister, Théophile Delcassé, meant the receipt of state subventions. Still, this agency was small and but semiofficial in character. As the war lengthened, the arguments for greater initiative strengthened. They triumphed at the end of October 1915 when Aristide Briand succeeded Delcassé as foreign minister. In a matter of months, and with the help of his principal assistant, Philippe Berthelot, Briand unveiled a more comprehensive information service. Located near the ministry, the new Maison de la Presse would prove to be a key development in France's wartime propaganda experience. Indeed, it was to become a general "clearinghouse for all the government's propaganda effort," thus surpassing the role originally assigned to the war ministry's information service.[7]

It was here, at 3 rue François Premier, that the Maison opened its doors, telephones, telegraphic services, reading rooms, and in situ post office to the domestic and foreign press. For the latter, it meant better facilities and easier access to official information, as well as working space and reception rooms suitable for exchanges among members of foreign and French press associations. For the masters of the house, it meant more assured ministerial control of information, and substantial budget increases, from 8 million francs in 1915 to 25 million in 1916 and 1917.[8] It is to the creation and wartime evolution of this key agency that we now turn, before exploring its operational methods and the premises that underpinned its propaganda strategy.

The mission of the Maison was ambitious. It aspired to control the distribution of all ministerial news and documentation, all radio broadcasting and, in an uneasy alliance with the war ministry, all dissemination of photographic and cinematic materials. It also claimed direction of all privately run propaganda associations in France—another subject to which we must return with greater care.[9] Given the breadth of their mandate, the Maison's personnel were recruited from many different public and private sectors, although most were either diplomats, journalists, professors, or military officers, ably supported by mainly army-supplied typists, telephonists, telegraphists, messengers, and sentries.

Structurally, the Maison comprised four departments, or *sections*, each of which was organized by geographical as well as functional responsibilities. The Section diplomatique, for example, looked after the daily press conferences for French and foreign journalists. Its own research office, the Bureau d'études, generated the ministerial press releases and documents; and its press inquiry service, or *enquêtes de presse*, wanted information suitable for propaganda purposes abroad, an interest that explained its control of foreign-addressed, radio news releases from the Eiffel Tower station or from another based in Lyon.[10]

The Maison also included a Section militaire, an office charged with liaison with the war ministry and general staff and, in particular, with the army's ever more important photographic and cinematic department. At the same time, agents in this office also dealt with French and foreign journalists on matters directly relating to the military campaign, and were responsible for arranging press visits to the front lines. The third section, the Section de traduction et d'analyse de presse étrangère, required agents of more scholarly talents, linguists who read most of the world's principal languages and thus could translate key articles from the foreign press for the edification of planners and decision makers in Paris. Others in this same section did more in the way of intensive research—including studies more time-consuming than either the diplomatic or military sections could afford—and in the preparation of weekly, in-house bulletins on diverse subject matter.

The Maison's fourth department carried the explicit title Section de propagande. Like the others, it reflected geographical zones of responsibility, although the governing concept remained political. Was a given country an ally, an enemy, or neutral?[11] This section, as its title implied, was the most active in the generation and distribution of materials deemed most likely to influence public opinion abroad. It published books, brochures, and articles, all suitably translated for their intended markets; and it was a principal distributor abroad of the army's photographic and cinematic products. It also was responsible for the provision of suitable lecturers, men and women who could be sent abroad to speak authoritatively on behalf of France. Finally, this was the office that was expected to coordinate the propaganda efforts of many private organizations and religious groups—including the Alliance Française, the French chambers of commerce, and various Catholic, Protestant, and Jewish associations.[12]

So ends this cursory survey of the foreign ministry's principal information and propaganda office during the early years of the war. From its very birth in late 1915, the Maison was criticized for its potential to subvert the freedom and independence of the press; and for the following two years, until the Clemenceau ministry of November 1917, it would endure many a complaint from press and politician, as well as some significant structural revisions. That later stage of its history can be examined in subsequent pages. For the present, however, it seems advisable to look beyond the structures of the early war period to the actual work of the Maison and to the prevailing premises upon which it approached the question of information service and propaganda. Especially information destined for American consumption.

One might begin with the German invasion of France in August 1914 and the attendant atrocity stories. Within weeks of the war's outbreak, reports were circulating in the world's newspapers about the bestial behavior of German troops on French and Belgian soil. Rape, pillage, mutilation, and murder—acts of unspeakable violence against women, children, the elderly, and other innocent civilians—were all attributed to the kaiser's uniformed marauders. Whatever their degree of accuracy or exaggeration—and the debate remains lively—such charges had gospel-like authority for a credulous French public whose sons and husbands were defending the Marne, and were credible even to many of their sympathizers overseas.[13] But more significant for our purposes are the implications of this early controversy. On the one hand, the French war ministry had been concentrating more on the denial of information than on its provision. On the other, in the absence of any flow of measured information, the newspapers had had an imaginative field day on which one lurid account competed for distinction with another. At first blush, of course, the Germans were certainly made out to be the beasts of the reporters' intentions; but at second, reflective readers soon detected overwrought imagination and deliberate exaggeration. Underneath, they sensed lies, or at least accounts calculated to provoke outrage; and from that sense of rational design there emerged an early cynicism.[14] It was a cynicism that was, in reality, provoked not so much by manipulation of news as by the state's early resolve to keep the public ignorant. Ironically, it was this backlash that helped convince war and foreign ministry officials that the careful release of information might be preferable to the musings of journalists deprived of information.

It was this conclusion, drawn from the early months of the war, that became a leitmotiv of French propaganda from World War I to World War II. It was expressed a thousand times, in various forms, by men and women entrusted with French propaganda efforts between 1914 and 1940. Keep calumny to a minimum, for someone will turn your hate to the enemy's advantage. Avoid hyperbole, for someone will conclude that it is intended to deceive. Above all, avoid lies, for many will judge your cause deceitful and dishonorable. Such, certainly, was the dictum of the long-serving French ambassador to Washington, Jules Jusserand. Early in the history of the Maison de la Presse he counseled his superiors in Paris to be "extremely discreet" when it came to propaganda activities in America. The Germans, he advised early in 1916, were far too obvious in their rhetoric and in the spending of money designed to influence public opinion. But they had lost their dignity in a torrent of words, just as France had retained its own by comparative silence. What was needed, more than anything, was to be truthful and sincere with the Americans. By that he meant, remind them of France's life-and-death struggle with German barbarism, remind them of French heroism and military prowess, and remind them of France's unbroken association with a higher culture, one of the book and of art.[15]

Although tensions were to arise between proponents of Jusserand's subtle strategy and those attuned to the liabilities of restraint, in 1916 the ambassador and the Maison seem to have been closely aligned. Apart from its crafted subtlety, that strategy had two principal components. The first was a reliance on cultural propaganda, which is to say a program designed to educate and remind Americans of France's especial association with values intellectual and aesthetic. As one Americanist expert in the Maison put it in early 1916, the boldfaced German strategy had made Americans apprehensive of even the word *propagande*. Accordingly, he believed, there was great merit in the continued emphasis on France's cultural contribution to the world. Such, for instance, was how both he and Jusserand viewed France's participation in the San Francisco Exhibition of that year. Not so much propaganda as *éducation*. And certainly that was the thrust of the close working relationship between the Maison and the Beaux Arts department at the ministry of education. What was needed, both ministries agreed, was a ceaseless celebration of France's literary, artistic, scientific and medical genius.[16]

The second component of the foreign ministry's America-targeted, wartime propaganda was a reliance on American volunteers. On this point Jusserand was adamant.[17] There was, he had long since discerned, a lengthy list of potential cadres in America, men and women of the educated and cultural elite, who were not only prepared but also eager to defend France in whatever way they could. It was their words that would carry the most weight with fellow citizens, partly because they were such an articulate class, partly because, as manifest volunteers, they were not on the payroll of a foreign power. This approach, it should be said, was not the brainchild of the Maison. Indeed, the idea not only predated the Maison, but also was at least partly American in inspiration. More precisely, in November 1915, two prominent American Francophiles—independently of each other—urged Philippe Berthelot to recruit men and women like themselves for the purposes of propaganda in America. Behind their initiatives, certainly that of the architect, Whitney Warren, was an apprehension that the French propaganda effort, while more subtle than the German, lacked the energy to have the desired impact on American public opinion.[18]

It is impossible to provide the names of all those unpaid, but not unrewarded, American agents who labored to tell the French side of the story between 1914 and 1917. And were it not so, it would be untenable for even the most patient of readers. Instead, let me offer a profession-based selection of these early volunteers. Predictably, many were in the press corps, Paris-based journalists and writers, notably for the *New York Times* and the *Chicago Tribune*, men such as Wythe Williams, Robert Herrick, Owen Johnson, Frank Simonds, and Frank Munsey and evocative female writers such as Gertrude Atherton, Edith Wharton, and Carolyn Wilson. Take the case of Richard Harding Davis, who, in February 1916, pledged himself to serve France and her people, "a people so entirely splendid, and sane, loyal and indomitable." Or that of Edward Marshall, of the Curtis Brown News Bureau, a veteran journalist who also pledged to support the Allied cause and to combat German propaganda in the American Midwest. Or that of Edith Wharton, who, in 1917, pledged herself if necessary "to get up out of my grave" in order "to witness for France."[19] Publishers, too, were among those who supported the Allies from a still-neutral America: Ralph Pulitzer of the *New York World*, Adolph Ochs of the *New York Times*, and James Gordon Bennett, owner of the *New York Herald*.[20]

French relations with the latter paper, and its 125 affiliates, provide a particularly instructive example of the foreign ministry's cultivation of foreign newspapers in the early years of the war. It helped, of course, to have a sympathetic managing director as well as a like-minded publisher. The former, Kent Cooper, proved a willing accomplice, assuring Vice-Consul Gustave Heslouin in March 1916 not only that all the papers associated with the *New York Herald* were "completely at our disposition," but also that every care would be taken to avoid any public association with the French government. The ideal was to create the impression for their readers that most Americans were behind the Allied cause—when in fact Cooper believed otherwise. German propaganda, he told the vice-consul, had seduced most Americans, with the notable exception of the intellectual elite. Now it was time for a two-pronged counteroffensive, one through a series of favorable pieces on the French political leadership, the other through a collection of photographs and drawings illustrating the physical damage inflicted on northeastern France and depicting the indomitable will of Germany's victims never to buckle.[21]

Americans from other walks of life were eager to magnify the voice of France in America, some of them using the newspaper press in their own right. One thinks of prominent educators, for example, Dr. Charles W. Eliot, former president of Harvard University; Nicolas Murray Butler, president of Columbia University; George B. McClellan, distinguished professor of economic history at Princeton; Vassar professor Jean C. Bracq, specialist in French literature and author of a book subtitled *Fifty Years of German Aggression*; and John Finley, commissioner of education for the state of New York, as well as a senior editorial writer at the *New York Times*.[22] There were also prominent names from the financial world, people such as Paris-based residents James Hazen Hyde, Henry Oscar Beatty, Edward Tuck, and James Stillman, as well as New York–based Cornelius Vanderbilt, J. P.(Jack) and Anne Morgan, and Otto Kahn, all of them Francophile supporters of the Allied cause. Indeed, it was Kahn, a wealthy New York businessman who, in late 1916, was a principal if surreptitious figure behind the creation of an American Propaganda Committee for the support of the Allied cause.[23]

The appearance of this committee testified to two correlated trends: one, a new resolve to propagate the Anglo-French viewpoint; two, a growing conviction that the Germans were winning the propaganda war in America. Certainly none of these principals, French or American, suffered under the illusion that America was steadfastly pro-ally. The single presence of William Randolph Hearst's powerful International News Service was enough to dispel any such notion, for Hearst and his numerous papers were much more sympathetic to the Austro-German cause.[24] That is why, with the war seemingly determined to continue forever, pressure mounted on France's own would-be agents of propaganda in America. By late 1916 doubts were surfacing that the measured, subtle strategy insisted upon by Jusserand and supported by Berthelot was the equal of Germany's more overt and more richly financed efforts in America. In part, at least, doubts such as these were behind the dramatic new initiative to create a French High Commission in the

United States, once the latter had proclaimed its decision to enter the war in April 1917. Until then, however, the old structures and strategies remained in place, and beneath them some of the older French interpretations of America and Americans.

Such interpretations, examined at greater length in Chapter 2, warrant here a quick review. Americans, as seen through the collective lens of the French foreign ministry, were an industrious, hospitable, generous, openly curious people, a people genuinely democratic and republican, a people well instructed in the shared early histories of their republic and that of France. But they were now largely indifferent to European affairs, their lack of engagement springing from the topsoil of ignorance and an underlying loam of limited education. Most read little beyond the first page of a newspaper and showed limited powers of discernment beyond that invested in local issues. That was why, in the opinion of one *missionnaire* to America in 1916, film propaganda had such potential. Americans, he ventured, were rather like children, naive viewers who easily confounded images on celluloid with reality. The same naïveté, he surmised, was behind their gullibility when it came to associating France with dirty books and dubious public and private morality. So it was that Americans posed such a challenge, and such a hope. Given their limited horizons and blinkered optics, they really required "a complete re-education." But given those limitations, and the attendant shallowness of current views, their opinion was susceptible to cultivation—again ideally, not so much by French propaganda agents in America as by some of America's own intellectual elite.[25]

Ambassador Jusserand, France's chief principal propaganda agent in America, considered the foregoing conclusion as sacred text, however much he might have softened the lines of the characterization from which it was taken. He was genuinely fond of Americans, among whom he had traveled for over a decade; and he was well attuned to their sensitivities. In particular, in the middle of a European war, they were highly cautious about foreigners' attempts to sway their sympathies. By his reading, that was why German propaganda was proving counterproductive. It was too transparent in its goals and too clumsy in its means. Conversely, he believed, all that was needed to maintain American sympathies for war-torn France was a low-key campaign of accurate information. And one did not have to spend buckets of money, either on newfangled press-clipping and cable services to monitor American press opinion, or on any kind of financial compensation for positive press reports. Indeed, he regarded the latter practice as a seamy tactic employed only by countries with "something to hide and someone to deceive."[26]

Others involved in the campaign of messages for America knew what Jusserand meant, and sympathized with the ideals of this gentleman and scholar. But by the end of 1916 others had grown anxious. Gustave Heslouin, vice-consul in New York and future officer at the American desk in the Maison de la Presse, reported in March that only the intellectual elite remained steadfast behind France and, in June, that German propaganda was gathering speed.[27] Six months later the foreign ministry received another disturbing report, this time from the French government's Financial Office in New York. The Germans were making progress. More and more Americans were beginning to believe that France was deliberately drawing the war out, and that she had got involved in the first place only because of her alliance with autocratic Russia. Indeed, Maurice Casenave suggested, it was precisely this gathering momentum that had inspired people like Otto Kahn and Paul Cravath to organize their own pro-Allied propaganda committee.[28]

In fact, the government in Paris already had taken a new initiative to expand its information services in America. In October 1916 the foreign ministry notified Jusserand that a new office was about to be established in New York, under the direction of the former editor of *Le Matin*, Stéphane Lauzanne. The latter's role was to provide a liaison service between the various agencies of the French state in America and the American press. Complicating the task, however, was the admonition that the office be "unofficial" in character—a constraint that was consistent with the old proscription against interfering in American politics, but one that troubled Lauzanne for months to come.[29] Indeed, it was not until the summer of 1917, after America had become a de facto ally, that he was able to add a final line to his already congested letterhead: "Rooms 817–18 Vanderbilt Hotel, New York," followed by an impenetrable second line: "The Effort of France, of her Allies, and of Her Friends. The French National Committee." A third line now read: "The Official Bureau of French Information," an office that he was to direct until the end of the war.[30]

Lauzanne's first six months in office were not easy. Forced to deny any official status, a denial reiterated by an ambassador in Washington who was more afraid of propaganda backfiring than convinced of its utility, the new arrival had to struggle against the odds. The biggest problem, he reported, was simple ignorance. Americans still did not grasp the issues surrounding the war in Europe and were disturbingly ignorant of the statistics and data that were indispensable to any understanding of France's position. So it was that he and his assistant Marcel Knecht, a medical doctor by training, wrote articles for the press, provided text and numbers to American journalists, granted interviews, and responded with their own published letters to editors. They also lectured, sometimes far from New York, and more and more often in English—their use of that language being a sore spot for people like Jusserand and Lauzanne, who had hosted far too many unilingual French speakers in America.[31] Significantly, they agreed, too, on a matter of principle. No money was to be exchanged between those who represented France in America and those who presented France through the American press. Faced with a suggestion that his office buy twenty-five hundred dollars worth of advertising in the *Evening Post*, in order to support the costs of an illustrated issue on France, Lauzanne roundly condemned the very notion of "publicité payante."[32]

In addition to the information services provided through the embassy in Washington, the consulate in New York, and Lauzanne's offices at the Vanderbilt Hotel, there was also a torrent of officially sponsored *missionnaires* to America. Two of these are discussed below as further illustration of the foreign ministry's reading of the propaganda situation in America in 1916. More are considered, but sparingly, to illustrate the myriad fronts on which their propaganda campaign was conducted.

The first detailed illustration is provided by the marquis Melchior de Polignac, who arrived in America in May 1916 ostensibly for a Washington exhibition of military artifacts from the western front. In fact, he was out to test the waters of American opinion. Initially, he discerned the demons of Jusserand's nightmare, namely, that inept propaganda efforts could do more harm than good. Indeed, in early July the American press had reported on the French parliament's recent decision to allocate 25 million francs for propaganda in neutral countries. Writing to Berthelot, Polignac stressed the "deplorable impression" that such reports had made in America, the more so as France's long-standing disavowal of opinion manipulation had won her much sympathy among propaganda-shy Americans. Jusserand must have applauded, but only until December. It was then that Polignac submitted a second, and less sanguine, assessment. Now, he told Ernest Guy in the propaganda section of the Maison that the campaign in America was "in full crisis." The German ambassador, Count Johann von Bernstorff, was making huge inroads in American opinion. What was needed, and needed urgently, was a "Big Man" in the United States, someone with a prominent name, a sweeping authority, and an understanding of how to reach the right press and diplomatic circles.[33]

One month earlier, another French *missionnaire* arrived in America, at the behest and on the budget of the Quai d'Orsay. He was Pierre de Lanux, a writer and a senior representative of the French Red Cross. Ostensibly, his mission was to assist in the work of the American War Relief Commission, headed by Anne Morgan. In fact, he, too, had been charged by the Maison to appraise American opinion, in particular that of America's literary and politically aware youth. Predictably, given the target group, he found reason to be encouraged. The better educated, he reported, especially those from the New York–Boston region, were more cognizant of European issues and were culturally connected to educated, well-to-do circles in England and France. At the same time, and less happily, they had a fuller appreciation of the implications of American involvement in the war and were therefore hesitant to commit themselves to the cause of intervention. Far more hesitant were the young men who were part of the 4-million-strong immigrant communities of the Midwest, half of whom had come from German-controlled lands, and most of whom were simply indifferent to the war in Europe.[34] On balance, therefore, the apprehension expressed in the de Lanux appraisal was similar to that detected by de Polignac. Both visitors seemed to feel that France needed to intensify her propaganda efforts. And they were not alone. As President Woodrow Wilson slowly steered a course toward an announcement of American intervention in March–April 1917, Lauzanne's associates on the French National Committee in New York now began to press for more explicitly anti-German releases on the one hand, and more clear-cut pro-French releases on the other.[35]

As for the second kind of illustrations, those of the diverse fronts on which the propaganda war took place, I can but offer a sampling. To do otherwise, once again, would be to exhaust the reader's patience. But whom to choose as samples? Educators? For example, Professor A. Geouffre de Lapradelle, who held a visitor's chair in French studies at Columbia, kept in close touch with French diplomatic representatives in America, and understood that "the best propaganda was that which was not open to the accusation"? Or perhaps one of his predecessors in the same chair—a man such as the literary historian Gustave Lanson, who, in the summer of 1916, was sent by the French education ministry to explore ways of strengthening relations between French and American universities? Or someone like Professor Gilbert Chinard, another historian, one who resumed a teaching career at Berkeley in 1917, after an extended tour of duty at the American desk in the Maison de la Presse? Or perhaps a living legend like Henri Bergson, an internationally famous philosopher who was enjoined to do an American lecture tour in March 1917, and to publish a series of articles in the Sunday *New York Times*, a series—so appropriate to wartime—on the subject of democracy. Ambassador Jusserand was delighted, the more so because he believed such a contribution was more valuable precisely because it was not "propagande directe."[36]

Should it be artistic or literary people? People like Jacques Copeau, who, early in 1917, led a cast from the Théâtre du Vieux Colombier on a three-month American tour, three months of Claudel, Corneille, Marivaux, Molière, Racine, even Shakespeare. Or the New York resident and artist Baron Charles Huard, who became a principal organizer of French art exhibitions for the consulate in New York? Or the watercolorist Charles Duvent, whose works were used, early in 1917, to help raise funds in New York for the American Ambulance Corps in France? Should it be military men such the popular Lieutenant Zinovi Pechkoff and the former University of Chicago student Captain Paul Périgord, who became two of the Consulate's most effective speakers on the European campaign? Or should it be musicians, for example, those of the orchestra called Les Instruments Anciens, a group that toured America with some frequency and whose music gently associated France with the beautiful and the benign?[37]

Speaking of groups, the foreign ministry's early wartime propaganda effort was closely allied with that of many independent, or at least semi-independent, associations. The latter, for the most part, were not products of the war, nor creatures of the French state; wartime circumstance had brought them all to a patriotic pitch, just as wartime circumstance had inclined the government to support them. Accordingly, together they financed and published a huge number of lectures, speeches, articles, pamphlets, books, photo albums, and poster collections, all of which were conceived as propagandistic devices. Apart from the common patriotic link, they were a diverse lot.

Some were inspired by religion: the Comité catholique de propagande française à l'étranger, and its homologues, the Comité protestant and the Comité israélite. Some were primarily scholarly by conception, whether the literary-minded Société des gens de lettres and the Comité du livre, the lecture-minded Société des conférences, or the linguistic-minded Alliance Française. Some, like numerous *chambres de commerce*, though primarily economic in orientation, could appreciate the need for wedding patriotism and profit. Others seemed to have had a more narrowly patriotic base from the outset, essentially such wartime associations as Amitiés françaises, L'idée française à l'étranger; La Grande ligue internationale contre l'Austro-Pangermanisme; the Comité de la propagande chez les alliés, the Comité de la propagande chez les neutres, and the more broadly based Union des grandes associations françaises contre la propagande ennemie. Finally, and of particular import for this study, there was the expressly Francophilic Comité France-

Amérique, a prewar association that continued to be a key instrument in the promotion of Franco-American relations throughout the war and the subsequent interwar period.[38]

All these devices, and more, were used by the French government, through the Foreign and Education Ministries in particular, as part of its wartime propaganda strategy in America. And central to the education ministry, of course, at least until American intervention in April 1917, was the prescription never to forget the two great constants: America's neutral status, and the long-standing resolve of her people not to be hoodwinked into someone else's war. To that end, and especially in light of Jusserand's unrivaled authority as resident expert, the Quai d'Orsay used money and polemics sparingly and was more disposed to employ American volunteers than its own agents. For the first year of its existence, roughly until the late autumn of 1916, the Maison de la Presse seemed satisfied with its campaign and confident that words used subtly and sparingly would have more effect than those used coarsely and to excess.

Not only words, of course. Between them, the embassy, the consulate, and the Lauzanne office cooperated in the distribution of the photographic and film collections produced by the war ministry and the tourist section of the commerce ministry. Books and pamphlets were similarly distributed, some to educational establishments, some to organizations such as the Alliance Française, the American Committee for Propaganda, and the Committee for Relief in Belgium, and some to newspapers, magazines, and learned journals. There were charity bazaars to be supported, in New York, Chicago, Boston, and Baltimore—four principal ones between June 1916 and March 1917 alone. And there were innumerable gardens to be cultivated and nourished. Among them were those of the press: such individuals as Wythe Williams of the *New York Times*, Lincoln Eyre of the *New York World*, Scott Mowrer of the *Chicago Daily News*, and Edward Marshall of the Curtis Brown News Agency. Every prominent American who visited France was a tiny potential garden, whether a man or woman of science, politics, literature, art, or education. So was every American who resided in wartime France and worked on sundry charitable committees: the American Clearing House, the American Fund for French Wounded, the American Hospital, the Commission for Relief in Belgium.[39] All these and, again, more, were part of the vast field in which French propagandists labored to seed goodwill for their country during the first two and a half years of the war.

As was anticipated by all, much more could be done, and more openly, once American intervention in the war had been decided. It was this development, in April 1917, that signaled a more ambitious and aggressive French propaganda strategy, this one carried out largely under the auspices of a revamped organizational structure in both France and America. As for the former, there had been a crescendo of domestic complaints against the government's propaganda strategy in 1915–1916, starting with the portrayal of the Maison as the headquarters of deceit and as a menace to the freedom of expression, and extending full circle to its denigration as old-fashioned and ineffective. It therefore came as no surprise when, in the spring of 1917, the new Alexandre Ribot cabinet scrapped the Maison and replaced it with two new *services,* one for *information diplomatique,* under Albert Legrand, the other for *information à l'étranger,* under Louis Steeg. In fact, however, while the name Maison technically disappeared, its only somewhat reduced staff continued to operate from their old offices on the rue François Premier. Which is where they remained, even under the sweeping shakeup of May 1918, when the Clemenceau government created a Commissariat général à l'information et à la propagande, under the leadership of the diplomat Anthony Klobukowski, but under the direct authority of the premier's office.[40]

As for changes in America, the shift from neutrality to de facto alliance prompted the French government to raise its profile by creating a full-fledged High Commission to the United States, under the direction of an able and high-profile commissioner, André Tardieu.[41] The latter, who had begun the war serving as an information officer for the war ministry, arrived in Washington on 17 May 1917, now *en mission* for the foreign ministry. Within a month the commission was installed on Fifteenth Street Northwest, and Tardieu had laid the groundwork for an organization that would eventually employ nine hundred French citizens and three hundred Americans. Premier Georges Clemenceau had seen to it that the commission would have a broad mandate; and Tardieu was determined to fulfill it in every respect. Tighter links had to be forged with the American army and navy. Money had to be raised from private and public sources. Contracts had to be negotiated for American exports that were vital to the French war effort—from textiles to armaments to food. Ever improved arrangements had to be made for the transport of goods and men by land and sea, as well as for the interdiction of German supplies by means of Allied blockade. And, of particular relevance here, new energy and initiatives were needed on the propaganda front.[42]

The intention was to centralize French information services under the direct control of the High Commission and its Service d'études et d'information, headed first by Professor Louis Aubert and subsequently by Professor Othon Guerlac, a Romance-language specialist at Cornell.[43] In that way—again the intention—there was to be some uniformity in the type and quality of information that was transmitted from France through the cerebral cortex that was the commission, and then disseminated by that agency's multiple limbs and appendages in America, including the embassy and consulates, Lauzanne's Official French Bureau in New York, the Federation of the Alliance Française, and the France-America Society. Such centralization also accorded with the French government's desire to work hand in hand with America's new Committee on Public Information and to cultivate the goodwill of sundry associations in America, in particular, the educational, religious, and ethnic.[44] Using a range of familiar devices—press conferences and press releases, books, pamphlets and lectures, photographs and films—the "Service Aubert" sought to impose a new measure of order on France's propaganda war in America and inject into it a new measure of energy. At the same time, it was this office that was entrusted with the task of monitoring American public opinion and, in particular, of appraising the impact of German propaganda.[45]

By the spring of 1917, as already witnessed, there was a sense in Paris and in French circles in America that the Germans had stolen a march on France. That concern, together with other worries, continued to attract the attention of foreign ministry personnel both at home and abroad. Undeniably, they were apprehensive about German propaganda, particularly as it exploited pacifist feelings in the United States, aggravated Irish American resentment of England—France's ally—and magnified the tensions between the Roman Catholic Church and a reputedly anticlerical, secularly minded French republic.[46] And one of the reasons why they worried was the shortage of resources. Compared to the Germans, the French seemed always constrained by too limited budgets, too little timely information from Paris, and too few up-to-date films on the theater of war. Even more disturbing was the discovery that many American schoolchildren were being taught French by teachers of German background and by means of French grammar texts issued by German publishers. Indeed, the only thing that seemed in surfeit was the endless parade of Paris-dispatched "missions" by visitors out to sample American opinion and undertake instant analyses.[47]

But competition with Germany was only part of the problem. France's allies were another, Britain in particular. For example, early in June 1918, the staff of the High Commission in Washington feared the American public just might conclude that the British army was fighting single-handedly against the German spring offensive; and they resented the way too many British speakers and writers almost dismissed France as an already prostrate victim.

Indeed, the whole notion of France as victim of German aggression and wanton destruction could be overplayed, for it implied that France was finished, exhausted, unable to carry on—unlike Britain, which not only fought on, but also could express its determination to do so in a language familiar to Americans.[48] What was more, there seemed a tendency in some French circles both to exaggerate France's suffering and to exacerbate matters by fawning over resource-rich America. As Stéphane Lauzanne wrote to Jusserand, one had to speak to Americans politely and sensitively, but also clearly and firmly. One needed to appeal to America's sense of friendship for France, not to its vanity—which, he judged, was already excessive. Rephrased, as Casenave wrote to Tardieu, newly returned to Paris to head the new Commissariat des affaires de guerre franco-américaines, France had to avoid any suggestion of an appeal to "American charity."[49]

The key to such avoidance lay in the projection of an image worthy of France, an image Americans would respect. For starters, as François Monod wrote to one congressional committee, the French were an industrious and thrifty people, trained from childhood to save, disciplined enough to forgo luxuries, and committed enough to invest their fortunes in government war bonds.[50] Furthermore, far from being bled white, their country still enjoyed such a large agricultural, industrial, and imperial resource base that postwar recovery would be rapid. So rapid, in fact, that foreign investors would be falling over themselves. Certainly it was no "second Belgium," some "poor cousin" who was going to appear cap in hand. And, as always, France had a natural association with civilization, with democratic ideals, and with republican sentiment, all of which explained an historic affinity between that country and the American nation. Unlike the Germans, who were practiced invaders, and whose atrocities against people and churches were still being enacted, and still recalled, the French were victims ennobled by an heroic struggle against aggression and barbarism. Under such circumstances, what was more natural than that that they should now insist on the return of the "lost" provinces of Alsace and Lorraine to the bosom of France? Not so much in retribution but in the interests of natural justice.[51]

As in the early war years, the French government floated its ideas on diverse media, its efforts including an America-targeted campaign by means of posters, ten thousand copies of which depicted a young Alsatian girl in mourning clothes. Below her sad figure was the simple inscription "She is Waiting." Effective, too, was the poster series based on the poignant drawings done by French schoolchildren. Photographically illustrated books and brochures also remained favorites: mass-produced editions, some issued in the millions of copies, that juxtaposed scenes of German-delivered devastation beside portraits of France's proud, unbreakable soldiers and civilians.[52] Simple textual material also had its uses: books such as English translations of Louis Madelin's *La Bataille de la Marne* or Gustave Rageot's *Ce que la France a fait pendant la guerre*, works, in short, that combined scholarly cachet with readability. Such was especially true of works authored by French press experts resident in the United States: *Young France and New America,* by Pierre de Lanux, or *Fighting France,* by Stéphane Lauzanne. On the less scholarly side, though for a reason, the Information Commissariat also published eighty thousand copies of the memoirs of Prince Lichnowsky, the prewar German ambassador to London, in hopes of riling readers in neutral countries.[53] There were also periodic bulletins such as that prepared and released each week by the High Commission's military affairs department, or the *Bulletin d'information artistique,* prepared by the education ministry and distributed through the diplomatic service; and press articles, either those derived from French newspapers and forwarded for republication in America, or pieces prepared by the Paris-based Information Commissariat for original use by some American publication.[54]

Still other ways remained open to the High Commission for projecting the French image in America, some of them more traditional than others. The traveling military exhibition was a great success, as Americans flocked to see the shells and tanks and flamethrowers with which their French allies were fighting the war. And a squad of wounded veterans who had been detailed to accompany such exhibitions ensured that the gravity of the war was not lost on the visitors. Neither was it lost on those attending the special Bastille Day celebrations on 14 July 1918, these comprising some two hundred events played out across the continent during which speech after speech was addressed to France's courage, its indomitable will, and the sacred bond between the French and American republics.[55] In other quarters, too, and on other occasions, the spoken word remained a propaganda staple. Whether at patriotic rallies, assemblies of the American Legion, university gatherings, or meetings of sundry Francophilic organizations, the public lecture remained one of the most common devices for expressing the mind of France in America. Indeed, between seven thousand and eight thousand public lectures were sponsored by the High Commission between May 1917 and December 1918.[56]

Not that tradition reigned everywhere. Increasingly, for instance, these lectures were accompanied by images shown by slide projectors, the images themselves distributed by the photographic section of Klobukowki's

Information Commissariat. Film, too, became more and more useful toward the end of the war, most of it produced by the French army's cinematic department—including "shorts" on such subjects as the air arm, women in the war, animals in the war, and the United States in the war. In particular, the Pathé Exchange in New York ensured that French-produced newsreel footage was a staple in countless American movie theaters.[57] By the later stages of the war, radio, too, was being used extensively, although principally as a device to pass information across the Atlantic from a government transmitter in Lyon to a government distributor, namely the High Commission in Washington. From mid-June 1918 a transatlantic radio-telegram service was in operation, a service that included one news bulletin per hour. The same technology also permitted transmission and receipt of dispatches from the government-supported Agence Havas, yet another service that daily attracted to the High Commission offices journalists from the Associated Press, the United Press, the Foreign News Service, and even Hearst's International News Service.[58]

The preceding invocation of message and media invites a return to the subject of propaganda agents and agencies, whether of French or American origin, and whether fully or occasionally engaged. As might be expected, the list of participants' names grew longer in the last year of the war, and the scope of their activities more broad. If that were somewhat less true of the Jusserand embassy, and of the consulates scattered across America, it was doubly true of Klobukowski's Information Commission at the foreign ministry, and of Tardieu's High Commission in Washington. The prolonged war effort, and the attendant need for more centralized control of information destined for friends, enemies, and neutrals, ensured that these two bodies would be indispensable to the propaganda war—they, as well as Lauzanne's Official Bureau of French Information in New York. Together, their stables of writers and lecturers, some of them directly involved with the American Committee for Public Information, worked laboriously to ensure that the French perspective received maximum publicity, and the French voice maximum audience.

Their task would have been more difficult had it not been for the sympathetic attention of many "upper-class" Americans, people in some cases "over-awed by London and Paris society."[59] If Hearst and his newspapers remained resolutely critical, others in the press world were more kind. To the names of journalists earlier identified for their Francophilic stance can be added Walter Duranty and Edwin L. James, both of whom worked in wartime Paris for the *New York Times*, as well as that paper's business manager, Louis Wiley; Floyd Gibbons of the *Chicago Tribune*, Scott Mowrer of the

Chicago Daily News as well as the sympathetic services of the Otis F. Wood press agency.[60] Other friends were concentrated in the France-America Society: among others, its president, Nicolas Murray Butler; its director, George F. Peabody; and Frank Pavey, an executive member of the Federation of the Alliance Française. There were bankers such as J. P. Morgan and Thomas W. Lamont, and lawyers such as William Guthrie, Frederick Coudert, and the former attorney-general George Wickersham. There were diplomats, notably Myron Herrick, a former ambassador to Paris and an assiduous writer of pro-French articles for the wartime *Chicago Tribune*, and there were such scholars as W. R. Thayer, twice president of the American Historical Association, who predicted that "for a generation to come, the very word *German* will be detested in the United States."[61]

While American luminaries within the France-America Society cultivated Francophilia on their side of the Atlantic, their French counterparts on the rue Cassette in Paris did the same. It was they, for example, who published an English translation of Louis Barbosa's *Devoir des neutres* and provided multiple copies for circulation abroad by the Quai d'Orsay.[62] For their part, French journalists continued to cooperate with their government, publishing, as they sometimes did, foreign ministry–prepared articles that had been explicitly designed to influence opinion.[63] By the same token, the work of the state-subsidized, Paris-based propaganda groups escalated toward the end of the war. The Comité protestant, for one, actively collaborated with American religious organizations by sending speakers to underscore the moral imperatives of the war against Germany, as did the Comité catholique with its much traveled president, Monseigneur Baudrillart.[64] The same was true of the Comité du livre, a state-inspired creation of 1916 that cultivated relations with intellectual circles around the world, including a network of correspondents in the United States.[65]

Indeed, even in the midst of a terrible war, there remained a familiar emphasis upon the aesthetic, and things of the mind. The foreign ministry continued to cultivate relations between its own National University Office and the American Bureau of University Relations, a liaison that annually provided French teachers for American schools and universities. It also provided, through the High Commission offices, large numbers of books and brochures for university libraries and for individual members of the Society of French Teachers. Just as it sponsored high-profile educational study missions to America, missions of the sort launched in October 1918 under the co-sponsorship of the ministry, the Institut de France, and the Ecole des Hautes Etudes Sociales.[66]

Similarly, the Quai d'Orsay did not neglect the battalions concealed in the fine arts. Articles and illustrations on French ceramics, literature, and painting were prepared for publication in the American magazine *The New France*. Money was found, including American money, for a project to open a French bookstore on New York's Fifth Avenue, one that would promote French literature and art. And still more was found, in conjunction with resources from the fine arts section of the education ministry, to send Louis Hasselmans to conduct the Chicago Opera and to see that French composers sparkled under his baton.[67] In sum, as Information Commissioner Klobukowski put it to his premier, it was essential that France highlight itself as the world's "intellectual nest," as much for the sake of its allies as its enemies.[68]

Messages such as these, dispersed through media such as these, doubtless contributed to the change in America's perception of France in the last year of the war. Those messages, underscored by American participation in the war and by the domestic propaganda efforts of George Creel's Committee on Public Information, were now finding more and more resonance among Americans across the continent. Reporting on an extended lecture tour of western cities in July 1918, Maurice Casenave was struck by the way the populace had rallied to the war effort. From Minneapolis to Seattle and Portland, from San Francisco and Los Angeles to Omaha and Saint Louis, Americans had thrown their support behind the Allied cause. And they had done so, he concluded, with demonstrable "Francophilic enthusiasm."[69]

Demonstrable, but not spontaneous. Behind the upsurge in favor of France was the success of French and American efforts to solicit more sympathy from the Roman Catholic Church in America, principally by focusing on the carnage visited upon French cathedrals by German artillery shells. The press, too, by Stéphane Lauzanne's assessment, had swung firmly behind the Allied war effort, excepting only the newspaper holdings of William Randolph Hearst.[70] And there was, too, the opinion-molding work of new war-born organizations in America, organizations such as the Union of French and Alsatian Societies, which—under the chairmanship of the prominent New York Francophile Daniel Blumenthal—prepared the ground for a postwar return to France of Alsace and Lorraine. More consequential still was the Committee on Allied Tribute to France, an umbrella organization that embraced well more than a dozen pro-Allied groups and that was directed by another prominent Francophile, the journalist Owen Johnson.[71]

This is not to say that French propagandists thought that all was well in America. They knew that old habits die hard; and they knew that the national mood swing was more inspired by Washington's decision to join the war effort than by their own attempts to educate the American public. Indeed, they still complained about the ignorance of that public, a condition they attributed partly to inadequate information flow from Paris—especially information translated into English—and partly to the financial and linguistic advantages that British propagandists enjoyed over their French allies. They knew, too, that their efforts to link the German people to the atrocities committed by the German regime had yielded limited results—which meant that Americans were unlikely to lend themselves to an appropriately punitive peace. Furthermore, because Americans did not fully share France's optic on the enduring German problem, they would be quick to reconcile themselves to a postwar situation. In particular, since "sentiment does not last long against material interest," French propagandists feared that the Americans and English would be only too anxious to reestablish commercial relations with Germany as quickly as possible.[72]

It was not long before such premonitions were put to the test. The war in western Europe ended with an armistice on 11 November 1918, a truce that formalized Germany's unconditional surrender. Before the end of that year, peace delegations were assembling in Paris with a view to building a foundation for the postwar world; and by the end of June 1919 the German delegation, now representing the new democratic Republic of Weimar, had been coerced into signing the famous Treaty of Versailles. From the beginning, the Germans hated it. They resented the manner in which it had been imposed; and they resented many of its terms, most notably the attribution of guilt for the outbreak of war in 1914 and for the ensuing four years of destruction. In short, they regarded it as excessively harsh. If not at the outset, before 1919 had run its course, Anglo-American opinion was drifting toward a similar conclusion—one fueled by an active German propaganda campaign.[73] And whether or not one judged the treaty too harsh in absolute terms, given the intensity of the German reaction, was it not an obstacle to international reconciliation and therefore to an enduring peace? The French, of course, had an answer. The problem was not with the treaty. The difficulty lay with the mounting hesitation of victors to enforce terms that had been called into being by a willful act of German aggression. Rephrased, security against future aggression was a prerequisite for peaceful coexistence. What that meant for the French was strict adherence to the treaty's terms. And what *that* meant for the British and Americans, as time went on, was an apprehension about French pugnacity and unreasonableness.

In fact, the fault line between France and its former allies, America in particular, was already visible before the Versailles treaty was tabled. Within weeks of the Armistice, the Quai d'Orsay had identified hostile articles in the *Baltimore Sun* and the *Pittsburgh Dispatch,* respectively. These articles struck two blows. They urged an early pullout of American troops and supplies from France, on the grounds that their continued presence would be used by the French to secure postwar aid. They also highlighted alleged French criticism of America's limited contribution to the war, the kind of allegation that was certain to drive a wedge between the former allies and, therefore, that was suspected of being a product of German propaganda.[74] Indeed, the threat represented by such German propaganda actually seemed to increase with the cessation of hostilities. The Germans were said to be buying up cinema houses in foreign countries, the better to ensure audience access to German film products; and in the very months when the peace conference was being held in Paris, the French Information Commissariat concluded that the Germans were accelerating their propaganda efforts around the globe. Evidence seemed to be accumulating, none more striking, sensational or—by the Hearst press—repeated than the reports on American military efforts to combat French venereal disease, or on how France had charged the American army rent for use of its trenches. And none more alarming than that of German propaganda directed at American military camps, hospitals, and troop ships, propaganda calculated to promote anti-French feelings among soldiers heading home.[75]

There were other warning signs, some of them transparent, others indirect and more subtle. In February 1919 François Monod alerted Tardieu to the trend in American public opinion. Americans wanted nothing more than to disengage from Europe as quickly as possible. Their government, having so energetically shaped opinion in wartime, had precipitately abandoned its educational role for the peace. Accordingly, the public remained ignorant about Europe, left in the hands of journalists who were themselves "ignorant, glib, . . . even hostile." All that, in combination with the undermining effects of German propaganda, helped explain why many Americans held France responsible for the deficiencies of the peace settlement. Furthermore, France itself was already scrimping on its own propaganda effort, which Monod now judged quite insufficient for the task at hand.

Such were some of the transparent signs of trouble on the postwar propaganda front. But this report also uncovered something more subtle, if potentially as damaging. Having given some prominence to American ignorance of conditions outside America, Monod proceeded to offer a rough psychological profile—one that might now appear a trifle patronizing. Reminiscent of a remark once made by his old boss, Tardieu, to the effect that the reading level of American sixteen-year-olds was comparable to that of twelve-year-old French children, Monod wrote the following. "American minds are like blank tablets, as quick to register something new as to forget it." Furthermore, so he judged, they were particularly susceptible to morally framed issues, the more banal and familiar the better.[76] Together, from his point of view, those two qualities provided openings for a new propaganda impulse from France. Together, and from ours, those discerned qualities may say as much about the French mind, and therefore about a recurrent obstacle to the work of French propagandists in America.

Closer to home, in Paris, the foreign ministry undertook exceptional efforts to accommodate the large press contingent that accompanied President Wilson to France. It requisitioned the Hotel Dufayel for the use of American journalists; it hired the American journalist George H. Peet to serve as a liaison officer between the French government and his compatriots in the press; and it ensured the daily provision of press releases and information bulletins from Klobukowski's Information Commissariat. Indeed, when it came to news, the ministry had to struggle with two competing needs—one to see that information was not leaked prematurely to the press, the other to educate an American press corps that it judged ignorant of matters European. Worse, some, like Hearst's agents, were seen as deliberate troublemakers. Worse still, one journalist for the *Washington Star* was summed up as "'a jackass,' en très bon Américain."[77] Little wonder that Commissioner Klobukowski was desperate to accelerate the information program, believing as he did that since 11 November the war was simply being waged in another form. In an angry response to suggestions that the need for propaganda had run its course, Klobukowski wrote Foreign Minister Stéphen Pichon: "No, Minister, the need for propaganda has not expired; and the time has not come to cut back on it. Much to the contrary."[78]

It was that same spirit that kept his officials determined to stay the course, despite the frustrations inspired by tight budgets.[79] While the peace conference delegates contemplated various blueprints for a postwar world, the foreign ministry did its best to keep pace with the Germans. Its High Commission in Washington ordered five hundred more copies of Joseph Bédier's *German Atrocities* and secured for a special magazine issue a formal statement by a French cardinal condemning the German shelling of the cathedral at Reims.[80] Its financial subventions continued to be distributed to a wide assortment of sympathetic groups and agencies, from the Comité du livre and the Effort de la France et ses alliés to the West Coast monthly *Le Franco-*

Californien.[81] It also continued to support the well-established public lecture system, although with increasing awareness of the need for English speakers who could radiate optimism in the future of France and address economics and finances as well as literature and philosophy. Similarly progressive was the ministry's commitment to a scholarship program for study in the United States, a program funded in part by the ministry's secret "fonds spéciaux" but distributed through the education ministry's National Office for Universities.[82] In view of such activities, it must have been particularly gratifying for the French government to read, in August 1918, a *Washington Post* article entitled "France and England Wisely Avoided Propaganda in U.S." Written by an "Ex-Attaché," a familiar *nom de plume*, the article contrasted French tact with German "tactlessness and brutality" and insisted that Tardieu's High Commission and Lauzanne's Information Bureau did not "undertake anything in the nature of propaganda."[83]

Breathtakingly inaccurate as this was, there is reason to wonder whether the American market could have used less subtlety and more verbal brawn. Certainly some observers sensed that France was again falling behind the Germans. It was not simply a matter of what the French had done, or not done. Part of the problem, increasingly, was President Wilson's insistence on incorporating provision for the League of Nations into the German treaty, a provision that Republicans in general and senators in particular found offensive.[84] Just in the process of extricating America from the European snake pit, many Americans wished to curtail, not extend, the country's international commitments. That said, there was a perception in other respects that France had become more of a problem than the now defeated Germany. At the very least, the French republic was seen as being bent on vengeance, a state of mind that seemed little calculated to ensure continued peace. At the worst, France was suspected of entertaining imperial ambitions in eastern Europe and abroad, a suspicion bolstered by the size of its battle-tested army and its new air arm.

Given such apprehensions, it proved no small challenge for the French foreign ministry to "sell" the Versailles treaty to the American people. Indeed, in the face of a president who refused to have a treaty stripped of the League of Nations, and a senate that refused a treaty which included it, the sale proved impossible.[85] To that extent, it is unlikely that a massive expenditure of energy, funds, and rhetoric by the Quai d'Orsay would have made any appreciable difference. Indeed, if Ambassador Jusserand were right, such a strategy might well have backfired. Ever cautious about appearing to meddle in American affairs, Jusserand reminded his superiors that *propaganda* was not a good word in America, and he took pains to transmit the text of an article from the *New York Sun* of 14 November 1919. That article read in part:

> Propaganda is the science or art of influencing public opinion in favor of, or against, an institution, a brand of soap, a school of art, a dynasty, a motor car, a political candidate . . . or anything else which engages the propagandist's energy. It is carried on by means of publicity obtained through motion pictures, letters to the editor, pamphlets, lectures, interviews, extracts from state papers and formal addresses by dignitaries in and out of office. . . . Some scoffers hold that most propaganda carried forward even under respectable and responsible patronage should be described by a shorter word. That word is bunk.[86]

In view of such straight talk, which Jusserand suggested was representative of American reactions to opinion manipulation, there seemed more proof of the merits of subtlety and understatement. French president Raymond Poincaré said as much a month later when he discouraged the foreign ministry from trying to force Wilson's hand on the matter of the league, invoking Jusserand's advice while doing so.[87]

So not for the first time, or the last, one of the great dilemmas of the propagandist surfaced in the immediate wake of peace. How brazen, how outrageous, could one afford to be? How reticent, and how modest? Influenced mightily by the practiced caution of Ambassador Jusserand, the French government pursued a propaganda policy characterized by restraint. At the beginning of the war, such a policy had required little discipline, for so little machinery then existed for the generation and dissemination of information for influencing opinion at home and abroad—a condition by no means confined to France.[88] With the passage of time, one year, then two, then three, the significance of information control became more and more manifest, and with it the need for more elaborate facilities. Even then, extra caution and restraint were needed for neutral countries, such as the United States, where more aggressive and overt German propaganda techniques were generally deemed to be failing.[89]

The entrance of the United States into the war in April 1917 reconfigured the war of words. Just as German propagandists were reduced to near silence in America, French propagandists and their American volunteers could be more outspoken and assertive—for about a year and a half, until the Armistice, when the propaganda environment changed once more. Thereafter, throughout the whole of 1919, during and after the peace conference in Paris, the ground seemed to shift perceptibly back in Germany's favor. By the end of November 1919 the American Senate had refused to ratify Wilson's treaty, and with that refusal came the unintended collapse of the Anglo-American guarantee of French security.[90] Neither development had much to do with foreign propagandists. The Germans, the principal beneficiaries of this twinned failure, were not behind the president's obstinacy; and the French could do nothing about it.

Words, images, and ideas had been part of the war effort, an important part. Those wielded by French propaganda agents certainly had been used to encourage America's slow transition from neutrality and to solidify the de facto Franco-American alliance after April 1917. But there were strict limits on the utility of words at any given moment and on the ability of their planters to bring in a harvest on demand. Neutrality did not suddenly vanish with the sweep of a verbal wand, any more than Allied solidarity could assuredly be preserved after the Armistice. The recent war experience made this clear to the French foreign ministry. Like cultivators worldwide, they understood as never before the imperative of regular seeding, the only certainty that existed amid all the chronic uncertainties of maturation and yield. That, metaphorically expressed, is why the Quai d'Orsay did not terminate its propaganda service with the end of the war, why it continued to stress the long-term benefits of a broad cultural propaganda directed principally at the American elite, and why its appreciation of the American "market" increased steadily from one war to the next.[91]

CHAPTER 4

From War to Peace, 1920–1929

❖

The hot war ended in November 1918. A cold war quickly ensued, despite the false promises and genuine hopes that surrounded the vision of a war-free future. In the twelve months that followed the Armistice, half of them dedicated to the making of the peace, the French foreign ministry made some key decisions about its peacetime propaganda strategy. First, it recommitted itself to a continuation of efforts to influence thinking and sentiment in foreign countries. Second, it would do so prudently, making public, reams of accurate information about every aspect of French policy and perspectives, and relying on sympathetic Americans to disseminate the data and to articulate a French point of view. Third, as Klobukowski observed at one interministerial conference late in the war, every advantage had to be taken of France's unrivaled intellectual and artistic reputation.[1] One could even expect to find an expansion of the cultural propaganda efforts once undertaken by the old prewar Bureau des écoles and more recently by the Maison de la Presse and its successor, Klobukowski's Information Commission.

The climate in which these decisions were taken, and these expectations nourished, was informed by several factors. One, certainly, was the conviction that the Germans had not reconciled themselves to their defeat. If anything, they had accelerated their propaganda efforts, especially in locations where the potential for success was greatest—as it was in the American Midwest, in particular. They would do their best to discredit France on every front, attribute to her the "spirit of revenge," and portray that spirit as the principal stumbling block to a viable and an honorable peace. And they would do their best to magnify and exploit tensions in Franco-American relations. Accordingly, this reading of German intentions inspired a new push from American Francophiles for France to intensify, rather than diminish, its propaganda efforts in the United States. Just as there had been wartime evidence of Americans urging the French on to more forceful deployment of the word, so there is evidence of American calls for more vigor in combating hostile propaganda in peacetime. Those of that mind decried their own government's decision to suddenly shut down the Committee on Public Information, and warned French agents in America that British publicity, as well as German, was overpowering anything from Paris.[2]

A second factor that contributed to the climate of the day arose from the interplay between Anglo-German constructions of the postwar world and certain academic reconstructions of the prewar period. A third was of a domestic nature, in the form of a collection of complaints and criticisms from the French media about American policies and American culture. A fourth extended the third, to the state of mind through which some prominent French observers interpreted the meaning of modern America. Finally, throughout the 1920s, there were some concrete policy differences between the two sister republics. In combination, these five factors presented huge challenges to those charged with the task of seeding, nourishing, and ultimately harvesting the bounty of healthy Franco-American relations.

Enlarging now on the first of these, one may invoke in greater detail the forces that were regarded as hostile to France and to the French point of view. One, predictably, was the propaganda engine of Germany's new Weimar Republic. Predictably, too, French observers remained divided over the efficacy of this Teutonic verbal onslaught. Still in evidence was the belief that German complaints regarding the peace settlement and the postwar world were so outrageous and so insensitive that their impact on Americans would be minimal.[3] That said, there was also evidence that some Americans had been softened by the heat of the German argument. The Hearst presses, true to form, were characteristically scabrous when it came to France.[4] Ambassador Jusserand's reports in 1921 on the scandalous charges thrown about by the *New York American* were but prologues for those submitted by his successor, Paul Claudel, or by postwar *missionnaires* such as Captain Zinovi Pechkoff. Whether from New York, San Francisco, or anywhere in between, the Hearst papers loved to snipe at anything from France's intransigence over the peace settlement and its "militarist ambitions," to her avarice and moral degradation.[5] Nor was this reaction simply attributable to Hearst. Even Frank Munsey's papers, the *New York Sun and Globe* and the *New York Herald*, were proving critical of France, of French domestic politics in particular; and the *Washington Post*, according to Claudel, had turned "systematically hostile." Even the normally sympathetic Edwin L. James, Paris-based correspondent for the *New York Times*, occasionally proved perverse and critical.[6] Then there were perceived pro-German politicians, senators such as Gilbert Hitchcock of Nebraska who made France out to be a militarist and imperialist power; Thaddeus Caraway of Arkansas, who called France the "spoiled child" of Europe and her premier a "puffed-up village undertaker"; and Robert Owen of Oklahoma, whom French observers thought to be "in perfect communion" with the German perspective.[7]

Still, irritating as were the former enemy's attempts to poison the well, they paled in comparison to the resentment triggered by Britain's anti-French propaganda in America. The postwar edition of British sniping had started early, with the 1920 publication of John Maynard Keynes's *The Economic Consequences of the Peace*. Keynes, a brilliant but disgruntled economist on the British delegation at Paris, was quick to point out the shortcomings of the treaty with Germany, shortcomings that he attributed to Allied greed and destructive vengeance. The book sold well in America, and thus was seen as more grist in the mill of American disenchantment with France.[8] But the peak of French resentment toward the British was not to come until 1922–1923, over the issue of naval disarmament; and it found no stronger expression than in the dispatches of the normally reserved Jules Jusserand. The English, he suspected, were trying to alienate France from America; and to that end, all concerns for the truth had been cast aside. Especially disturbing was his suspicion that some alliance of convenience had been forged between Britain and the Hearst press, evidence of which seemed to lie in that press's procurement of exclusive rights to an anti-French article written by the British wartime prime minister, David Lloyd George. The only saving grace in this campaign of distortion, Jusserand observed, was that such intemperate pieces, including a subsequent but equally damning article by H. G. Wells, only put Americans on their guard. For that reason, Jusserand counseled his superiors in Paris, it was important to remember the deleterious effects of clumsy propaganda.[9]

Adding to the sense that France was being maligned, not to say vilified, was the interplay between this Anglo-German factor and, our second, the early innings of an historical debate over the origins of the war just ended. Although there were scholars and publicists worldwide who remained faithful to the official verdict of German responsibility for that war, two American historians sounded early discordant notes. Basically, they found a disturbing simplicity in the Versailles attribution of war guilt to Germany, disturbing because the origins of the war now seemed so much more complex than what had been allowed for in Paris. Rephrased, responsibility for the war had to be distributed in some fashion, an argument that today may seem intellectually appealing but that the French at the time saw as a betrayal. One of the early salvos was fired in May 1924 when Harry Elmer Barnes of Smith College published, in *Current History*, an article that the French embassy regarded as part of an "insidious" propaganda campaign to exonerate Germany. They were less happy still when Barnes's book appeared two years later and enjoyed reported sales of one hundred thousand copies. Four years later still, a new book provoked more consternation. This time it was the work of Sidney B. Fay, a scholarly piece of great sophistication, but another that somehow reduced Germany's responsibility for the war and increased that of Britain and France. When a second edition appeared two years later, it was Paul Claudel's turn to vent his anger over the impunity with which a work of such "remarkable inexactitude" could be republished. Somehow, the once obvious fact that France had been invaded by Germany in August 1914 was being shaded at the victim's expense.[10]

A third factor that heightened the challenge to French propaganda in America—in addition to those represented by the Germans, British, and scholars who overlooked the obvious—was the static interference that regularly emanated from France itself. Every time a Paris paper ventured some criticism about American policy or culture, an American publication was sure to repeat the comment and quite possibly magnify it, and none more consistently and with less veiled delight than Hearst's ever vigilant International News Service. That is why concerns were exchanged between the Quai d'Orsay in Paris and the embassy in Washington about the downside of a free press. Neither the minister nor the ambassador was much pleased in February 1920, for example, when some French papers got close to labeling the ailing President Wilson as "pro-German." Whatever Americans thought of their president, they did not much like foreigners being vocal in their criticism.[11] Neither did they appreciate some of the satirical work by French caricaturists and popular song writers, work aimed at deflating American pretensions. For that matter, neither did Jusserand, who dismissed such mischief as the work of people who feared France might be short of enemies, nor his minister, Alexandre Millerand, who did what he could to counsel restraint on a headstrong French press.[12] And certainly in the 1920s, when France and America were arguing over wartime costs and associated loans, it did not help to read reports of a gambling explosion in the French capital, or of a speculative fever on the French Bourse, or of American flags being booed during the 1924 summer Olympics in Paris.[13]

A fourth factor at play, an extension of the role of the popular media, was the French perspective on postwar American culture. In many ways, of course, this was a continuation of the attitudes that had prevailed both before and during the recent war. And those attitudes were not monochrome. Generalizing, as we must, French writers saw much that was appealing in American society. Academics and nonacademics alike continued to praise the energy, the youthfulness, the openness to novelty, the efficiencies, the vast human and material resources, that accounted for that country's great power status by the time the war had ended. More than that, people like André Maurois found an intellectual vibrancy as well, in circles where ideas were respected and where truly "cultivated" Americans and French were each other's equals. America, he proclaimed, was more than a culture of "bathrooms, central heating, and refrigerators."[14]

The distinguished academic André Siegfried obviously agreed. A frequent visitor to American university campuses, he admired much of what he found in the United States, including a productive process that was unrivaled anywhere in the world. That said, however, Siegfried has also been seen as illustrative of French perceptions of America as essentially a "process," an assembly line driven by production and consumption.[15] Another Franco-American champion agreed. The eminent Cardinal Baudrillart, for all of his efforts to court Catholic opinion in America, secretly found most Americans to be loud, insecure, ignorant, materialistic, and machine obsessed. Others, often inspired by their own visits to the New World in the 1920s offered new chapters of criticism. These included Lucien Romier's *Qui sera le maître*, Georges Duhamel's *Scènes de la vie future*, and the unequivocally titled *Le cancer américain,* by René Aron and Arnaud Dandieu. Through them all ran apprehensions about a mechanistic, philistine culture, which had limited appreciation of things cerebral and aesthetic. Also present was an underlying fear that this was indeed the way of the future, the rest of the world trailing in America's wake. As Baudrillart confided to his diary, since there was so little to learn from Americans, it would be a mistake to try to imitate them.[16]

Finally, and of an entirely different order, the foregoing collection of attitudes and perceptions have to be contextualized within a range of specific financial and political issues. Here we have the fifth factor, or the fifth set of challenges, that confronted French opinion shapers in the years following the war. These, together with the previous four, complete the complex and fundamentally distressing conditions within which French propagandists were obliged to work in the early postwar period.

Issues arising from the Paris Peace Conference were certainly central to the troubled peacetime atmosphere. Entering the process as de facto allies,

French and American participants soon stumbled upon several fields of friction. The former were more intent on affirming German responsibility for the war, more determined to exact stiff financial reparations from their defeated enemy, more resolved to ensure their future security through strict enforcement of Germany's disarmed condition. The Americans, in the form of their president, Woodrow Wilson, were more attuned to the risks of poisoning the future peace with too much emphasis on guilt, fiscal compensation, and armed deterrence, and to the promise of setting up an international organization capable of ensuring the peace through negotiation and compromise. And just as French observers had predicted even before the end of hostilities, the Americans were anxious to restore prewar economic prosperity by reestablishing trade relations with defeated enemies and by recovering the massive amounts of private and public capital that they had invested in the Anglo-French military effort since 1914.[17]

Neither set of expectations lacked a rationale. No sophisticated discussion of collective responsibility for the war could erase the fact that France had indeed been invaded in August 1914. Nothing short of casuistry could conceal or minimize the extent of material damage to northeastern France, where hundreds of tiny villages had disappeared along with churches and factories, schools and hospitals, mines and rail lines. The costs of reconstruction alone would be immense, even before one had to address the heavy charges associated with the enduring work on behalf of orphans and refugees, with pensions and medical care for millions of disabled veterans, with compensation for war widows and their children. These, on top of the astronomical sums spent on the war itself, meant that the Third Republic entered the postwar period on extremely tenuous financial ground. Already warindebted to the United Kingdom and to the United States, and reluctant to impose too heavy a postwar tax burden on a citizenry that had suffered so much, after November 1918 the government compounded its fiscal plight by further borrowing from abroad. By 1920 France owed between 3 billion and 4 billion dollars to the United States.[18]

Most Americans, it seems, thought that the debt should be paid, and in a timely fashion. Inspired by an intense desire to put the war behind them, some by a determination to stay out of European affairs forever and others by a belief that the League of Nations was the only means with which to avert future war, no American knew the visceral feeling triggered by a powerful, border enemy. This Atlantic-wide sense of security made it easier for them to contemplate accommodation with the Germans, especially with the new democratic regime of Weimar and, at the same time, to nourish frustrations with a France too fearful and recalcitrant. Neither did they appreciate the Paris-floated arguments that France warranted special treatment because of its enormous material and human sacrifice to the Allied cause, or that her debt payments should be contingent upon receipt of German reparations. A debt, after all, was a debt. Nor did they like the French government's efforts to shut out foreign contractors from the lucrative tasks of postwar construction. In all, therefore, it took little time before the Franco-American wartime "association" found itself under intense postwar American scrutiny.

It was under French examination as well. In Paris, they attributed the steady decline of the franc to a combination of national indebtedness, Germany's sluggish reparation payments, and hard-line creditors in America; it was a decline that decreased not only their purchasing power for imported goods but also, ironically, their capacity to pay France's debts. Neither did they appreciate the escalation of American tariff policy, a strategy designed to protect American producers from foreign competitors with "the highest trade barriers in American history."[19] André Tardieu, former high commissioner in wartime America, articulated much of this resentment in a hard-hitting book of 1927. Drawing upon his personal experiences in Washington, Tardieu was positive about many things American, but not all. America, he said, had become the principal beneficiary of the war, a nation that had profited financially during the period of neutrality, the period of engagement, and the period of peace. Lest there be any doubt, "everything that Europe lost, America has gained." But that was not all. Given France's heavy indebtedness to the United States, 60 percent of Germany's anticipated reparation payments to France would be funneled to France's creditor, America—which was to say that monies destined for repair of France's devastated regions would end up in the hands of the "richest and most prosperous of the belligerents." And if that were not enough, French citizens were subjected to patronizing counsel from America to the effect that a smaller army, a higher tax base, and a more modest lifestyle were the answers to their financial plight. That is why, he ventured, Europe "has not a kind word for the United States. . . . Once the idol of Europe, she is today without a single worshipper."[20]

The notion that France's military establishment was even partly to blame for that country's predicament was especially abrasive to authorities in Paris. Not only were the army and navy alleged to be too large and expensive in their own right, but they were now implicated in the nation's alleged imperialist ambitions in Europe and abroad, its exaggerated fear of Germany, and its suspected determination to exact revenge for 1914. Given repeated French denials of any wish for *revanche*, or for territorial expansion anywhere, every whisper to the contrary met with an even louder denial. Truthfully, the Americans were less concerned about the size of France's continental army than about the strength of her high seas fleet, a concern that peaked during the Washington Naval Conference of 1921–1922. Although part of a broader disarmament strategy designed to avert a postwar naval race, the formula worked out in Washington seemed to be particularly disadvantageous to the French. Or so it seemed to the Quai d'Orsay. When it came to capital ships, not only was France to be nudged into fourth place, behind America, Britain and Japan, but she was reduced to sharing that place with Italy—a resolution that the French regarded as particularly humiliating.[21] Conveniently overlooking the ascent of the Japanese, French diplomats and media observers easily discerned the subtle and malicious hand of "les Anglo-Saxons"—still further evidence, in their eyes, of the ungrateful and uncomprehending spirit that seemed to have infected British and American attitudes toward their former ally.

In sum, there was no mistaking the fact that the postwar world seemed to the French to be almost as hostile as when the guns had been firing. Germany, the former foe, was unrepentant and was as interested in inflaming Franco-American relations as was Britain, a former ally. Some Francophiles apart, Americans seemed increasingly indifferent to French security but increasingly alive to an apprehended state of French belligerence. The postwar costs looked astronomical, especially in the light of a foundering franc that made imports more expensive; and what benefits a weaker currency might have had for exports were nullified by American tariff legislation. Finally, there was the growing uneasiness with the power of American capital, American technology, and American production techniques and, broadly, with the intrusiveness of American culture. All that, from debts to culture, was raised for public discussion, complaint, and ridicule by a French press mindful of national pride and the imperative of selling papers. And all that, in turn, was duly reprised by American press syndicates equally mindful of pride and profits.

As if such were not enough to confound the promotion of healthy relations between France and America, there was yet one more enduring complication that, since it was not peculiar to Franco-American relations, is addressed here as prologue to a discussion of propaganda. Tersely put, that complication was postwar cynicism about the "news" and about the agencies that had controlled and delivered it. The fact was that wartime experience, early in France, later in America, had taught many lessons to the recipients, as well as to the manipulators, of information. As the French had learned in the first year of the war, sometimes it was more damaging to stifle news than to manage its release, especially when no news from official quarters might mean its fabrication by unofficial quarters. Thereafter, the central issue became one of determining how much information ought to be released, when, and to whom.

In America, even during the period of neutrality, one could trace a growing skepticism about the reliability of information that had passed into the public sphere and about the motives behind that passage. In particular, there had been a widespread fear that foreign propagandists might dupe Washington into entering the war. After 1917, with that fear partially substantiated by American engagement in the war, the mood hardened against foreign maneuverings, a mood to which the ever cautious Jules Jusserand made constant reference. But the cynicism hit full-blown when postwar revelations made it clear just how energetic and ambitious America's own Committee on Public Information had been. It was in the 1920s that Americans learned how their minds had been marshaled and their emotions aroused in the interests of a united war effort. And they learned that their government, media, educators, and clergy had been complicit in that national cause. However accepting most may have been of the end result, with America out of the war, victorious, in a year and a half, the clock would never be turned back. From the 1920s onward, everyone would encounter, and themselves repeat, the phrase "You can't believe a word you read." So widespread was this black sentiment that one scholar has found it appropriate to attribute the "debasement of the word" to experiences between 1914 and 1918; and to that end he quotes one jaded British propagandist, the celebrated writer Rudyard Kipling, father of a son killed in the war: "If any question why we died. Tell them, because our fathers lied."[22] All told, practitioners of the word were going to have a difficult time in the postwar world.

So much for the field of obstacles that confronted postwar propagandists in general and, in our case, those of France in particular. How, then, did they address the central issue of promoting healthy Franco-American relations in the 1920s, and what stratagems and devices were used to surmount the obstacles? To answer those questions, one must first return to the foreign ministry's evolving institutional infrastructure, the machinery that was put in place to implement a national public relations strategy.

World War I left the foreign ministry unchanged in only one respect. The minister, and his personal cabinet, remained at the apex of the bureaucratic pyramid and served as the critical link to the premier and other government ministers. Thereafter, change abounded. It was in 1915 that there had appeared the office of the secretary-general, an office awarded to the ministry's highest ranking civil servant. Between 1915 and 1940 four men occupied this office: Jules Cambon, Maurice Paléologue, Philippe Berthelot, and Alexis Saint-Léger Léger; and it was to each of them in succession that responsibility fell for the day-to-day affairs of the ministry. Beneath them, in turn, was a collection of different *services* and *directions*, the most important being the Direction des affaires politiques et commerciales. The latter, a prewar creation, had a total of three directors in the 1920s, all of them career diplomats. Those three were Emmanuel Peretti de la Rocca, Jules Laroche, and Charles Corbin; and under their charge operated four geographical *sous-directions*, one for Europe, a second for Asia-Pacific, a third for Africa–Middle East, and a fourth—central to our purposes—for all the Americas.

In 1920 two new services were created beneath the level of the four subdirectorates. One was the Service français de la Société des nations, an organism charged with responsibility for the nascent League of Nations. The other, and pivotal to this study, was a replacement for the prewar Bureau des écoles, and the two wartime agencies, the Maison de la Presse, and the Commissariat for Information. This new body, created by decree in January 1920, was awarded the title Service des Oeuvres françaises à l'étranger. It was, in fact, France's latest edition of a propaganda service. Or rather it was a principal component in the government's plan to preserve the propaganda momentum in peacetime, with the help of certain allied agencies within and beyond the Quai d'Orsay. As for the personnel of Oeuvres, they were expected to work in close liaison with their own ministerial colleagues in the newly structured Service d'information et de presse, an agency that reported directly to the minister's office and that had two responsibilities.[23] One was to provide reliable information to the foreign press, either directly to journalists based in Paris or indirectly through the services of the embassies and consulates abroad. The other was to monitor and analyze foreign press coverage of France, with a view to ensuring informed ministerial decision making in Paris.[24] As for allied agencies outside the foreign ministry, Oeuvres personnel expected to work with the education ministry's new Service universitaire des relations culturelles avec l'étranger, with the ministry of fine arts' Service d'action artistique à l'étranger, and with the tourism department at the ministry of commerce.

Given the reaffirmed, postwar emphasis on the importance of cultural propaganda abroad, the Service des Oeuvres was the command post of the foreign ministry's promotional efforts abroad and the crucial link with similarly charged departments in other ministries. Commencing its history with a staff of twenty, including one *chef du service*, this agency comprised four sections based on function and geography. One, the Section universitaire des écoles, assumed responsibility for educational interests abroad. A second did the same for matters artistic and literary, as did the third for matters relating to tourism, sport, and cinema. A fourth section, abbreviated to Diverses, attended to subject areas that were not obviously part of the duties of its sister sections—areas, for example, such as religious and charity functions abroad. Each section, in turn, included a number of geographical desks, roughly corresponding to the four geographical divisions within the Directorate of Political and Commercial Affairs. Housed on the rue François Premier, once the headquarters of the now defunct Maison de la Presse, Oeuvres fell under the directorship of four career diplomats in the 1920s: Albert Milhaud, Jean Giraudoux, Emile Naggiar, and Fernand Pila.[25]

Their mission, it must be emphasized, was far removed from that which has been called "black" propaganda. Following the by-now-traditional strictures of senior voices such as that of Ambassador Jusserand, the men and women of Oeuvres engaged in no lies, or even in immoderate exaggeration. True believers in the particular virtues of French culture, they saw their role as primarily an instructional one, namely, first to teach the world about, and then to remind it of, France's especial genius. To that end, Oeuvres would be a "center of advice and support" for artists and intellectuals worldwide, an objective that explains its four-part internal structure. And to call it a "mission" seems perfectly apt, given the beliefs that animated it:

> Our literature, our art, our civilization of the intellect, our ideas, have exercised across the ages a powerful attraction on other nations. Our universities and our schools abroad are veritable centers of propaganda for France. [This] intellectual penetration abroad [amounts to] one of the most powerful forms of influence we have worldwide.[26]

Inspired by this conviction, French propagandists trusted that the steady promotion of France as the cultural capital of the world, as a country committed to ideas and aesthetic pursuits, was the best way to plant seeds of goodwill. Differences, ephemeral ones over frontiers or trade or armaments, among nations were bound to arise and dissipate, but underneath the differences there might always be a deep layer of respect and, ideally, of admiration.

While that aspiration certainly applied to France's relations with the United States, it was not confined to it. The mission, indeed, was global in scope; and from what fragmentary evidence exists, there is reason to believe Oeuvres budgets in the 1920s gave higher priority to European and Asian countries than to the United States.[27] Whether such ranking reflected a reluctance to recognize the arrival of America on the world stage, or whether it had to do with the costs of an enterprise in which the franc had suffered against the dollar, is difficult to say. Nonetheless, the presence of America certainly had made itself felt, both as wartime ally and postwar creditor; and of this the Quai d'Orsay was fully aware. While concerns were expressed in Paris, and among American Francophiles, about the sluggishness of France's propaganda campaign, those expressions also reflected a determination to address the issue. Two Paris-based, state-supported, religious organizations proved particularly adamant about the need for the foreign ministry to combat German postwar propaganda in the United States. On the one hand, while war-experienced Catholic propagandists decried the ongoing "campaign of horrible lies spread by German-American Catholics," their counterparts in the Comité protestant de propagande française à l'étranger continued to circulate their own postwar *Bulletin* in America, a publication frankly if privately defined as "un instrument de propagande." Without such initiatives, these organizations believed, German propaganda would continue to have a field day in America.[28]

But it was far more than a question of will. Part of the problem in America in the early 1920s was that there were too many chefs in the kitchen. Jusserand remained at his post in Washington, apprehensive about hostile propaganda but determined not to stoop to the level of France's antagonists. What happened in the nation's capital he could largely control, but New York was another matter. There, a bewildering collection of state-sponsored agencies competed with one another over rights and responsibilities for propaganda work in America. Lest this text appear as complex as the reality it seeks to engage, we can confine ourselves for the moment to a simple identification of those agencies. One was the office of the consul-general, a man named Gaston Liebert, and a man with very pronounced propaganda ambitions. Another, for a time, was the Office of French Services in the United States, a postwar successor to Tardieu's High Commission. Under the direction of Maurice Casenave, this office sought to coordinate French propaganda activities in the United States, principally through its own information service run by Marcel Rouffie, another veteran of French promotion in America. But the High Commission had left more than a single heir, including a restructured Official Bureau of French Information under Marcel Knecht, and a French Press Bureau under Henri-Martin Barzun.[29] Together, though rarely in tandem, these multiple offices and officers displayed greater taste for direct action than did the cautious Jusserand in Washington.

For his part, this long-serving ambassador understood the challenges confronting France in America, challenges intensified by the work of foreign propagandists. Some of the latter enjoyed close links to the 5-million-to-6-million strong German American communities. It was no secret, he reported in September 1920, that this immigrant vote was likely to go to the Republican presidential candidate, Warren Harding, and against Wilsonian Democrats. Neither had he missed the intense activity of British propagandists, whose efforts were backed by better funding and more personnel than that available to French agents. And had he done so, the destructive impact of British propaganda before and during the Washington Naval Conference of 1921–1922 would, in itself, have sufficed to dispel any remaining doubts.[30] Indeed, again and again the ambassador pleaded for more resources: better and more timely information from Paris, a well-qualified financial adviser for the embassy, and some relief for what he called the ministry's "distressing parsimony." Of particular importance, he observed, was the need to consolidate the diverse and competing agencies that operated in New York.[31]

That said, there remained the danger of an overreaction. The truth was, or so he believed, that subtle and understated information provision remained more effective than messages that were crude in content and obvious in delivery. Throughout 1920 and 1921 he reminded his superiors that much of the American press, from Washington to Kansas City, was fully mindful of German treaty violations and of German defaults on reparation payments; and he took heart from an early interview with President Harding's new secretary of state, Charles Evans Hughes, who said that his public utterances on behalf of France actually understated the strength of his affection for that recovering country.[32] However, returning to a familiar refrain, Jusserand warned that there were reasons for France's measured success. First was the message. She had presented herself as firm but fair, as dignified in peace as she had been in war, industrious in her efforts to rebuild, prudent in public expenditure.[33] Second, under his watch, she had done everything to avoid the appearance of unseemly pressure on American authorities or inappropriate manipulation of American public opinion. That was just as well, he reminded his minister, for in 1922–1923 there had been a domestic crescendo against the activities of foreign-inspired propaganda. Hughes himself had publicly condemned citizens who seemed bent on reintroducing European squabbles to American soil; and the Republican National Committee had issued a similarly critical statement on the risks implicit in propaganda from abroad. That was why it was so important that France avoid any reckless word or deed.[34]

It was also one of the reasons why the ambassador was so upset with the consul-general in New York, Gaston Liebert. There had been a history of little abrasions between the two, most of them about oversights and minor indiscretions detected by the ambassador. But there were also some substantial matters, including Jusserand's belief that consuls-general were to confine their work to commercial relations and not interfere in the conduct of diplomacy.[35] More serious, however, was Jusserand's identification of Liebert as the principal local critic of French propaganda strategy in America. One of the ambassador's reports to Paris proved a measure of his exasperation. In January 1923 he used a positive article on France by the *New York Times* as evidence of the baselessness of Liebert's complaints about inaction. Indeed, Jusserand went further, accusing Liebert of deliberately misrepresenting American press coverage in order to strengthen his case for bolder propaganda initiatives.[36]

Whatever truth there was in the latter charge, it was clear that Liebert openly dissented from Jusserand's views on propaganda. The consul-general not only believed that energy was lacking, he also thought that too much reliance had been placed on American Francophiles. In accordance with that view, he had pushed aggressively for a New York–based information service that could counteract German and British propaganda.[37] By early 1923 he had his wish. One postwar creation, the Official French Information Office, had been wrapped up; he had been named director of a new French Information Bureau located on Madison Avenue; and two New York papers, the *Times* and the *Sun*, promptly complained. France, they feared, was turning reckless, abandoning its formerly judicious approach to information provision in favor of "official propaganda," an accusation that Liebert believed had been inspired by a hostile informant in Washington.[38]

The bureau, he told the *Sun*, was, if anything, the negation of propaganda. Indeed, if the latter were the equivalent of poison, accurate information was its only effective antidote—the provision of which, he protested, was the bureau's only purpose. Likening it to the British information service in New York, Liebert proclaimed that he would be putting "true, real, indisputable . . . facts and figures" before the American public. *Facts, Figures, and Weekly News*, indeed, became the bureau's official bulletin. A form letter that accompanied the first issue notified recipients that the information contained therein had been prepared "from a purely objective point of view" and without the slightest intention of influencing public opinion "in any way." All that its authors wished to do was inform American newspapers and magazines, American business institutions, and the American public at large.[39] To that end, from the spring of 1923 until at least the autumn of 1924, the bulletin sought to inform its readers on every subject central to France's interests, from the diplomatic and military to the economic and technological. But there was no mistaking its edge. Readers often were treated to reminders of German wartime atrocities and to fact-filled denials of Germany's inability to pay reparations.[40] Conversely, France received a much better press, of the sort that assured Americans of France's unblotched record as a colonial power. Drawing upon the language of an unimpeachable source such as the French colonial minister, *Facts and Figures* assured readers that France had "brought with her wherever she spread herself . . . a tradition of humaneness and justice, inspired by her racial temperament, a Christian spirit, and a total absence of race or colour prejudice."[41]

Within a year of the bulletin's creation, messages such as these were being sent out to some two thousand organizations in the United States and some eight newspapers and magazines; and by June 1924 the figure had risen to three thousand recipients, including those in Canada, Mexico, and Cuba. As proof of its effectiveness, in January 1924 Liebert provided numerous examples of items from the bulletin that had been reproduced by papers ranging from the *Troy Times* and *Providence News* to the *New York Times* and the *Christian Science Monitor*, some of them relying heavily on the text of the original articles. Nor was Liebert content to rely solely on the impact of *Facts and Figures*. Individual items, such as translated texts of ministerial speeches in France, were also dispatched to a wide assortment of American media, including the *Wall Street Journal*, the *Literary Digest*, and *Forbes Magazine*; and detailed data were placed at the disposal of Francophile academics setting off on lecture tours of the United States.[42] Indeed, university professors across America—in Ohio, Michigan, Illinois, Minnesota, Rhode Island, and Massachusetts—were often recipients of the bureau's information, sometimes at their own request, sometimes not. The end result, Liebert maintained, was that his work was constantly providing a "corrective" to the often inaccurate information that kept appearing in the American media. It was the bureau, he insisted, that offered Americans the only English-language periodical delivered from a French perspective, including the exaltation of France's literature and art.[43]

But not everyone was impressed by Gaston Liebert and the French Information Bureau. Until the end of his posting in late 1924, and his subsequent retirement, Jules Jusserand remained apprehensive about the new wave in propaganda. Some of his confidantes shared those views, including one American who reckoned the consul-general was a "damned fool" who had "more brains in his shoes" than in his head. Others decided that the bureau was too expensive for the results it produced, and that it was a prime target for accusations against French propaganda in a country grown sensitive to foreign influences.[44] One prominent, and public, critic was Frank Pavey, president of the Federation of the Alliance Française in the United States and Canada, who feared that his organization of two hundred chapters and eighteen thousand members might be associated with the perception of the bureau as a propaganda agency.[45] Writing to Liebert in June 1924, Pavey said bluntly that the bureau's "status is fundamentally and inherently wrong in principle. No foreign government ought to be allowed to maintain any such office within the limits of the United States." To which Liebert, not one to turn away from an argument, responded with a complaint that Pavey had long resisted efforts to accelerate France's information service, and with a retort that he had never, ever, meddled in American politics. There was nothing, he said, of the "occult" in the bureau's activities.[46]

There was more truth to this defense than to the claim that the bureau was objective in its perspective. Nevertheless, Liebert's time had run out. Early in 1925 he was sent off as French minister to Havana, to the great pleasure of one Wall Street Francophile, who judged disastrous the whole history of the bureau. But for a short time, the disaster loomed even larger. In late May, word appeared that Liebert's successor would carry the title of director of French propaganda services in the United States, an exceptionally incompetent appellation given American sensitivity about propaganda. In fact, nothing came of it. The bureau met a quiet death, partly as a result of outraged complaints from other New York Francophiles. Early in June, the vice president of the France-America Society wrote to Emile Daeschner, Jusserand's successor.[47] The very idea of publicly proclaimed propaganda was folly, declared Frederick Cunliffe-Owen, a man who knew something about subtle communication. If it was to be done at all, it had to be done à la Jusserand, without "drum or trumpet" and with "enormous tact and supreme delicacy."[48] But in the end, and for awhile, the ministry decided against running an information service independent of the embassy and consulates. Instead, it undertook a time-consuming, two-pronged survey of French propaganda in America—one headed by Gaston Bergery, the other by Raymond Patenôtre—and in the interim reendorsed the prudent strategy and method of the retired Jusserand.[49]

Central to both, strategy and method, was a continued reliance on the sympathetic understanding of prominent American Francophiles, many of them active members of the France-America Society, and Anne Morgan's New York–based American Committee for Reconstruction of Devastated France.

Throughout the 1920s, there was a constant Francophilic effort by names familiar to us from the war years, even the prewar years: Nicolas Murray Butler, Frederick Coudert, John Finley, William Guthrie, J. P. Morgan Jr., George Peabody, George Wickersham, and Louis Wiley. Academics, lawyers, journalists, financiers, these were men of proven loyalty to healthy Franco-American relations. But there were others among this same cohort of Francophiles, some, such as Myron Herrick and Thomas Lamont, who worked with Coudert, Finley, Guthrie, and others in the American Society of the French Legion of Honor; and others still, such as Gilbert Chinard, James Hazen Hyde, Frank Pavey, Felix Weill, and Leroy White, who devoted their energies to the continent-wide Federation of the Alliance Française.

Nevertheless, such organizations and individuals represented but the tip of the iceberg, for legion were the names recorded in Paris of men and women whose sympathy for France was enduring. A few examples must suffice. There were men such as Laurence Adler, a journalist with the *North American Review*, who had defended France's occupation of the Ruhr Valley in January 1923, as had the retired secretary of state, Bainbridge Colby. There was Frederick Allen, a New York lawyer who in May 1924 delivered a Francophilic speech to the American Academy of Political and Social Science. There was Edward Bell, political editor of the *Chicago Tribune*, and Otis F. Wood, head of a prominent press agency and prime mover in efforts to construct a brand-new commerce-and-culture-focused "Maison Française" in the heart of New York City. There was Samuel Gompers of the American Federation of Labor, who, in January 1924, published an article defending French action in the Ruhr and warning of German capitalist incursions in America. Employers could be equally sympathetic. Take, for example, the business promoter Julius Bache, whose *Bache Review* supported France's stand on reparations, or the president of Detroit's Packard Motor Company, Henry B. Joy, who, unbidden and at his own expense, published a volume of pro-French articles. Churchmen, too, could be equally outspoken about their positive feelings for France, among them Monseigneur Curley, archbishop of Baltimore; Abbé Ernest Dimnet, a priest long associated with Yale University Press, and Dr. Charles Macfarland, general secretary of the New York-based Federal Council of Churches.[50]

Women, too, proved themselves eager volunteers in the service of a country for which they obviously felt great affinity: Mrs. Charles H. Max, a key figure in the founding of the postwar French Hospital in New York; Mrs. Keyes, wife of Harvard-educated New Hampshire senator Henry W. Keyes, who had written a sympathetic piece in *Good Housekeeping*, not coincidentally with data provided to her by the French embassy; Miss Marjorie Nott, the daughter of a university president, who in 1924 volunteered her services as propagandist; Mrs. Minor, the general president of the Daughters of the American Revolution—an organization that Jusserand regarded as a "precious asset for friendship with France."[51]

And there were still other American-run organizations and agencies that worked to combat the forces of Francophobia, whether indigenous or foreign. These included the New York State Chamber of Commerce and, particularly, the French section of the New York Bankers' Trust. Frequently, another source of support was the American Legion, an organization of veterans whose distrust of the recent German enemy remained active throughout the 1920s. In April 1927, early in his ambassadorship, Paul Claudel described that body and its 3-million membership as "one of the most reliable forces" on which France could count.[52] And then there were the educational and cultural agencies, American-run but with missions to promote a knowledge of French civilization. These, too, were numerous, but worthy of special mention in this decade would be the on-campus Maisons Françaises at Columbia University in New York and at the Universities of Chicago and Wisconsin. It was in such facilities that French-language libraries could be found, information bulletins published, residence provided, and—in the case of French nationals studying in America—financial resources located. Of similar instructional thrust was the Institut Français in New York, an organization founded in 1911 and destined for a major expansion in the course of 1924–1925. Like the campus-based *maisons*, the institute offered its members a wide range of activities and information, including lecture series on French subject matter, library resources, a French-language bulletin on the latest news from France and, as part of the postwar expansion, an art gallery highlighting local and touring French art.[53]

In addition to these American-run organizations, from France-Amérique to the French Institute, there were other agencies that operated in the United States but did so with personnel who were more directly linked to French officialdom in Paris. There was, for example, Gustave de la Jarrie, editor of the English-language *French Colonial Digest*, a bulletin produced under Liebert's French Information Bureau; just as there were Firmin Guego and H. P. Sampers, journalist and publisher, respectively, of New York's French-language and France-subsidized paper, *Le Courrier des Etats-Unis*. More obvious still were the tireless Monseigneur Baudrillart and Abbé Monod, of the government-subsidized Comité catholique and Comité protestant, respectively, as well as Monsieur J. Perret, director of the French Tourist Bureau in New

York, and thus the person responsible for that body's monthly bulletin *Le Voyageur en France*. Less obvious, but clear enough, were French academics— people like Bernard Fay, Albert Feuillerat, and Charles Cestre—who voyaged frequently between France and the United States, executing cross-continent lecture tours or taking up longer-term residence in institutions such as Columbia, Harvard, Stanford, or prestigious women's colleges, among them Vassar, Bryn Mawr, and Wellesley.

Indeed, the foreign ministry certainly continued to express a belief in the power of the spoken word, particularly when delivered by people whose names were known in America. Between 1920 and 1926 Americans were treated to a succession of visiting French personalities, not one of whom missed an opportunity to clarify France's perspective and massage its reputation. There were marshals and generals, for example, Fayolle, Nivelle, Taufflieb, and Foch, as well as the veteran America-observer Captain Pechkoff. There were ex-premiers—Briand, Clemenceau, and Viviani. And there was an endless train of other officially sponsored, and subsidized, visitors: concert musicians such as Mme Ganna Walska McCormick and Nadia Boulanger; such editors as Georges Lechartier of the *Journal des Debats*; French-language teachers, among them Marguerite Clément; and Jean Sapène, representing the Société des films de France.

Indeed, whatever its belief in the power of words, through lectures, press articles, and interviews, the Quai d'Orsay was also mindful of the importance of visual imagery. In an early postwar note on the need for an improved propaganda agency in America, one that would specialize in photographs and cinema, Edmond Ratisbonne warned the cinema section of Oeuvres that time was pressing. French films, in particular, were already losing ground to American film products, a condition that would worsen unless the bare-bones facilities in New York were expanded. Himself a veteran of the army's wartime photographic department, he urged the diplomats to acquire materials from the war ministry—slides, photographs, and films—that could be distributed to American schools, universities, museums, and Francophilic societies, and published in the country's newspapers and magazines. Well-chosen images of every aspect of French life, he said, had the greatest potential for satisfying the ministry's need for "discreet propaganda."[54]

It appears from the archival record now extant that these pleas had some effect. By October 1921 a restructured Bureau de cinématographie et de projection was operating in New York under the familiar figure of Maurice Casenave and his superiors at Oeuvres in Paris. With a view to avoiding any hint of malevolent foreign propaganda, the bureau put forth the operational premise that all the materials supplied by Paris were either for rent or for purchase by Americans who knew what they were doing.[55] But it is apparent that the bureau experienced growing pains. In early 1922 it was placed under the authority of the consul general in New York, and the experienced Edmond Ratisbonne was asked to provide its daily direction on a monthly office subvention of seven hundred dollars. Thereafter, in the mid–1920s, the history of this photographic-cinematic service becomes murkier. All that is clear is that the tide of American film production and distribution was rising faster than that of its French competitors.[56] And with it, too often, came a waterline of anti-French detritus. *Beau Geste*, Hollywood's scathing impression of the French Foreign Legion, was a case in point, one that prompted a polite embassy appeal to Will Hays, president of the Motion Pictures Producers and Distributors of America, for cuts in the film. Ambassador Claudel was more outspoken. Without naming the film, Claudel publicly condemned what he called the "abuses" committed by the American film industry and characterized some filmmakers as both "ignorant and malevolent."[57] It was a cry that would be repeated again and again as French diplomats squirmed under the weight of an ever more popular, foreign-dominated medium that too often, they thought, indulged in unhelpful caricatures of France and its people.[58]

Struggling to compete in a field so heavily influenced by American, British, and German capital, struggling with a national currency that was foundering until the second half of the decade, and struggling with the task of resolving competing propaganda priorities around the globe, the foreign ministry stuck to its time-tested strategy in America. Its Service d'information et de presse in Paris provided American journalists there with opportunities for daily interviews and with sheaves of data and analyses prepared by ministerial experts. Its Oeuvres offices ensured hospitable receptions for visiting Americans from the fields of arts and letters and for students registered in French educational institutions. Oeuvres also controlled the number and level of subventions that would go to individuals and organizations operating under its mandate.

Once again, it is not possible to provide a complete list of those subventions; however, a judicious sampling will suggest something about the range of its activities. In 1921, for example, money was found to support the operation of two American publications. One was an illustrated, French-language magazine called *La France*. Another was a monthly bulletin, published by a group of Francophile financiers, called the *Fortnightly Review of French Economic Conditions*. In 1922, one of the recipients of ministerial money was La Bienvenue Française, an organization aimed at promoting international intellectual exchange. The following year the ministry funded the trip of Abbé Viollet to attend a national conference of social work in America, partly on the grounds that this churchman had worked with American organizations during the war and had been invited to the conference by the American Red Cross. And every year, the Federation of the Alliance Française could count on substantial financial support from the Quai d'Orsay—an enduring support that reflected the belief of people like Claudel that there was no better investment for French propaganda in America.[59]

Meanwhile, the ministry's ambassador in Washington, and consuls across America, did their best not only to follow the course of events there, but also to influence both elite and popular opinion in subtle but enduring ways. Solicited meetings with journalists, editors, and publishers were designed to put France's best foot forward, as were corrective letters to editors, the granting of interviews, the provision of formal press releases, and the distribution of officially endorsed publications from France. To the ambassador and consuls fell tasks great and small, from the reception of their own prime minister on American soil, to the tracking down of a suitable French tenor for the Washington opera. To them was accorded responsibility for the official face of France in America; and to that end, personnel from the embassy and consulates attended one public function after another: anniversary celebrations of the Daughters of the American Revolution; chapter meetings of the Alliance Française in St. Louis, or San Francisco, or New Orleans; banquets of France-Amérique; national celebrations on 4 and 14 July; conventions of the American Legion; openings of an art gallery in Chicago, or of an opera at the Metropolitan in New York; the awarding of prizes and medals to American students who had excelled in the French language. In short, there was an endless stream of public occasions when the presence of a French diplomat, the ensuing photograph in the local paper, and the text of his address to the assembled gathering were all efforts to underscore the bond between the two countries. This, indeed, was what it was all about, the goal of trying to keep Franco-American relations stable and positive below the continuing surface eruptions over such matters as debts and disarmament.

By 1927 there were signs of some recovery in those relations. It is doubtful, however, whether a great deal of credit should be attributed to the French propaganda campaign—a campaign that authorities in Paris knew was still being troubled by underfunded information services in America.[60] Rather, the hint of improvement derived from an apparently dramatic idea. In the spring of 1926, Premier and Foreign Minister Aristide Briand had first floated the notion of an international agreement to outlaw any future resort to war; and given the growing importance of the United States in world affairs, as well as the suspicions still entertained there about France's alleged militarism, he proposed that this commitment be expressed by means of a bilateral Franco-American convention. By the time of Paul Claudel's arrival in America, early in 1927, an opening of sorts seemed to be in the works. And it was a timely one, for the consul in Chicago was worried about the anti-European sentiment that seemed to have settled over the American Midwest. Except, that is, in the case of Germany, which enjoyed a privileged position.[61] The Briand proposal, Claudel believed, had the potential to improve the situation because it allowed France to remind Americans just how much France hated war. As he said himself in a public address that autumn, "[W]ar is for us what yellow fever once was for South America, and earthquakes are for Japan." For us, he said, opposition to war is "relentless and passionate."[62]

The evolution of what came to be known in France as the Briand-Kellogg Pact, however, was not trouble free. Frank Kellogg, the American secretary of state, encouraged by his president, Calvin Coolidge, was apprehensive of an exclusively bilateral accord with France and delayed negotiations until it was agreed that a multilateral convention was the ultimate goal.[63] For a while, early in 1928, those delays incurred the wrath of the French media, which, in turn, prompted Claudel to complain of journalists who willfully set out to irritate America at a time when precisely the opposite was France's goal. Enough, he pleaded, of this "stupid criticism."[64] Happily, however, the crisis passed. A Franco-American arbitration treaty was signed in early February and dispatched for ratification by the French parliament and by the American Congress. Claudel's mood improved. For the following eleven months, until the American Senate ratified the treaty in January 1929, the ambassador's reports on American opinion were much more optimistic. By May 1928 he had detected an appreciable change in the way France was regarded; indeed, he went so far as to say that France was now "unanimously respected in the United States." Gone was most of the criticism of French militarism, and in its place was an esteem for France's pacifist commitment.[65] France suddenly had become the darling of the American media, a development that reflected widespread admiration across American public opinion. Even in the State Department and the White House, the frowns, whenever France was mentioned, had turned to smiles; and President Coolidge, despite his apparent distaste of Europe in general and of France in particular, was talking about the mutilateral renunciation of war as if it had been his own idea.[66]

This did not mean, as Claudel well understood, that the layers-deep residue of resentment over French war debts had been swept aside. Any illusions on that score would have disappeared in late 1928 as Coolidge was preparing to hand the reins to Herbert Hoover. In a particularly nasty speech to the diplomatic corps, the outgoing president attacked both Britain and France for their foot-dragging on war debts and naval disarmament, accusing them of ingratitude and bad faith.[67] Still, the critics of the Franco-American pact had become a minority, though a vociferous one, led by the Hearst chain and the *Chicago Tribune*; and when Senate ratification was announced in mid-January 1929, Claudel was satisfied that the critics had been discredited, especially in the eyes of the American public.[68] Indeed, there was now even reason for the ambassador to have second thoughts about the departing Coolidge, whose public remarks in February 1929 were much more conciliatory than those of three months before to the diplomatic community. The president, Claudel reminded his superiors, really had been central to the conclusion of the Franco-American accord; and whatever maladroitness one detected in his manner was probably a result of simple inexperience. The same was not true of Herbert Hoover, who, nonetheless, presented himself to French observers "not as a lion, but as a sphinx."[69]

Had the ambassador known the future, he would have chosen the current uncertainty. For the moment, the mood in mid–1929 America had improved, and France was a beneficiary of the change. But trouble was brewing again, and his resources for heading it off were limited. As for the latter, money remained tight and American sensitivity to the risks of foreign propaganda remained as high as ever. And whatever reprieve France now enjoyed in American eyes, key media voices remained shrill and unrepentant on many matters relating to the Third Republic, loud Continental voices heard in such newspapers as the *Washington Post,* the *Chicago Tribune,* and the *San Francisco Examiner*. Events in October 1929 offered grist for their mills. Briand, a tough politician recast as an apostle of peace, left the foreign ministry, and took with him a good part of France's recent reputation as a pacific power. Days later came the Wall Street crash, a massive financial failure that sent shock waves through the American and, subsequently, the global economy. Overnight, money became tight, as creditors either recovered their money by calling in their loans, or did not, and thus became debtors. Governments, like individuals, had to address the crisis; and like their citizens, they demanded a settling of accounts. By late 1929, France and America again seemed destined for a collision; and it seemed improbable that any word or image could ward off the inevitable.

CHAPTER 5

The End of the Postwar Period, 1930–1935

❖

The onset of the world Depression marked a new and painful chapter in the history of postwar Franco-American relations, a chapter that brought with it a host of arduous challenges for the propaganda agents in the French foreign ministry. The euphoria inspired by the Briand-Kellogg accord soon evaporated, leaving behind a collection of enduring irritants. Unsurprisingly, given the mounting economic crisis, money was the most abrasive of them all. The already decade-long combination of reparation issues, war debt issues, and trade issues remained as contentious as ever—indeed, more so, in the minds of now cash-strapped American taxpayers and American investment houses. And as if money questions were an insufficient impediment, there remained the still sensitive issue of international disarmament—the most obvious solution, in the eyes of its partisans worldwide, for averting another major war. But as had been the case for a decade, a distant and isolationist America was much keener on seeing a general reduction in European armaments than were the Europeans. While Americans saw armaments as a potential cause of armed squabbles on the Continent, Europe regarded them as symptoms of long-standing, historically confirmed tensions. For the Europeans, serious disarmament demanded a prologue, not an epilogue, of sustained political and economic reconciliation.

There were, to be sure, other issues that added more venom to this toxic mix. They may be regarded as secondary in nature, as long as the word is used with caution. For the fact is that divisive issues, like debts and disarmament, were repeatedly brought to the boiling point by unrestrained, public commentaries in both countries. Of greatest substance were the lingering cultural perceptions that informed so many appraisals of the other's policies.

Some French public commentators were adept at whipping up their readers, on matters such as French debts to the United States, by portraying a heartless, money-driven, self-serving America. In short, it was not simply a matter of the dollars owing, but rather the failure of Americans to recognize France's huge wartime sacrifices, or to admit that those sacrifices had saved Western civilization from Teutonic barbarism. Conversely, some American commentators, the perennial, sharp-tongued critics of French postwar policy, were no less adept at stirring their own readers. Why, they asked, should American taxpayers assume the costs of public loans to France, particularly when French taxpayers were being treated so lightly by their own government?[1] Finally, lest this already complex mix be left too simple, there were shouts and whispers from players who were neither French nor Americans. British, Germans, and Italians, whether politicians, diplomats, or media people, were—for a variety of reasons—not at all interested in improving Franco-American relations. With all these, the issues and the *provocateurs*, French propagandists had to contend.

From the French point of view, ever since 1919 there had been an obvious symbiotic relationship between the reparations that Germany owed to France, and the war and postwar reconstruction debts that France owed to America. If Germany's were paid promptly and, eventually, in full, so too would France's debts to her creditors—barring, one should add, a negotiated reduction in those debts as a recognition of France's huge demographic and material sacrifices during the war. Instead, however, what allowances had been made in the 1920s on the subject of reparations had been made to Germany's benefit. The Dawes Plan of 1924, and the Young Plan of 1929, both brokered by Americans, had effectively lightened Germany's financial obligations, in some cases by extending the period of payments, in others by reducing the interest rates on monies owing.[2] One might argue, as proponents did, that a more sustainable payment schedule in fact increased the likelihood of France being paid; but the spreading and lessening of payments were not entirely in France's best interests—especially if America maintained its pressure for full and timely payments on French war debts. For a decade, therefore, French irritation over German bad faith on reparations, and French irritation over American inflexibility on debts, ensured an underlying state of resentment in Paris.

Regrettably, it was matched, measure for measure, by resentment across the United States. There, majority opinion, official and public, had never been willing to recognize a relationship between Germany's obligations to its former enemies and France's obligations to a former ally. Each was a separate transaction to a different creditor. Furthermore, it did not help matters when it was pointed out, as it frequently was, that American postwar loans to Germany—in the interests of promoting German economic recovery as well as future returns on American investments—were being used to fund that country's reparation payments. That meant, effectively, that a substantial part of German obligations to France—as much as half—were being covered by American investment dollars.[3] Thus, from an American perspective, their money was paying for reparations, in amounts substantially greater than those hitherto paid to the United States by Britain and France for war debts.

Neither did it help to know that by the late 1920s, on the eve of the Depression and into its early years, France's fiscal situation was exceptionally healthy. Unemployment was low, the gold reserve was second only to that of the United States, and the franc had regained its status as a powerful international currency. In short, French foot-dragging on the matter of war debts seemed to be a reflection more of will than of means. As Claudel observed, the image of a "fabulously rich France" defaulting on her debts inspired genuine indignation in the United States.[4] That perception strengthened in America in the wake of two events. The first was the refusal of the French parliament to ratify what Americans regarded as the generous Mellon-Bérenger debt agreement, which had been negotiated in April 1926.[5] The second was the unenthusiastic French response to President Hoover's proposed one-year moratorium on reparations and war debts in the summer of 1931. Given that response, partly determined by the suddenness of the announcement and partly by the cavalier way in which undertakings agreed upon in the Young Plan were to be shelved, this apparently generous gesture proved to be more irritant than balm in Franco-American relations. Indeed, the eventual collapse of the moratorium proposal, a collapse widely attributed to French intransigence, marked one of the lowest points in Franco-American relations in the interwar years.[6]

As such, it fit well into the frequently troubled ambiance of trade relations between the two countries. On the positive side, France ranked fifth in world trade with the United States, behind only Britain, Canada, Germany, and Japan. By 1927 France accounted for some 13 percent of American exports and had granted favored-nation status to several hundred American products. Conversely, the United States was the fourth-largest consumer of French exports. In these respects, then, there was a significant compatibility between the two economies as well as a certain stability. Still, there were shadows, which were to lengthen considerably after 1930. Not unnaturally, both nations wished to protect the efforts and the profits of domestic producers. Not unnaturally, both resented the efforts of the other to do so. The Americans still rankled over the difficulties they had encountered in the early 1920s when it came to participating in reconstruction projects in postwar France, just as they resented the competitive advantage that French imperial territories enjoyed in the metropolitan marketplace. Indeed, despite their avowed wish for an improvement in Franco-German relations, they were not happy with the preferential trade agreements that those two countries had worked out for themselves in the 1920s.

If the State Department deplored France's "exorbitant quota licence fees, high duties, sales . . . taxes and discriminations against American commerce," the French resented American insistence on valuing imports on the basis of American, rather than French, prices; and they were outraged by the use of especially stringent health standards on foreign agricultural imports, standards they suspected were simply disguised protectionist devices.[7] Still, they were no happier in June 1930 when the Smoot-Hawley Act erected an undisguised, high protectionist wall around the United States, a measure that encouraged France and other countries to adopt similar measures in a Depression-dampened world economy.[8] Increased protectionism, aggravated by the enduring tensions over reparations and war debts, ensured that Franco-American relations were in for some very tough times early in the 1930s.

And differences over money were only part of the problem. Another was contained in the word *disarmament*. Without addressing for the moment the collection of attitudes and perceptions that underlay both nations' approach to the disarmament issue, it can be ventured here that their respective positions had changed little since the days of the Versailles settlement and the Washington Naval Conference. Americans could see little justification for a large French military establishment, especially given Germany's disarmed condition and France's heavy financial obligations to the United States. What they chose to see, instead, was evidence of French militarism and French imperialism, neither of which was calculated to endear an American public.

For their part, and at best, the French regarded American pressure to disarm as evidence of naïveté. Secure in their transatlantic bastion, too forgiving of German wartime aggression and postwar recalcitrance, too indifferent to France's concerns about naval competition from the British, Italians, and Japanese, Americans were content to promote simplistic solutions. Very simply put, that is why the French refused to become full partners in the naval accords concluded by the Americans, British, and Japanese at the London Naval Conference of 1930, and why they, among others, approached so warily the World Disarmament Conference that opened in Geneva in 1932. Again, and as always, they insisted on the implementation of adequate security assurances as an essential step to making further cuts in their army and navy. Such, at least, is the simplest way of articulating the critical difference between France and America on the thorny issue of disarmament.

But formal policy positions on specific issues and at specific moments were themselves products of more deeply established states of mind. From the French side, the long-standing ambivalence about America and its culture remained intact and, if anything, sharpened at the end of the 1920s. Its wealth and resources, its industrial efficiency, its technological innovativeness, remained sources of wonder, even admiration, for some French commentators. Some, indeed, thought they saw the Future in America and rushed to embrace it. Others remained appalled by the prospect, for the Future they perceived had Mammon for a god. What was different by the late 1920s, however, were the reinforcements brought to the latter camp by the collection of thorny policy issues addressed above. Resentment over the American position on reparations, war debts, trade, and disarmament had given rise to outright suspicion about America's intentions. It was, therefore, more than straightforward policy disagreements. In large measure, it was a matter of detecting malevolent motive beneath the surface talk of international reconciliation and economic recovery.

Sequentially and selectively assembled, America's behavior toward the postwar Third Republic was open to criticism. It had not ratified the Versailles treaty with Germany, a refusal that conveniently had freed it from the undertaking to guarantee French security. The same refusal had liberated it from the obligation of joining the League of Nations and thus from participating in Geneva-based efforts to ensure collective security. But it had been central in attempts to address some of Germany's reparations grievances, partly out of a perception that the treaty itself had been too harsh, partly that French efforts to enforce the treaty's terms had been too rigorous. Related perceptions seemed to account for complaints that France was exaggerating the German threat as a way of preserving its military and imperial power in Europe and abroad—a reading that then underwrote the American demand for a limitation on global naval expenditure, including that of France. And anticipated French savings on armaments, again conveniently, might then be funneled into French war debt payments to the United States. Thus selected and assembled, it was not surprising that by the late 1920s, an increasing number of French observers had detected something calculated and sinister in American policy. That dark form was an emergent American empire, one more of capital than of territory. In short, the older, more abstract fears about America's growing cultural influence were now sharpened by readings of her international and economic policies throughout the 1920s. As one French writer put it, imperialism does not always come "armed and helmeted." Sometimes it appears "in the guise of the banker and teller."[9]

Such remarks were but momentary flashes in the storm that crackled through Franco-American relations in the early 1930s. But they, like the illustrations that follow, were mild by comparison with acrid press commentaries of the sort that described America as a country that had evolved from barbarism to decadence without having experienced civilization.[10] Even the centrist, government-associated *Le Temps* had no choice but to give voice to mounting French misgivings about America. "More and more," one editorial proclaimed, "whether she intends it or not, the great American Republic appears to other nations as an empire crammed with riches, nourished on pride, its solitude held aloft in defiance." American protectionism, the paper maintained, actually impeded other countries' capacity to repay war debts, just as its promotion of disarmament—sound theoretically—was indifferent to political realities. While France insisted on security first, before disarming, America secured for itself naval parity with Britain, the number-one naval power in the world. Such hypocrisy, combined with presidential press releases issued as if from some "new Mount Sinai," was offensive; but no more perhaps than the paper's accusation that American propensity for excess, and their madcap stock speculation through 1929, had been a major cause of the global economic collapse from which everyone now suffered.[11]

Even attempts at damage control could be tricky. André Géraud, for example, reviewing Georges Duhamel's new *Scènes de la vie future* for the *New York Times*, found it impossible not to reiterate the author's ideas: namely, that America was a material civilization divorced from a moral one, shorn of deep historical roots, committed to "the extreme development of urban life and the use of machines." Although distancing himself from the author's conclusions, Géraud had no compunction about calling the book "a vehement statement for the prosecution . . . against American civilization."[12] Precisely the same stance, reflecting the same problem, was taken two years later, in 1932, when the pro-American Gabriel Hanotaux reviewed the Aron-Dandieu book called *Le cancer américain* for *Le Temps*. One might dissent from the book's arguments, as Hanotaux did, but not before he laid out, publicly again, those same arguments. Compared to abrasions such as these, French propagandists might only have sighed at statements of an entirely opposite nature—those in which French artists and writers had proved so eager to applaud American innovation that they only succeeded in disparaging and diminishing France in American eyes.[13]

If public statements such as these complicated the life of the French propagandist in America, they were but a portion of the problem. For the fact is that America had in abundance its own prominent counterparts, each perfectly capable of turning up the heat. Once more, the most reliable among them were consistent Francophobes, people who thought France had overplayed the card of innocent victim in 1914, and with it, her appeals for special dispensation on war debts. For them, it was her *revanchisme* against Germany that was not only the principal stumbling block to lasting peace, but also a major impediment to resolving issues of reparations, debts, and disarmament. Conversely, for Ambassador Claudel and the man who succeeded him in March 1933, André de Laboulaye, such bleak readings of France constituted impediments of quite another sort. Again and again, through the early 1930s, they were forced to confront a succession of hostile images and texts, many of them publicized across America. Most of this material, predictably, came from the press, and with a frequency too great to survey here. Instead, and following earlier precedents, it should suffice to mention some of the press materials that caught the eye and stirred the anger of the French embassy in Washington.

The topics, of course, were as varied as were the media. No matter the subject, Ned McLean's *Washington Post* was seen as a reliably hostile force, at least until the paper was acquired by Eugene Meyer in June 1933. The same was generally true of Colonel Robert McCormick's *Chicago Tribune*, whether it was addressing France's "frivolity" and "irresponsibility" in and out of the London Naval Conference, the France-linked "vindictive statecraft of Versailles," or France's December 1932 decision to default on war debt payments despite a gold reserve almost as large as that of the United States. Clearly, one *Tribune* editorial observed in the spring of 1933, it was time for "Plain Talk to France."[14] The *Saturday Evening Post* was another publication that seemed inclined to target France, an inclination that the embassy took seriously, given its 2.5-million sales circulation and an actual readership estimated to be four times greater. Two articles, in particular, incensed them. In April 1930 the magazine published a damning indictment of French reception of American tourists in Paris; and two years later, the same author contributed a very critical piece on French propaganda efforts in the United States.[15] As for the remainder, with one notable exception, it was more a matter of sporadic criticism, whether it was the *Magazine of Wall Street* addressing French financial policy in 1932, the *China Weekly Review* examining French imperial policy in 1933, or *Fortune* appraising French disarmament policy in 1934.[16] For that matter, even the *New York Times* had no choice but to report the most Francophobic remarks when publicly delivered—including Senator Reed Smoot's unhappy characterization of France as a Shylock out to extract the last pound of German reparation flesh.[17]

The exception, of course, was the Hearst press, for it did nothing by half measures. Like McLean and McCormick, but more so, William Randolph Hearst seemed to delight in baiting France. By the 1930s he had refined this particular art to such a degree that he was actually expelled from France for illegal possession and publication of a government document pertaining to naval disarmament. It was he, whom the Washington chargé d'affaires called a "singular specialist of malevolence," who was responsible for the *San Francisco Examiner*'s outspoken editorials on France.[18] The paper had no qualms about attributing the disarmament impasse to "Militaristic France," and to her "perennial" goal of "fortify[ing] her continental position with the aid of other nations." It mocked the notion of "Poverty-Stricken France," and openly laid the charge of dishonor against Britain as well as France for the failure to fulfill their financial obligations to America. As powerfully, if not more so, the paper published one devastating cartoon after another, each trained on Anglo-French duplicity. They were called the "Pampered Pair" and were graphically derided for the fortunes they allegedly were sacrificing to the gods of war—instead of paying their debts; and in a deliberate invocation of the German treaty violations in August 1914, the paper portrayed a wealthy France tearing up its war debts agreement as "Just Another Scrap of Paper."[19] Indeed, as a measure of how egregious French observers found the Hearst presses, the normally constrained Paul Claudel confessed to his ministry: "I normally don't bother reporting on the Hearst papers," given the "vulgarities, lies and calumnies which they never cease vomiting on France."[20]

So it was that the challenges confronting French propagandists in America were multiplied not only by authentic and substantive policy differences between the two countries, but also by the respective *mentalités* from which had grown the policies. That is why public figures in both countries, particularly politicians and journalists, were so instrumental in articulating those differences in policy and psychology to their respective reading publics. Although there was indeed a counterforce to these negative and divisive readings of each other, in the form of French agents and their American allies, what we have done to the present is outline the desperate need for a Francophile offensive in the early years of the Depression. And that need was determined principally by French and American players on both sides of the Atlantic.

However, there is one additional factor that warrants brief consideration.

If some French commentators who were adept at getting the American wind up, and some Americans only too eager to reciprocate, there were others who subtly incited and tried to sustain the incongruence of France and America. Leading the field by the early 1930s were the agents of Germany's Weimar Republic. They, too, magnified the task of. French propagandists, the more so as their strategy by 1930 was reminiscent of that of France—namely, an inoffensive, primarily cultural campaign, in this case to rehabilitate the image of Germany in America. For the time being, gone were the days of strident declamations and accusations, and in were the days of information provision and prospective cultural exchange. One report, prepared in the summer of 1932 and dispatched to the foreign minister's personal *cabinet*, was produced by a professor at Yale who was candid about the success of this German strategy. German propaganda, he said, was recording great success. It, abetted by historical works such as that of Sidney Fay, had managed to take most of the sting out of Germany's alleged guilt for 1914 and had helped swing American opinion against France. The German embassy in Washington served as the conductor of this new symphony, but an "invisible" one that avoided the sensational and the exaggerated in favor of good and substantial information on German achievements in the arts and sciences. By such discreet means, it had patiently cultivated a garden of Germanophilia, out of which had come an increase in American tourist trade to Germany, increased numbers of American students traveling to Germany, and an increased interest in all things German on American university campuses—all, it seemed, at the expense of France.[21]

A year and a half before this report found its way from the United States to Paris, the Service des Oeuvres had conducted its own activity assessment for 1930, the first full year of the Depression. Given its timing, this report provides both a summary of ministerial efforts and a forecast of what could be expected in the years to come. The principal goal of Oeuvres, since its inception in 1920, was to expand the "moral and intellectual influence of France throughout the world," and by so doing to serve as an arm of French diplomacy. Its means for accomplishing this were geographically and conceptually ambitious but financially still constrained. Indeed, in 1930 it drew almost a quarter of its budget from funds raised through the government's sports and gambling commissions.[22] Oeuvres was responsible for a range of broadly cultural activities worldwide, from radio broadcasting and cinema distribution; to sports competition, tourist promotion, and philanthropic work in the fields of medicine and charity; and finally, of course, to education. Indeed, it was the latter responsibility that ensured that the foreign ministry, through Oeuvres, would work in tandem with the education ministry, as well as with the latter's National Office for French Universities Abroad. In sum, this propaganda strategy continued to eschew tactics dependent on fraud or exaggeration, in favor of those that prized accurate information and genuine intellectual and artistic achievement. As such, it was addressed to the long term; it was indirect and undramatic. Indeed, at times it was so "obscure," that neither the French media nor parliament paid it much attention. And when they did on occasion, so these authors avowed, such propaganda rivals as Germany and Italy were quick to learn from the French example.[23]

While there may be some truth to the claim that France was a pioneer in the field of subtle and inoffensive propaganda, there is a great deal to the assertion of Oeuvres's eclecticism. By the early 1930s it had developed not only a complex network of services, but also a corresponding network of interministerial contacts that made possible the provision of those services. In short, propaganda work in America, or anywhere else, was to a considerable extent conditioned by arrangements, financial and otherwise, worked out in Paris. While there certainly were occasional instances of collaboration between Oeuvres and most other ministries—army, navy, agriculture, colonies, public works—and while all were dependent upon the largesse of the finance ministry, the foreign ministry's most important collaborators were the ministries of commerce and education. As for the former, commerce supervised its own labyrinth of offices, a number of which turn up in the records of the foreign ministry for the early 1930s, including a sprawling network of Chambers of Commerce at home and abroad, a National Committee for Foreign Trade, a National Committee for Counselors of Foreign Commerce—with its own Office of Economic Propaganda—a National Office for Tourism, and the state-supported steamship company known as the French Line. In each instance of contact between any one of these entities and the Quai d'Orsay, what was always at issue was both the promotion of France's image abroad—a principally diplomatic objective—and the advancement of its commercial interests either at home or abroad—the principal mandate of the ministry of commerce.

Oeuvres's involvement in matters of education was even more extensive, and its nature even more complex. Some of its work was conducted through formally funded government agencies such as the National Office for French Universities Abroad, and the Paris-based offices of the Alliance Française. Some of it involved cooperative liaison with a host of government-approved agencies, for example, Jacques Lebel's Center for Documentary Information, on the rue Notre-Dame des Victoires; and Senator Jean Philip's

French Committee for the Development of Intellectual and Economic Relations Abroad, an organization that operated from number 25 Avenue Victor Emmanuel III.[24] The latter's location was significant, for essentially next door to it, at numbers 9–11, were the offices of two America-focused organizations: the parent body of the France-America Society, and the Institute for American Studies. Together, whether explicitly America-addressed or not, these organizations lent their expertise and facilities to Oeuvres's ongoing efforts to promote in the United States an appreciation of French intellectual achievement across the ages.

As one might expect, the means for doing so were varied and, once again, far more extensive than a few examples can illustrate—although further evidence of Oeuvres educational activity will be explored as our focus shifts from Paris to America itself. Central to those efforts was facilitating the passage of French students and French teachers to America, as well as the passage of American students and teachers to France. To that end Oeuvres, in close concert with the French Line, the Compagnie Générale Transatlantique, regularly arranged travel subventions for French academics recommended by the ministry of education, and for Americans selected by the New York–based Institute for International Education.[25] Significantly, however, in an effort to avoid American criticism of French propaganda efforts in the United States, the involved ministries ensured that the distribution of travel monies for Americans was handled by the Paris-based Society of Friends of the University. In a word, it was a deliberate subterfuge, the use of an apparently arms-length body to conceal the French government's role in funding the education of Americans, and thereby—in the words of one contemporary writer—"infusing their soul with French humanism."[26]

Financial subventions of quite another order were also central to Oeuvres's efforts in education, although the precise distribution channels for those monies are less clear. In point of fact, the foreign ministry provided annual grants to a number of America-based schools, colleges, and exchange programs. While the sums involved appear to have been modest, they were provided on a regular basis to such organizations as the Franco-American University Exchange; the College of the Marist Fathers in San Francisco; the Kansas-based Notre Dame of Sion; as well as the Assumptionist-run College in Worcester, Massachusetts; and the School of Commerce in Woonsocket, Rhode Island. Additionally, with funds provided by the National Office of Universities, Oeuvres monitored the progress and provided support for French scholarship holders in America—a group that numbered thirty-two men and women in 1931.[27] American students, too, were beneficiaries of the ministry's promotion of things French in the United States. Not only were their school and college libraries supplemented by donations of French-language books, and their own academic performances in French rewarded by gold, silver, and bronze medals furnished from Paris, but their campus-located Maisons Françaises were likely to receive an annual financial donation through the schools and universities department of Oeuvres.[28] Finally, on a slightly different educational level, Francophilic organizations across America were recipients of direct funding from the offices of Oeuvres in Paris. These included, between 1930 and 1933, the France-Louisiana Alliance, the Los Angeles–based France-America Institute, the French Institute at Emory University, and the French Institutes in Washington and New York.

Individuals, as well as institutions, were recipients of Oeuvres's educational funding. In the period under consideration there is direct evidence of travel subventions for a series of prominent French visitors to America, all of them with a mandate to promote closer educational and cultural relations between the two countries. These included Jules Bois, former president of the Société des gens de lettres; Pierre Mortier, president of the Fédération des Sociétés d'écrivains et revues littéraires; and Gaston Rageot, president of the Fédération internationale des Associations professionelles des gens de lettres.[29] Gilbert Chinard, a French national but by 1930 a professor of history at Johns Hopkins, was—through the French Institute in Washington—another regular recipient of ministerial funds, much of which went to defray the costs of publishing his work on France's historical presence in America.[30] And circumstantial evidence certainly allows one to conclude that ministerial support of one sort or another went into Marcel Aubert's and Albert Feuillerat's visiting lectureships at Yale, Joseph Bedier's and Daniel Mornet's at the University of California, Raoul Blanchard's at Harvard, and Antoine Meillet's at Columbia.[31]

The ministry-supported Alliance Française rested on yet another educational plane. Founded in 1883, it was designed first and foremost to promote the French language, an objective eagerly embraced when the Federation of the Alliance Française in the United States was created in 1902.[32] The federation was the inspiration of the Harvard-educated and long-familiar Francophile James Hazen Hyde, who made immediate provision for the French ambassador—originally Jules Cambon—to serve as honorary president. At its creation, the federation comprised thirty-three chapters in America, a number that when its affiliate Cercles Français is included, had risen to 286 by 1933. By then, it seems clear, the most active chapters of the Alliance were to be found in New York, Massachusetts, New Jersey, Pennsylvania, and

California. Certainly these would appear to have been among the principal beneficiaries of the funds annually awarded by Oeuvres's Section diverse to the New York–based federation, notwithstanding supplementary subventions awarded directly from Paris either to individual chapters or to individual visitors from France who would speak or perform on the request of those chapters. Such occasions, together with French-language classes, concerts, and exhibitions, represented yet another way in which French civilization was to be kept alive in the consciousness of Americans. And the foreign ministry was behind the effort every step of the way, as was every ambassador from Jules Jusserand, Emile Daeschner, Henri Bérenger, and Paul Claudel in the 1920s, to André Lefebvre de Laboulaye, Georges Bonnet, and René Doynel de Saint-Quentin in the 1930s.

On those occasions when musicians, novelists, and artists were prospective visitors to America, the foreign ministry often became involved in a subvention system of another order. And another one calculated either to conceal its hand from the inattentive or at least to make its involvement appear at arm's length. In concert with education and fine arts' Service d'action artistique à l'étranger, directed by Philippe Erlanger, Oeuvres quietly provided an ongoing series of grants to a publicly identified organization called the Association française d'expansion et action artistique.[33] Nominally, it was this body, with Erlanger also acting as its secretary-general, that distributed the funds to worthy applicants or to those recruited in advance by either of the two ministries. However, by the early 1930s the key decision-making body, the Administrative Council of Action Artistique, was presided over by Senator Henry de Jouvenel, with Erlanger and Jean Marx, Oeuvres director, as the principal executive voices. It was they who, along with representatives from the artistic and intellectual world of the French capital, accepted or rejected the applications for financial subsidies—usually on the basis of recommendations from the various subcommittees which composed the Comité d'Action Artistique: including those for literature, music, theater, art, radio, and cinema.[34] This eclecticism, the reader is reminded, was magnified many times over by the global nature of this enterprise. America was but one of its spheres of interest and, apparently, as yet a secondary one compared with Europe and the Middle East. Still, and despite a very fragmentary record for the early 1930s, it is clear that in 1932 and 1933 this Action Artistique was responsible for the subsidized diffusion of French films in America, frequent lecture tours by the novelist Lucie Delarue-Mardrus, a concert tour of the United States by a group specializing in antique musical instruments, the

American appearance of cellist Madeleine Monnier, and that of guest conductor Daniel Lazarus with the St. Louis Symphony.[35]

By the 1930s, there was something quite traditional in a strategy based on the propagation of language, ideas, and aesthetics. Jules Jusserand would have approved, just as he would have applauded other familiar tactical efforts to keep the name and image of France bright before Americans. The philanthropic work carried out by Oeuvres's Section diverse was one such example. For instance, in 1930, financial subventions were provided through Oeuvres to French benevolent societies in Chicago, New Orleans, New York, and Philadelphia; and certainly the French Hospital in New York was accustomed to an annual donation. Although neither intellectual nor artistic in bent, support such as this was similarly calculated to advance the good name of France in America. Different, again, in thrust, but traditional in nature, was an ongoing series of special promotions calculated to endear Americans to France. Such promotions included the Paris opening of the Maison Américaine at the Cité Universitaire in April 1930; tireless publicity for the activities of the Franco-American Museum at Blérancourt, itself a monument to the joint efforts of World War I; annual trans-America celebrations of Bastille Day, centered around the embassy and every consulate between Boston and San Francisco; and well-publicized preparations for the opening and functioning of the French pavilion at the Chicago World Fair of 1933.[36]

Yet another time-tested device for projecting positive images of France in America was active engagement with that country's media. Sometimes, particularly after the rise to power of Adolf Hitler early in 1933, it was a matter of taking the initiative. We have, for example, the admission by Charles de Fontnouvelle, consul general in New York, that his offices had prepared entire, positively framed articles destined for American periodicals, articles that appeared, however, under the signatures of prominent Americans. We also know that at least one particularly positive *New York Times* editorial, this one entitled "The Laboulayes," came in the wake of a congenial luncheon shared by the ambassador and three friendly editorial hosts: John Finley, Louis Wiley, and Edwin James.[37] Quite often, it was a matter of reacting to, and attempting to redress, damaging pieces in American newspapers and magazines. In this connection we have examples of Philippe Berthelot instructing the embassy to secure a retraction of a critical piece that had appeared in the *Baltimore Sun*, and of Fontnouvelle successfully asking the *New York Times* for an opportunity to respond to what his superiors deemed to be anti-French materials furnished by the German consulate in New York. Of similar cast was Ambassador Claudel's successful intervention at the State Department, in the interests of securing a retraction and apology from the New York magazine *Liberty* for a scurrilous attack on the French Foreign Legion—and eventually of an offer to publish an embassy-inspired corrective.[38]

Nor was it always a question of being reactive. Sometimes interventions could be more preemptive in nature, as was the case when the Quai d'Orsay arranged for an article in *Foreign Affairs* by the French journalist Wladimir d'Ormesson, an article initiated by its editor, the Francophile Hamilton Fish Armstrong.[39] More delicate, and risky, was the practice of providing operational subventions for French-language publications in America. How widespread the practice was is difficult to say, but sometimes the evidence is unequivocal. The San Francisco–based *Courrier du Pacifique*, with a circulation of some five thousand, regularly received subventions from the Quai d'Orsay, in some cases for the specific purpose of supporting the paper's public sponsorship of recent French films.[40] The Chicago magazine *Chanteclair* received annual subventions, as did, apparently, *Le Messager de New York* as well as that city's *Revue Franco-Américaine*. But the largest recipient of French funding was another New York publication called *Le Courrier des Etats-Unis*. Said to have a circulation of more than twelve thousand by 1935, the paper seemed to be in a constant state of financial crisis and on the brink of collapse. Yet it survived—with cautious verbal support from the embassy in Washington, textual support from French writers such as Maurois and de Lanux, subscription fees from some two thousand universities and colleges, advertising revenues from the likes of Pierre Cartier, the New York jeweler, and monthly financial subsidies provided by the Quai d'Orsay's information and press service.[41]

While to this point we have emphasized the continuity of French propaganda strategy and of the tactical devices employed to satisfy it, there were signs in the early 1930s of new, or at least newer, initiatives on the part of the French foreign ministry. Perhaps the newest, so far as one can tell from the extant records, was a form of contractual arrangement with America-based publicity agents. One of them was a convinced Francophile by the name of Mrs. Moon Jones, who, between 1930 and 1932, offered a range of press services to the foreign ministry, the French Line, and the New York offices of Foreign Commerce and Tourism. Supplier of press materials to some two thousand American publications, her company distributed across America positively couched articles on France, articles that carried the French government's stamp of approval. Furthermore, she did so in full awareness that her provisioning had to be done in "an extremely discreet" manner.[42]

Another, and of greater duration, was the ministry's arrangement with Thérèse Bonney, yet one more American Francophile, and one with a doctorate from the Sorbonne. Bonney's field of expertise was French art in general, and photography in particular, interests early inspired by undergraduate studies at Berkeley, Harvard, and Columbia; and her one-woman press-service operation based in New York clearly earned the admiration of principals in Oeuvres and the ministerial press and information service. Like Mrs. Moon Jones, she was instrumental in providing press copy, both text and photographs, to various media outlets in America, just as she became increasingly involved with the ministry's attempt to promote French art in the gallery of the recently opened Maison Française at Rockefeller Center, as well as in the form of traveling exhibitions. Predictably, given her métier, much of her funding came from the Quai d'Orsay through the intermediary services of the Association française d'expansion et action artistique. Recommended to the latter by Oeuvres's Fernand Pila, Bonney's offices were described as "the principal French photographic propaganda in the United States."[43]

Thérèse Bonney's work on French premises at New York's Rockefeller Center brings to mind yet another important development in France's propaganda efforts in America. One of the original objectives of Senator Jean Philip's Committee for the Development of Intellectual and Economic Relations, founded in October 1930, had been to ensure that a Maison Française would be included in the plans for the new Rockefeller Center. By 1932 several contentious points had been resolved. The French premises would provide for a range of activities, both commercial and cultural; and the cultural projects, enabled by facilities for concerts, lectures, exhibitions, and cinema, would thus become a major force in French propaganda efforts in America—despite the persistent reluctance of the Quai d'Orsay, and its Washington embassy, to accept financial responsibility for the Maison's activities. Rather, they believed, the costs ought to be assumed by the commercial participants and by the privately run Maison Française Corporation, directed by a Mr. I. Frenkel—a man with direct links to Jean Philip's committee in Paris. All the ministry had been willing to do with respect to the operating costs of the facilities was pay the rental charges of office space for its consulate general, an obligation that it had assumed before the end of 1933.[44] Special events were another matter. In the course of 1934, plans were afoot to mount several exhibitions at the Maison, with energy and expertise provided by Bonney, and with funding by the foreign ministry as well as by the Maison-installed offices of the French Line and those of France's National Railway.[45]

Other media were also being explored by the ministry in the early

1930s, in gradual recognition that radio broadcasts and movie theaters were going to play a greater and greater role in molding public attitudes on any subject. But effective broadcasting to America from France, or by France's advocates in America, was still sporadic. In March 1930 Jules Henry of the Washington embassy did participate in a series addressed to foreign diplomats by the Columbia Broadcasting System, during which he stressed French efforts at stabilizing the franc, at promoting economic and political reconciliation with Germany, and at undertaking significant reductions in the country's armaments. And two years later a speech broadcast from Paris by the elderly and failing Jules Jusserand was said to have attracted "millions" of American listeners. Certainly it impressed the editors of the *New York Times,* who not only agreed to publish the text of the address but also provided a commentary that underscored France's legitimate security concerns and acknowledged America's partial responsibility for French protectionist policies.[46] Overall, however, there was some agreement that France, by January 1935, was running behind its English, German, and Italian competitors, all of whose short-wave transmissions to some 20 million American receivers were more frequent, better advertised, and of better quality.[47]

Cinema, too, contained promise and peril, mostly the latter for an industry dwarfed by Hollywood and constrained by a foreign language. Some, among them Ambassador Laboulaye, recognized that film had the potential to be the single more effective propaganda instrument in a country's arsenal; and certainly no opportunities were missed for glittering debuts of French films, attended by diplomats and a Francophilic elite, such as happened in New York in February 1931 for *Le collier de la reine.* But, on balance, the ministry was always at a disadvantage. France's film distribution system in the United States still left much to be desired, muddled as it was by too many participants from the embassy and consulates, the National Office of Tourism, and the French Line, as well as from private distributors. The end result was that French films were not effectively marketed, and inquiries about them—principally from schools and universities—were not answered in timely fashion. More damaging still was the frequent uproar over Hollywood's portrayal of things French and, conversely, what was seen in America to be France's absurd overreaction.

Given what was seen from Paris to be an American cinematic proclivity for maligning France, the most desirable solution was to contain the problem right at the studio level. To that end, and for a while in the early 1930s, the embassy succeeded in getting one Valentin Mandelstamm hired to the staff of Will H. Hays, the executive officer of the Motion Picture Producers and

Distributors of America. The idea was that Mandelstamm would head off problems that might be developing on either side of the Atlantic. They might include, and certainly did, a French determination to suspend the distribution license for a Fox film called *Hell's Belles*; a decision by Paramount to show an American dog, in a sector occupied by American troops, being awarded a French *croix de guerre*; or one by Fox to have an unmistakably French peddler engaged in selling pornographic pictures.[48] But the contagion was beyond the resources of one man, even of one country. In July 1932 Claudel had to protest against the release of a film entitled *Indecent*, which was based on Flaubert's classic *Madame Bovary*. A year later the French consul in Los Angeles was instructed to secure a title change for a new film called *The Worst Woman of Paris*. On a happier note, however, Ambassador Laboulaye was able to offer Paris some reassurance in February 1934. Not only had American film coverage of the street riots in Paris avoided any scenes of violence, but the Hays organization had reaffirmed its commitment to the French government not to misrepresent France by means of lurid imagery.[49]

Images, however, whether broadcast verbally or projected graphically, still remained secondary in the preoccupations of French propagandists. While betraying some awareness of their potential, the ministry's agents were less concerned about their shortcomings in the field of the new media than they were about deficiencies in the older field of published text. And by 1930, in the face of Depression-strained Franco-American relations, there was a re-kindled interest in investing France with some kind of official information office in America. That project, a variation on the old wartime bureaus and Gaston Liebert's information service of the mid–1920s, took some years to develop, inspired as it was by the success of Weimar Germany's propaganda efforts yet constrained as it also was by a new wave of American hypersensitivity to foreign propaganda.

The momentum in favor of creating a new information service in America began to pick up steam early in 1932, just at a time when France was coming under increasing criticism for its stance on disarmament. And as had happened before, the initiative was to come from disturbed American Francophiles. People like the Columbia-educated William Guthrie clearly were becoming frustrated. The prominent New York lawyer was certainly prepared to continue his own efforts on behalf of France, projects that, with the collaboration of Louis Wiley, recently had included the translation and publication in the *New York Times* of an official French statement on armaments. But he wanted a much better information service close at hand, one, especially, that could distribute materials in English. As it stood, he warned French diplomats, there was an "incalculable misunderstanding" about France that was spreading across the United States. At the same time, however, Guthrie recalled and reendorsed Jusserand's oft-repeated qualms about "systematic propaganda" and affirmed that what was needed in America "would not be a propaganda agency in the objectionable sense of the word."[50]

Whatever the sophistry involved, the proposal seemed to carry with it the force of the obvious. However, it was not without obstacles. One of them seemed equally self-evident to Jules Henry in the Washington embassy. There was little point in creating a discrete information office in America until the Quai d'Orsay had multiplied its capacity to furnish such an office with up-to-date and extensive English-language texts. Not to do so would mean "putting the cart before the horse."[51] Another was a lack of consensus on how acute was France's plight. Paul Claudel, back from a tour of the American Midwest, concluded that France's cultural propaganda strategy was paying off, the more so as it was completely invulnerable to charges of prevarication; and so far as he could tell, there was no evidence of an ugly anti-French campaign richly funded and manipulated by Germany. But, as had been the case before, the New York consul general was less confident. Compared to the voices of England, Germany, and Italy, that of France was muted; and in the presence of such silence "the most fantastic" charges were being leveled against that country, not only for its stance on disarmament, but also for its contribution to Germany's economic collapse and the weakness of the pound sterling. Simply put, French efforts could not compare with those mounted by the British Library of Information in New York or by the well-financed and skilled services located in the German consulate general.[52]

A third impediment to early redressment of the situation arose in connection with the manner in which some new French information service should be created. Should reliance be placed on the work of private publicity agents, the method chosen by the Russians and Poles? Should there be an expansion of the duties and information facilities of the embassy or consulate general, along the lines of the German model? Or should there be an entirely new information bureau in America? Abbreviating the discussions that took place in the course of 1932, one can say that the private model drew few adherents, apparently despite the efforts of Mrs. Moon Jones. The embassy and consular models also had limited support, partly owing to recollections of the earlier Liebert experiment, when the "official" nature of his position with the French government had opened France to charges of foreign propaganda. Certainly the American department at the Quai d'Orsay remained mindful of Jules Jusserand's constant prescription, namely that every effort had to be made to "scrupulously avoid" any hint of government propaganda. The same was true of the ministry's information and press service, which in 1933 actually chastised the Agence Havas for being too visible abroad and thus too easily accused of being a tool of the government.[53] Instead, but slowly, the foreign ministry gravitated toward a solution of a freestanding information service, one that could deny any direct affiliation with the French government and one that, ideally, would be directed by Americans.

If prudence remained the watchword, the need for action became ever more apparent. At the end of 1932, Premier Herriot warned his diplomatic agents worldwide that France was being victimized by "a campaign of systematic denigration," a campaign that drew new inspiration from parliament's recent decision to suspend payments on the American debt. And in the United States, in particular, opinion on France was described as worse than it had been for many years.[54] For awhile, at least, there was worse to come. In California, the French consul in Los Angeles reckoned that 99 percent of West Coast Americans were sympathetic to Germany, a reflection of that country's heavy investment in propaganda services. But elsewhere, too, in New York, St. Louis, Cincinnati, and Houston, the mood against France was ugly. "We are portrayed," one report by a senior diplomat claimed, as "stuffed with gold, imperialistic, corrupt, as indifferent to treaties as we are to our own word."[55] There was little doubt that the need for action was there; but just as that need intensified, something happened in Europe. At the end of January 1933, Adolf Hitler became chancellor of Germany and animator of a regime that had an inherent belief in the power of word and image to shape popular perceptions to its liking. Both at home and abroad. While ultimately, and paradoxically, that belief would be turned to France's advantage, in the early months of 1933 it further complicated the question of an accelerated French information service for America.

Within three months of the Nazi takeover in Germany, a new wave of anxiety swept across the United States; but by no means was it inspired solely by the Germans. Long suspicious of French activity in America, in April 1933 certain newspapers were quick to alert their readers to a lively discussion in the French Chamber of Deputies. That discussion had centered around a report by Adrien Dariac on foreign ministry spending, a report that both noted the need for an effective French counter propaganda campaign worldwide, and drew a connection between that need and the paltry sums that France was spending on information services compared to those of Britain, Germany, and Italy. The deputy, however, made a concerted attempt to stress that salvation lay solely in the form of accurate—as opposed to fraudulent—information.

But his care was for naught. It did not stop the *Chicago Tribune* from running an article under the title "France Plans Big Propaganda Campaign in U.S," or the *Washington Post* from prophesying a one-million-dollar campaign in America. Even worse, the *Post*'s correspondent framed his article in the context of France's corrupt journalistic practices, explaining to his readers that the intended campaign only made sense to a French public accustomed to press behavior that was "honestly and candidly corrupt." Americans, he affirmed, would have none of it, and would not tolerate being manipulated by anyone's press. In the crash of waves like these, few would have noticed more generous retorts such as the one written to the *New York Times* by a city resident. The fuss about French propaganda, he wrote, was entirely misplaced, for its nature was strictly cultural. Educated people worldwide were familiar with French classics, whether literary, musical, or artistic; and to promote such familiarity was really a service to civilization. "If that be 'propaganda,' the writer concluded, "let's have more of it."[56]

Although few Americans may have been quite as magnanimous toward France as the letter writer, many more were showing their apprehensions about developments in Hitler's Germany—including nearly 2 million New York Jews. Within a month of Hitler's appearance in power, they were expressing deep misgivings about his anti-Semitic measures, misgivings that members of the French foreign ministry believed were exploitable within the influential Jewish community of America. "In an instant," Ambassador Laboulaye judged, the Nazi regime had forfeited the sympathy of most Americans. Within four months, some American papers were claiming that the considerable success of Weimar Germany's propaganda efforts in America had been all but erased by the clumsy hands of a Nazi-appointed ambassador and consul general.[57] And for the remainder of the year French readings of the damage inflicted by the Nazis on Germanophiles in America became more optimistic. In July, *New York Times* editor Louis Wiley wrote a private letter to the recently widowed Mme Jusserand, assuring her that Hitler's damage to Germany was already "irreparable" in American eyes. Nazi anti-Semitic measures alone were enough to provoke other countries to place "an iron ring" around Germany. In December the Quai d'Orsay had in hand two articles from the Chicago papers. One, from the *Chicago Tribune*, was based largely on a piece originally published in Paris by *Le Petit Parisien*, exposing instructions to German diplomatic officials on how to corrupt the presses of North and South America—principally in the form of bribery. The other, published by the *Chicago Daily News*, was of similar ilk and addressed German plans for disguising propaganda under the cover of "news," for concealing the German provenance of materials being distributed in America, and for resorting where possible to the bribing of American journalists.[58]

As hopeful as these developments certainly were from the French point of view, they also were responsible for heightening American anxiety about foreign propaganda from whatever source.[59] And it was French awareness of that fact that reduced to a crawl any movement toward a new information service in the United States. The need for having such a service, however, seemed ever more transparent, despite the self-destructive work being done there by the Nazi regime. For the fact was that the world's temperature was rising under the rhetorical flame applied by the minions of Hitler, Mussolini, Stalin, and the emperor of Japan. The Germans, Italians, and Japanese spoke of war as a virtue and seemed bent on preparing themselves for military confrontation. Mindful of these hostile gestures, both verbal and material, the French were experiencing increased anxiety about their national security, an anxiety that focused attention on their frontiers and on the search for potential allies, of which none, at least in the long run, was more promising in resource base than the United States of America.

There was, however, not even a hope of recruiting American services in the immediate future—not in a world still largely free of war, and in a country committed heart and soul to remaining detached from active involvement in other nations' squabbles. The best hope in the short run was to continue the decade-old strategy of tilling the soil, sowing good seed, weeding regularly, and praying for a bountiful harvest. That meant exchanging musicians, artists, novelists, teachers, and students. Indeed, Oeuvres's activity in cultural propaganda remained the "fundamental" element in the ministry's efforts to secure its minimal objective, namely America's "moral support" in peacetime.[60] But it also meant a smooth and constant flow of reliable information both in the interests of France's image and of an understanding of its perspective. For that, one needed an expansion of the ministry's information infrastructure both in Paris and in America. All that, however, obvious as the need seemed by 1933, had to be reconciled with the equally urgent need to avoid alienating Americans with overdone and overly obvious propaganda. And old as the issue was, it was not getting any easier to resolve in the early Hitler years than it had been in the past.

Ambassador Laboulaye remained firmly in the tradition of Jules Jusserand, consistently reticent about an information office outside the confines of the embassy and consulates. Indeed, if paradoxically, it seemed preferable to confine information provision to the country's official diplomatic agents—whose role and interests were obvious to all—than to rely on an

office whose avowed independence from government control would only ag-
gravate American suspicions. Repeatedly, throughout 1933 and 1934,
Laboulaye warned his superiors that any "active, direct, and systematic propaganda campaign in America will only have disastrous results." The least
faux pas, he said, could compromise the success of the entire endeavor, with
nothing being more dangerous than information that was not completely accurate, especially in a country already worked up about German and Japanese activity on American soil. The remark was portentous. In December
1934, a French budgetary provision for "allowing France to make herself better known abroad," was met with hostility by the American press and characterized as a commitment to disguised propaganda.[61]

Still, the fact was that by December 1934 clear progress was being made
toward the creation of a privately run French information office in New
York—one that would have no formal or fiduciary connection with the government of France, no political affiliation or overtly propagandistic function,
indeed no objective save the provision of reliable information to interested,
inquiring parties in America. The initiative, so far as one can tell, came from
René de Chambrun, a French-born New York lawyer. It was he who assembled
the cumbersomely titled Association for the Creation of a French Information Office in the United States, and presumably he who recruited many of
its founding members on both sides of the Atlantic. For an organization without "official" status, it had a blue-ribbon cast, beginning with its president,
Philippe Pétain, marshal of France and, until very recently, war minister in
the cabinet of Gaston Doumergue. Prominent compatriots added their luster
to the membership rolls, including Chambrun's father, General Jacques de
Chambrun, the politician Paul Reynaud, the banker Philippe de Rothschild,
the car manufacturer Louis Renault, and the writer André Maurois as well as
names from state-connected bodies such as the French Line, the Bank of
France, the French National Railways, and the University of Paris. Not to be
outshone, the American membership included a galaxy of prominent names,
many of them familiar to Francophile circles in America: the Morgans, J. P.
and Anne; John D. Rockefeller Jr.; Cornelius Vanderbilt; Eugene Meyer, the
new owner of the *Washington Post*; Louis Wiley of the *New York Times*; Ogden
Reid of the *New York Herald Tribune*; and old standbys like Whitney Warren, William Guthrie, Thomas Lamont, and Frederic Coudert.[62] Founded in
December 1934 and registered in January 1935 in Paris, where its council
offices were to be located, the new association would devote the whole of
1935 preparing for the opening of the New York office early in 1936. By then,
four years of debate and indecision had elapsed since the debt and disarma-

ment questions had soured Franco-American relations enough for the need for redressment to become manifest.

So it is that the period here under examination yields a collection of mixed trends, most notably the interwar nadir of Franco-American relations and the beginning of their recovery in the course of 1933. Through both decline and revival, the tension remained palpable between the need for a great propaganda effort in America, and the counter need for greater prudence in a country now so alive to foreign propagandists. So, too, while there was a recognition of the need to do more in the mass-audience fields of radio and cinema, priority was still being given to improving the supply and formatting of textual materials destined for circulation in America. And this choice doubtless reflects an underlying theme of French propaganda for more than two decades. Textual material was primarily aimed at America's educated elite, just as was the sustained emphasis on France's cultural achievements in art, music, and literature. It was because of that target, and its response, that Paul Claudel expressed more optimism than might have been warranted early in 1932. A recent tour of Kansas and Missouri, strongholds of German immigrants, suggested that Oeuvres's subtle educational and cultural efforts were paying dividends; and new evidence from the editorials of some of the New York papers, the *New York Times* in particular, also indicated that France was holding its own in the propaganda wars. It had its own brilliant public defenders, in the form of the Francophile community in New York and sympathetic journalists such as Walter Lippmann, Percy Philip, and Edwin James. We are not popular in America, Claudel observed. Americans "mistreat, wound, libel us, but they also admire us."[63] At least the elite did so, a distinction made three years later, early in 1935, by Claudel's successor, André de Laboulaye. It was gratifying, the latter reported, to see the "profound sympathy" in which France was held by the American elite; but the fact was that popular opinion had been colored far more by the Hearst presses, which seemed to attribute all of America's problems to the decision to get involved in Europe's war in 1917.[64]

This qualified, somewhat apprehensive appraisal was endorsed, and indeed surpassed, by a much lengthier assessment of the same year. Its principal author was Ernest Pezet, a member of the French Chamber of Deputies, and one of a small handful of parliamentarians who had demonstrated a sustained interest in the subject of French propaganda. His book, entitled *Sous les yeux du monde*, was the product of a long report that the Chamber's foreign affairs commission had submitted to parliament in February 1935 and that was addressed solely to the issue of French performance in the field of international propaganda.[65] On balance, the commission members—of whom Pezet was one—expressed considerable dissatisfaction with the current state of affairs, judging France's performance to be well behind that of the other principal European powers. While it roundly endorsed the long-standing emphasis on cultural propaganda, both educational and aesthetic, it lamented the paucity of human and financial resources. What was needed, the commission stressed repeatedly, was some kind of centralized command of all state propaganda abroad, by which all ministerial efforts would be coordinated through a single national committee, and funded—more liberally— through a single propaganda budget. Enough, they said, of paltry sums distributed by understaffed personnel in various ministerial departments and sporadically supplemented by unregulated, "secrets funds." Enough, too, of reliance on the well-intentioned but uncoordinated campaigns conducted by a surfeit of "private" groups, organizations, and associations—a condition that they thought was remediable through the creation of a general secretariat specifically dedicated to implementing the decisions of the central committee.[66]

This emphasis upon an improvement of the nation's propaganda infrastructure, in terms of both money and personnel, evidently appeared much warranted to informed observers in 1935. And it was a conclusion from which the foreign ministry could hardly dissent. Neither were the diplomats inclined to argue with the recommendation, clear but not terribly forceful, that more attention needed to be paid to media such as radio and cinema. Furthermore, the reaffirmed importance of cultural propaganda and its implicit target of foreign elites was entirely consistent with Quai d'Orsay thinking both past and current. On all of these matters, commission and foreign ministry were in broad agreement. But the one thing that had remained so central to the ministry's approach to America was not given much attention by the commission or by Ernest Pezet. While all agreed that any propaganda worthy of France was, by definition, a propaganda of truth, a propaganda of precise, accurate, and complete information, the commission was silent on how a foreign audience alert to outside interference was to be convinced of this benign intention. And that, of course, was the principal obstacle to propaganda in America, an obstacle so enduring that it took Nazi excesses to highlight French moderation. Indeed, it was that, not merely a resolve to spend more, that permitted an escalation of France's propaganda efforts in the United States in the years preceding World War II.

CHAPTER 6

From Peace to War, 1936–1939

❖

There is something grandly ironic in the fact that it took the Nazis, the last century's most vaunted propagandists, to revive France's propaganda fortunes in America. Ironic, not illogical. For the fact is that, although Hitler's regime tried to conceal its inherently aggressive nature beneath a peaceful vocabulary, neither the substance of its policies nor the manner of its propaganda was consistent with those professions. At home, it had been quick to repress any sign of resistance. Employers and workers, Catholics and Protestants, educators and farmers, either sympathized with the campaigns against socialists and Jews or were cowed into acquiescence—cowed, on the one hand, exhilarated on the other. For it seemed transparent to all that this new regime was bent on national revival. Freedom of speech sacrificed for order did not seem that bad a bargain to a population not fully released from the Depression and never allowed to forget the humiliation of Versailles. Step by apparently calculated step, the Führer was dismantling the settlement of 1919. No to German disarmament. No to restrictions on the size of the German army. No, in 1935, to the prohibition against a German air force. No, in 1936, to a demilitarized Rhineland. No, again, in 1938, to the restrictions against an Austro-German unification and to the consignment of Sudeten Germans to the Czechoslovak republic. And again no, in 1939, to the twenty-year-old provisions for an independent Polish state. No, finally, to peace, an answer about which the German population was more, but belatedly, ambivalent.

Curiously, while Americans were more determined to remain aloof from war—especially one triggered by enduring European squabbles—in the course of the 1930s, they were becoming less and less impressed by Herr Hitler. Some of this unease, eventually, had to do with Nazi foreign policy, as each year seemed to bring one more demand from Berlin, and one more promise that it would be the last. More of it had to do with the regime's domestic policies, especially the anti-Semitic measures that had commenced within months of Hitler's installation in January 1933. And American alarm mounted with the measures against Hitler's secular and religious opponents, and as the country slowly became one "Big Jail"—a phrase used by the outspoken American correspondent Dorothy Thompson, after her expulsion from Germany in August 1934.[1] There was also the matter of the regime's work in America, its efforts to manipulate opinion, perhaps even its desire to subvert the very democratic process that had been extinguished so successfully in Germany.[2]

Whatever their particular source of apprehension, attentive Americans slowly reappraised Franco-German tensions and slowly retreated from the notion that Chancellor Hitler was a reasonable man. By mid–1937, French Ambassador Georges Bonnet, Laboulaye's successor, was reporting that American opinion had become exasperated with Germany, partly, he said, because it was hostile to any form of dictatorship, and partly because it had become so disturbed by domestic repression of the Nazi variety. Two years later, the Washington embassy was satisfied that the vast majority of American newspapers had become critical of Germany and of the terror that Hitler seemed about to unleash on the world.[3] The truth was that Germany had actually increased French chances of currying favor in America. Rephrased, Hitler's excesses in the 1930s, both political and moral, gradually obscured American recollections of earlier French transgressions.

If Hitler, in his own way, proved an asset to France, so too did Franklin Roosevelt. Elected president for the first time in November 1932, Roosevelt had been early identified by French observers as a Francophile, and one with growth potential. Two years before his election to the White House, while still governor of the state of New York, he had been judged "very positively disposed to France."[4] And so, it would seem, he was. A classic example of America's eastern seaboard elite, the president had learned French from a childhood governess, studied the language at Groton and Harvard, honeymooned in Paris in 1905, and returned there with some frequency for reasons of both career and family. While evincing no very marked interest in French high culture, like Harold Ickes, his secretary for the interior, he admired the French as a people—on whose wartime sangfroid he had favorably commented—and took a special interest in Franco-American relations.[5] Certainly in contrast to Herbert Hoover, who, too often, had exhibited "an unmitigated scorn" for France, FDR was quickly categorized by Ambassadors Claudel and Laboulaye and former prime minister Paul Painlevé as decidedly "pro-French."[6]

Conversely, Roosevelt had no natural affinity for Germany, a country in which he had spent considerable time as a youth and whose school discipline had left unpleasant memories. Adulthood had brought no tempering of view. Not only had he advocated postwar prosecution of German war criminals, but he regretted the fact that the 1919 peace conference had not taken place in Berlin, as a reminder to Germans of the consequences of aggression. As for the Nazis, he early concluded that they were a form of evil incarnate. In 1933, having compared a translation of Hitler's *Mein Kampf* with its German original, the president remarked on the specious and misleading nature of the English version. "Hitler," he told Ambassador Claudel in the same year, "is a madman and his advisers . . . are even crazier than he," an impression he subsequently confirmed by branding the Führer a "visionary maniac" who likened himself to Julius Caesar and Jesus Christ, and who paced the floor "like a madman." Given the way most Germans had taken to the regime's bellicose talk, the president told the Washington press corps, and given French concerns about the demographic imbalance between France and Germany, "I would be scared too."[7]

If, between them, Hitler and Roosevelt were to widen the avenues for French propaganda efforts in America, yet a third force was rapidly coming into play. This was an indigenous French force, one that derived from public and official responses to the mounting threat from a rearming Germany. Clearly, greater effort was needed on all fronts, including that which faced the battalions of Nazi propagandists in America. Hardly more than a year after Hitler's accession to power, French observers were remarking on the deleterious effects of German propaganda in the United States. The number of American tourists disembarking at Le Havre had dropped appreciably, thanks, it was believed, to a sustained anti-French campaign in leading American magazines and newspapers.[8] Films, books, and student exchanges, too, were also part of the German offensive, one that by 1936–1937 was being executed by a film agency called Le Tobis, by the Westerman House bookshop, and by the Karl Schurz Foundation, all of them New York based.[9] Although there seemed to have been a waning of German interest in cultural propaganda in the late 1930s, there was none when it came to Nazi basics—at least as these were detected by French observers. First, the Nazis had secured control of all German media, thus tightening the grip on their own citizens. Second, they selected suitable pieces from one foreign press to feed to another, in the hopes of inflaming relations, say, between Britain and France, or between France and the United States. Third, they combed the foreign press for pieces sympathetic to Germany—but published by non-Germans—a search often satisfied in the columns of the Hearst newspaper empire. Fourth, into each such mission they poured vast amounts of money, on a scale never approached by France. Such, at least, was the way contemporary French observers perceived the propaganda front in the mid-to-late 1930s. And the conclusion they drew was unavoidable. The Third Republic had to do two things. Second, it had to commit more resources to wage this silent war. First, it had to develop a "mindset for propaganda."[10]

Sharpened awareness and improved opportunities, however, were only part of the difficult equation confronting the French foreign ministry and its agents in Paris and America. For the fact is that there remained a series of obstacles to any acceleration of their offensive in positive words and images. Indeed, the same obstacles reduced the entire course of Franco-American relations to such a snail's pace in the mid–1930s that one scholar has characterized the period a "diplomatic vacuum."[11]

One of those obstacles, familiar enough, was the sustained grip of American isolationism, a grip that only seemed to tighten before the prospect of another European imbroglio. If distaste for Hitler's regime had grown in proportion to Germany's unslaked appetite for territorial expansion, and to its savage domestic repression, such distaste had not been translated into a determination to risk American involvement on that troubled continent— the less so as tensions mounted in the Pacific between the United States and Japan. Indeed, in August 1936, President Roosevelt reiterated his intention of honoring the Neutrality Act of the previous year, that is, of keeping America free from the conflict virus apparently endemic in Europe, or—in the words of his colorful ambassador in Paris—of building an ark called *The United States of America*.[12] Furthermore, the suspicions remained that the Nazi phenomenon owed something to an unjust peace—"foolishly tough and humiliating"—and to an inflexible France. There was also an enduring suspicion that America somehow had been hoodwinked into war in 1917 by Anglo-French misrepresentations. So whatever improvement had been recorded in Franco-American relations during Roosevelt's first years as president, the French embassy was rightly doubtful that America would stand with France in the event of war. The popular mood, as well as that of Congress, remained resolutely hostile to any new entanglements in Europe.[13] And the idea that French propaganda could alter that state of mind carried its own liabilities.

If German policies raised the specter of war, and thus dissipated any American temptation to risk intervention, German propaganda work had a similarly neutralizing effect. Given their practiced distrust of foreign propaganda, in war and peace, Americans reacted to Nazi efforts among them by condemning all foreign attempts to manipulate domestic opinion. Reworded, the more alive they were to Germany's heavy-handed propaganda campaigns—in America as well as elsewhere—the more sensitive they were to any sign of foreign interference, including that directed from Paris.[14] Again and again, throughout the 1930s, those who monitored the distribution of French information in America kept returning to the point long reiterated by the vanished Jusserand. Whether expressed by Jules Henry in 1936 or by Jacques Kayser in 1939, the need for prudence and discretion remained uppermost in French minds. The latter's report, in particular, is worthy of remark. Americans, he said, had developed a "propaganda psychosis." It was this state of mind, he judged, that had inspired both the June 1938 law requiring all foreign-employed lobbyists to register with the State Department and the 1939 creation of a congressional committee to investigate anti-American activities—in particular, those waged by communists and fascists. With the stakes higher than ever, Kayser had no hesitation in recommending to his superiors continued reliance on the good offices of American Francophiles.[15]

The mutually supporting combination of American isolationism and American apprehensions about foreign propaganda was further reinforced by certain policy differences between France and America. In the mid–1930s, each continued to be aggravated by the other's Depression-sharpened protectionist measures ranging from cinema to cereals.[16] Another abrasion derived from monetary policy, and yet another from the issue of disarmament. Although FDR was more tolerant than many Americans of the French decision to defer war debt payments to the United States, he was less patient with French criticism of his decision to take the United States off the gold standard. That decision became the occasion for an open confrontation that occurred between the two countries at the London Economic Conference in the summer of 1933 and that led to extremely bitter feelings on the part of both delegations. It was there, and then, that William Bullitt, future American ambassador to Paris, described Georges Bonnet, future French ambassador to America and future foreign minister, "as cooperative as a rattlesnake." As for the long-enduring problem of disarmament, the divide between the two countries remained wide, and for a time wider when, that October, Germany withdrew from the discussions in Geneva and cited French intransigence as its justification. Although there is no reason to believe that Roosevelt regarded France as solely, even primarily, responsible for the impasse, he was certainly irritated by Paris press criticism of his perceived inability to understand France's point of view.[17]

Less able by far, and less willing, were America's seasoned critics of France, whether on the more defined ground of policy or the impressionistic ground of cultural perception. Leading the charge, and constant as ever, were the Hearst presses across the United States. In February 1934 the *San Francisco Examiner* had a field day with the street riots in Paris, playing up the use of black troops to quell the disorder and speculating on the possibilities of civil war. On the other side of the country, the *New York American* kept its own readers alert to the threat of a French propaganda onslaught and to the sundry ways in which profligate France continued to spend its money—instead of paying its war debts.[18] But on 5 April 1936, Hearst and the *American* plunged to new depths, or so French monitors fathomed the descent. France was simultaneously excoriated as the "Constant Menace to European Peace" and dismissed as the "Sick Woman of Europe." Not only had France been responsible for war in 1914, it was about to precipitate a new one, and one with its newfound ally, the communist regime of Russia:

> France repudiates her debts and obligations and then accuses others of doing so. France continually plots war and conquest, and then denounces others for desiring equality and independence. France is the disturber of the peace of the world, the destroyer of liberty, the betrayer of trusts, the repudiator of obligations, the Judas among peoples, the Cain among nations, and with the mark of Cain on her brow she wickedly and foolishly precipitates more . . . universal and unending slaughter. The Republic of France was born in the shadow of the guillotine and will end there.[19]

Little wonder the embassy was apoplectic, characterizing Hearst's efforts to sway millions of readers as "calumnious" and Hearst himself as the "megalomanic and malignant old man of San Simeon."[20]

Other voices joined with that of Hearst in alerting Americans to the futility of defending an honorless and self-depicted victim—even if, by contrast, they were sotto voce. Early in 1933, for example, the *Washington Post* carried a headlined article, "French Journalists Depend on Graft for Livelihood," with a subtitle reference to France's forthcoming propaganda campaign in America. French journalism, author Westbrook Pegler allowed, was "honestly and candidly corrupt," a profession that he likened to a poorly paid waiter who received tips for good service. Perhaps that was why, he might have surmised, an uncomprehending French public was behind its government's position on disarmament—a position that the *Post*'s editors saw as central to the impasse in negotiations at Geneva.[21] The *Chicago Tribune* was more critical, particularly when the left-leaning Popular Front was in power between 1936 and 1937. Articles addressed to French social turbulence were common, as were eye-catching headline references to a country that "Fears Red Revolution." But strikes and other forms of social disorder, the paper's editors opined, were hardly justification for the "dictatorship" being constructed by the socialist premier Léon Blum. Anticipating a receptive response from readers educated to detest tyranny and socialism, they summarized the premier's experiment, and his ambition, quite simply: "He has spent too much money; he has dislocated the economic life of the country. Bankruptcy impends. . . . Blum and his Popular Front government have put France in a deep hole. He says that only as dictator can he save it."[22]

Still other voices, and other conduct, raised higher the barriers to closer Franco-American relations. Not all of them American. In March 1936 the French Information Office in New York lamented the effect of a lecture given by Gabriel Rémond, a past president of France's National Federation of Catholic Students. Quite inadvertently, but at one blow, the young speaker had managed to disparage France's governing elite—for having lost its moral bearings—and unnerve his audience by some inferred fascistic-sounding remarks about French youth and their passion for nation and self-sacrifice. More damaging still was a published interview with a visiting curator from the Louvre whose latent contempt for American tourists in Paris had erupted into a remark about "casting pearls before swine."[23]

On balance, therefore, the prospects for new propaganda initiatives by France in America were simultaneously improved and inhibited. The growing Nazi menace was steadily underscoring the need for renewed effort by France, but also the need for greater prudence in the United States. Although Roosevelt enjoyed "extremely cordial relations" with the Francophilic publishers and editors of the *New York Times*, and although his personal distrust of Hitler was at least partly behind the rearmament program that was under way in America by late 1938, he still lead a nation and a Congress that were isolationist in temperament and gun-shy about foreign attempts to manipulate American opinion.[24] Besides, he remained preoccupied by his ongoing efforts to dig the country out of the Depression through a bold but controversial vision of state-driven, New Deal economics. From the French point of view, caution continued to dictate the pace and character of the foreign ministry's propaganda efforts—patiently waiting for Hitler to alienate more

Americans, and for the president to translate that alienation into more moral and material help for Europe's embattled democracies. Patience, however, did not mean standing pat.

Leading the way in parliament was Ernest Pezet, veteran member of the Chamber's foreign affairs commission and veteran critic of the government's postwar propaganda efforts. In June 1936, he and Gaston Riou proposed legislation that would create an interministerial *conseil supérieur* for propaganda, as well as a revamped secretariat to serve that council's bidding. Justification for this initiative was identified as twofold. First, Hitler's Third Reich was way ahead of France in the field of propaganda. Indeed, the authors claimed that the two countries were already at war, with the more aggressive of the two employing "the mind, ideas, words, science, and all other forms of expression" as their arms and munitions. It was time, therefore, for France to respond with more energy and greater resources, enlisting the print media, cinema, radio, and the fine arts to combat this onslaught. Second, it was time because French efforts to date had been inadequate. Despite a litany of criticisms going back to the 1920s, successive governments had failed to connect diplomacy, national defense, and public opinion. Worse, they had failed because they had confused two things for one. Foreigners' views of France were not the same as the French view of themselves. "Unfortunately, we tend to forget that foreigners do not have the same mentality."[25]

With that in mind, the first essential step was to replace that verbal irritant *propagande*, with the word *information*. A second, more challenging, was to teach an inward-looking France to look abroad, so that its information program would respond not only to French concerns but also to those circulating in each foreign country. A third, in the interests of the second, was to combine more effective use of the new information technologies, such as cinema and radio, with a less "academic," more mass-based promotional campaign. A fourth, significantly, was to adhere to what had always been the French way in propaganda, namely the circulation of truth. "For us, propaganda is nothing but accurate information openly distributed." And that information, they advised, had to emphasize France's commitment to a peaceful, energetic, and modern future for its youth.[26]

Spurred on by such deputies as Pezet and Riou, the Popular Front government convened its first interministerial meeting in September 1936. Chaired by Camille Chautemps, minister of state, the meeting brought together representatives from the Quai d'Orsay, public works, education, and commerce, all of them involved in some way or another in French "propaganda abroad." Although nothing very concrete emerged from the gathering, those attending agreed on the need for better coordination of efforts and for increased financial resources. Of particular interest to this study were the remarks of Jean Marx, from Oeuvres, and of a Monsieur Cavalier, representative from the Department for Higher Education, both of whom spoke positively of the long-standing cooperation between their two ministries and their shared resources for work abroad.[27]

Five months later, Camille Chautemps had an opportunity to report on the progress of the French propaganda services, this time to the Senate's foreign affairs commission. And by then he was appearing not only as minister of state, but also as chair of a new, interministerial coordinating committee for "services d'information et d'action à l'étranger," a committee created the previous October. Introduced by Senator and former ambassador Henri Bérenger—who expressed a particular concern about how, in America, German and Italian propagandists were outstripping their French rivals— Chautemps acknowledged the pressing need for more effective effort in the United States. Indeed, he admitted that the French "information services"— an expression deliberately more delicate than that of "propaganda"—had their work cut out for them. While it was true that the foreign ministry had its press office; education, its university exchange program; and commerce, its promotional campaigns for tourism, the fact remained that there had been too little money for any of them and too little coordination among them. Redressment of these problems in coordination was now his responsibility. Somehow, he suggested, the government had to increase its financial commitment to these services—in the form of both public and secret accounts. It also had to ensure higher efficiency across the services by tightening the coordination of efforts, so that the press services in the premier's office and those in the foreign, interior, colonial, and national defense ministries were all on the same page.[28]

This effort at coordination during 1936–1937, it should be said, seemed to have had limited results. Perhaps ministerial territorialism proved too much for the Coordinating Committee—a body that itself seems to have met infrequently. Perhaps the high level of political and economic turbulence within France deflected concerns about the need for an information offensive abroad. Perhaps, too, as suggested in one note prepared in May 1938 by the foreign ministry's press service, what was needed was not so much a major structural modification—for instance, the attempt to create a propaganda ministry during Léon Blum's short-lived government of March 1938—as a major psychological modification. French decision makers really needed to believe in the power of word and image, and needed to believe with the same fervor as the dictators in the necessity of waging an energetic propaganda counteroffensive.[29]

While the strength of that argument became more obvious as the threat of another European war grew in the final years of the decade, so too did that for a change in structure. By early 1939, with the dangers of the Czech crisis so narrowly averted, Deputy Adrien Dariac was again calling upon the government for a major informational initiative—this time through a "brand-new" service for the coordination of propaganda. As proof of the need for prompt action, he pointed out that even the Americans, so long allergic to the scent of propaganda, had just created within the State Department a section for the dissemination of American ideas and culture.[30] Instructive as that point might have been, however, the French government had more immediate concerns; and it was the latter that triggered a series of initiatives over the following ten months.

While the Czech crisis of September 1938 had not produced a hot war, it had unleashed a cold war of words. The potential for armed combat was there for all to see, however much the language on both sides had been full of pacific, if disbelieved, assurances. Indeed, the use of language had been central to the crisis itself as well as its resolution, as had been the strict control of information pertaining to the deployment and readiness of any nation's armed forces. State censorship again had seemed a sensible device in a time of crisis; but in this case it seemed sensible even after the fact. Only days after the resolution of that central European crisis, and the effective takeover of the Czech lands by German troops, Premier Edouard Daladier tightened the French state's grip on all radio broadcasting. The *Christian Science Monitor* called it a regime of "virtual censorship" and advised its readers that Paris would vet economic and financial news as well as the strictly political. Within six months the grip had been further tightened, this time through a so-called antipropaganda law, a law aimed at foreign manipulation of French domestic opinion. Publicly declaring its intent to root out any media material designed and financed to divide the French populace, the government took aim at anyone "tending to stir up racial or religious hatred." Perpetrators, according to these parliament-backed decree measures, would be charged under the law, and if found guilty, would face possible fines, confiscation of property, or imprisonment.[31]

As the reader might have surmised, these intensified efforts at information control within France were reflections of recent developments beyond that country's borders. Not only were Franco-German relations deteriorating in the spring of 1939, in the wake of Hitler's decision to complete the takeover of Czechoslovakia, but so too were Franco-Italian relations, principally over land and sea rivalries in North Africa and the Mediterranean. As the relations with Rome worsened through the summer, and as the Reich's gaze focused on some kind of confrontation with Poland, pressure mounted in Paris for measures that would exceed the simple devices of press censorship. Jean Dariac's report of April 1939 was part of that campaign for a more sweeping propaganda initiative. So was a series of articles that appeared between 1937 and 1939 in the press magazine *Presse publicité*, appealing for greater vigor in France's propaganda efforts abroad.[32]

To that end, in late July 1939, Premier Edouard Daladier addressed a report to the president of the republic, Albert Lebrun. Rehearsing recent but more modest attempts to coordinate information flow from government ministries, the premier concluded that the time for something more ambitious had come. Drawing upon provisions contained within the parliament-approved July 1938 Law on the General Organization of the Nation in Wartime, Daladier announced the creation of an interministerial General Commissariat for Information (CGI). Reminiscent of the body that had been run by Antony Klobukowski in 1917–1918, the new commissariat was to coordinate all ministerial information agencies, and was to do so under the direct authority of the premier's office. Lest there be any doubt about its sweeping mandate, Daladier explained that the CGI's responsibilities would include control of both state and private radio broadcasting as well as cinema distribution. At its head he placed Jean Giraudoux, internationally known playwright, career diplomat, and seasoned public servant within the foreign ministry's Service des Oeuvres. Thus, only a month before Hitler's invasion of Poland, France was finally putting into place the nucleus of a wartime information ministry.[33]

Parallel with these broadly conceived structural developments in French information services were the ongoing efforts to cultivate American opinion— ongoing, and accelerating, but also familiar in strategic design and in tactical agency. As always, this was to be a campaign of subtle persuasion, conducted wherever possible by American volunteers; by goodwill ambassadors from France's arts and letters community; and by state-appointed, publicly identifiable officers whose official functions included supporting the efforts of volunteers, French and foreign. It is to this group of officers that we now turn for a contemporary reading of France's place in America's perceptions in the mid-to-late nineteen-thirties.

Prominent among them were Ambassadors Laboulaye, Bonnet, and Saint-Quentin, and the chargé d'affaires, Jules Henry. Although the former were optimistic about their country's improving image among Americans—

and what Bonnet called a "current of deep sympathy" for France—they were also at one with their government's new resolve to intensify its propaganda efforts.[34] But prudence remained the watchword, and maintaining it was an objective that, ironically, was the more attainable given the still-limited financial and human resources accorded to the embassy. As Henry tactfully pointed out to his masters in Paris, the upside of France's modest efforts was that few Americans really believed that France was meddling in their affairs.[35] And what they did discern, in ways precisely consistent with French propaganda policy, was an emphasis upon cultural affiliation.

Still, none was satisfied with the status quo. Some thought the French propaganda campaign too elite driven, focused on wealthy Americans rather than on the ordinary citizen of Main Street. Others doubted the very existence of a campaign. "Our propaganda in America," one soured observer noted with deliberate overstatement, "is nonexistent; and everyone knows it."[36] More diplomatically, Ambassador Bonnet urged the Quai d'Orsay to address a series of lingering obstacles. The complete texts of French ministerial addresses needed to be cabled to America, as a matter of course, for immediate dissemination to the American media. French film distribution in the United States was still inadequate, as were the content, frequency, and quality of French radio broadcasts to that country. More needed to be done in the field of Franco-American student exchanges, including better preparation for French students who were America bound. Although the latter were not intended to be anything quite as crude as "agents de propagande," their utility to France did necessitate a more thorough grounding in contemporary European affairs than was presently in place.[37]

The embassy's chargé d'affaires enlarged upon the ambassador's views in a series of reports dispatched between 1936 and 1938. Resigned, it would seem, to the unlikelihood of a significantly expanded embassy budget, Henry recommended a series of modest financial outlays. The embassy and consulates needed much stronger radio receivers in order to stay in closer touch with Paris and to be able to promote programs broadcast from France. They also needed reliable projectors in order to promote French film products, direct telephone lines to the United Press in order to strengthen links with the American media, and—though outside the government's strict purview—a larger French press contingent in America.[38] On a more ambitious plane, Henry wanted to see a French library in the city of New York that would be a facility for "intellectual diffusion" through the media of French literature, scholarship, and film. And in keeping with the continuing emphasis upon cultural propaganda, he remarked on the need to refurbish existing French collections on university campuses from Illinois to Louisiana and from Pennsylvania to California. Even the established libraries at the American-run French Institute in New York and at the American Union of Saint Jean-Baptiste in Woonsocket, Rhode Island, needed an infusion of recent French books and periodicals.[39]

In a way reminiscent of similar arguments current in Paris, Henry pushed for something else: coordination of effort. In 1937, by pure coincidence, the timing proved propitious. Preparations for the Paris Exhibition of that year provided a splendid argument for bringing together officials from the embassy, consulate general, tourist office, and national railway office with French representatives from the ostensibly private sector—principally the New York–based French Chamber of Commerce, the French Line, and the Information Office. Together they would work not only on facilitating a time-specific American participation in France, but also on the longer-range promotion of France among Americans.[40] Would, Henry mused, that such coordination were possible for the American-run, Francophilic organizations such as the Federation of the Alliance Française, the French Institute, the French Lycée, and the France-America Society. But their charters were all different, their executives were all American, and some of the latter—mindful of public appearance—were balking at French attempts even to provide books for their facilities. Frank Pavey, in particular, was proving especially obdurate on this point; so much so that Henry believed that the longtime president of the federation was inadvertently leading an "anti-French campaign." This human obstacle, compounded by a new generation of less distinguished leadership in France-Amérique, simply underscored the challenge of trying to magnify the image of France in the United States. Only at the French Institute of New York, under its distinguished president, Dr. Hamilton Rice, was there ground for optimism.[41]

That had been in the autumn of 1937. A year and a half later the mood had changed again, for the better. Hitler's moves against Austria and Czechoslovakia, combined with a more intensified campaign of repression against his domestic opponents, had taken their toll on American Germanophilia. No less important was an initiative taken by Bonnet's successor, René de Saint-Quentin. Picking up on the idea of the U.S.-based coordinating committee that had been created to promote the Paris Exhibition of 1937, the ambassador assembled in early 1939 a new Action and Information Committee. New York based, this committee comprised representatives from the embassy, the consulate general, the French Chamber of Commerce, the French Line, the French Railroad Service, the French Tourist Office, the French Information

Center, the French-American Banking Corporation, the French Lycée, the French Institute, Agence Havas, Agence Téléfrance, the French Broadcasting Service, and the French Cinematic Service. Committed to the principle of monthly meetings, this new committee assumed responsibility for coordinating the diverse promotional activities of its constituent parts, as well as for compiling a national directory of Americans of demonstrated sympathy for France—agents whose assistance might be solicited in a variety of ways.

By the late 1930s such a directory would have continued to feature the names of many prominent American individuals and organizations. And behind the names and titles of the agents themselves was a familiar pattern of priorities. Once more, a representative sample will have to suffice. From the world of the arts came a collection of men and women whose talents and generosity had been rewarded by nominations to or promotions in the French Legion of Honor: Sylvia Beach of Shakespeare and Company; Albert Bender, San Francisco benefactor of the Louvre; George Blumenthal of New York's Metropolitan Museum; John Dorrance and Georges Haardt, wealthy friends of the Gobelins Works; conductors Louis Hasselmans of the Chicago Opera and Walter Damrosch of the American Conservatory at Fontainebleau; and Chauncey McCormick, vice president of the Chicago Museum of Fine Arts. From the world of education came a succession of presidents: James B. Conant, of Harvard; Stephen Duggan, of the Institute for International Education; Frank Pierrepont Graves, of the State University of New York; A. Hamilton Rice and Forsyth Wickes, of the French Institute in New York; Hamilton Holt, of Rollins College; William Mather Lewis, of Lafayette College; Robert Hall McCormick, of the Chicago chapter of the Alliance Française; Anne Morgan, of the American Friends of France; Frederick B. Robinson, of City College, New York; James Brown Scott, of Washington's French Institute; and Walter Dill Scott, of Northwestern University.

The media world, too, offered a galaxy of those who were proven Francophiles: Edwin James, Percy Phillip, Nicholas Roosevelt, and Louis Wiley of the *New York Times*; Ogden Reid, Leland Stowe, and Walter Lippmann of the *New York Tribune*;[42] John Elliott of the *Tribune* and, with increasing frequency, of the *San Francisco Examiner*; Frank Knox of the *Chicago Daily News*; George Cameron, owner and director of the *San Francisco Chronicle*; Raymond C. Carroll, Paris correspondent for the *Philadelphia Public Ledger*; Colonel Frederick Palmer of the North American News Agency; Clare Luce, writer and part owner of *Life*, *Fortune*, and *Time* magazines; Clayland Morgan, publicity director for the French Line and subsequently a spokesperson for the president of the National Broadcasting

Corporation (NBC); Clark M. Eichelberger and James Shotwell, joint patrons of *The French Say*; Helen Harvitt, editor of the *French Review*; W. M. Hewitt, owner of *Le Courrier des Etats-Unis*; Augustin Lusinchi, editor of the *Courrier du Pacifique*; Fernand Merckx, editor of *Le Messager de New York*; Martha Levit, editor of *La Semaine de New York*; Frank Monaghan, Yale-based editor of the *Franco-American Review*; and Henry Gratton Doyle, Washington-based editor of the *Modern Language Review*.

These soloists, of course, found ample support from a chorus of seasoned Francophilic associations across America. Some had an historical thrust, for example, the American Friends of Lafayette, the Franco-American Historical Society, and the Association of Veterans of the Foreign Legion; and some a linguistic, among these the American Association of Teachers of French, Le Lien du Parler Français, the transcontinental Federation of the Alliance Française, and the intercampus networks of Cercles Français. Some, such as the New York–based French Chamber of Commerce and the French-American Banking Corporation, saw the business world as their best opportunity for the promotion of France; while others brought to the public eye that country's commitment to charitable endeavors—whether through its continued support of the French Hospital in New York and the Société de charité des dames françaises in Los Angeles or of numerous *sociétés françaises de bienfaisance* in Chicago, New Orleans, New York, and Philadelphia. On top of this group came the sundry, cause-driven, American-directed organizations such as the Amitiés féminines de la France, the Société alsacienne, the Athénée Louisianais, the Union Saint Jean Baptiste, the French Institutes of New York and Washington, and the Los Angeles–based Institut France-Amérique, or the American Association for the Assistance to French Artists, the American Society for the French Lycée in New York, and the 1938 reincarnation of a wartime propaganda group called French American Art.[43]

This representative sampling of principally American-born agents and American-operated agencies had a French counterpart, which is to say individuals and associations also volunteering in the cause of closer Franco-American relations in the Hitler era. Once more, the world of French arts and letters offered up modestly subsidized battalions of men and women to tour America and succor American eyes, ears, and minds. Among these were La Montagne St-Hubert, the artist; pianists Nadia Boulanger, Henri Casadeus, and Magda Tagliaferro; Madeleine Monnier, the cellist; Pierre Duvauchelle, the conductor; opera impresario Jacques Rouché; theater director André Barsacq; Mme B. Dussane, the actress; Maurice Barret, the architect; and writers Jules Bois, Eve Curie, André Maurois, and Jules Romains; as well as a stream of academics representing the sciences, social sciences, and humanities and making themselves heard as guest lecturers from Boston to Stanford: Pierre Auger, Marcel Aubert, Raoul Blanchard, Bernard Fay, Gilbert Chinard, Charles Cestre, Georges Duthuit, Albert Feuillerat, Paul Hazard, Antoine Meillet, André Morize, and André Siegfried.[44]

By the mid–1930s informal ambassadors such as these had a complex support system from which to draw, even before departing French soil. In the first instance, most continued to enjoy access to subsidized travel costs through monies provided directly or indirectly by the foreign ministry's Service des Oeuvres or by the education ministry. More commonly, when support was indirect, monies from both ministries were flushed through education's fine arts division, into Philippe Erlanger's Service d'action artistique, and out again to the Association française d'action artistique, of which Erlanger was secretary-general.[45] It was this association that publicly distributed the subventions on the recommendation of its Conseil d'action artistique, itself advised by a set of expert subcommittees.[46] But if money were one thing, information was another; and Paris now featured a collection of agencies capable of preparing French travelers for America. Quite apart from the information facilities available at education, foreign affairs, or tourism, or in the universities, there were now several offices capable of furnishing officially endorsed information on both countries. Those offices included the Paris headquarters of the Comité France-Amérique, on the avenue Victor Emmanuel III; the Office français de renseignements, on the Champs-Elysées; and the Center for Documentary Information, on the rue Notre-Dame des Victoires.[47]

Each of these offices in Paris had a companion facility in New York, to which such travelers, or indeed inquisitive American residents, could turn for assistance—the most notable by the late 1930s being the French Information Office, on Fifth Avenue. At the same time, the network of information agents in America extended far beyond the metropolis of New York, from the salaried French professionals in the Washington embassy and the regional consulates, to American correspondents in the far-flung empires of the Société des Gens de Lettres, the Association Française d'Action Artistique, and the Alliance Française.[48] While these first two organizations operated a network of literary correspondents in America, as elsewhere, the Alliance Française ensured publicity and audience for those who would speak or perform on behalf of France, many of whom traveled on the account of Action Artistique and also were accommodated and financially compensated by funds awarded to the Fédération des Alliances Françaises in North America by the Service des Oeuvres in Paris.

For their part, the professionals assumed the duties of their predecessors, ever seeking to enhance the image and magnify the voice of France. They were there, for example, to add their gloss to opening nights at the French Theater of New York—especially for performances conducted by the much subsidized, and thus much traveled, Paris company of the Théâtre des Quatre Saisons—or at the International Theater of Chicago, where the Paris-subsidized Georges Cauuet was the director.[49] The same was true for France's musicians, the living and the dead. Members of the embassy or the consulates made a point of appearing when Robert Casadeus played Vincent d'Indy with the San Francisco Symphony, or when the Paris Conservatoire's Magda Tagliaferro played with the New York Philharmonic, or when the curtain rose on Gustave Charpentier's *Louise* at the Metropolitan Opera.[50]

For them, the professionals, the representation of France was a mix of the habitual and the occasional. Prize-giving, for example, was an ongoing affair: silver medals for students of French at the American University in Washington; the Joffre medal for French oratory at Stanford; more medals still for high school students in California, Massachusetts, and Illinois; a *croix* in the Legion of Honor for an associate editor of *National Geographic*.[51] Also enduring was the unbidden celluloid war in which French diplomats sought to defend the *tricouleur* through either praise or protest. Recognizing that cinema was "the best instrument we have at our disposal," French diplomats tried to promote American awareness of the most recent film offensive from France and to convince themselves that French-language offerings, such as the 1937 releases *Mayerling* and *Club de Femmes*, really had strengthened France's reputation in the eyes of American critics.[52] But this was not necessarily so in the eyes of a public more accustomed to the silver screen of Hollywood. In the eyes of counteroffensive officers, California could never quite distinguish between liberty and license, between character and caricature, indeed between what was real and what imaginary. And so France and its people too often seemed distorted by the lens of willfully myopic cameramen and by filmmakers who cast aspersions on the honesty of French public servants, exaggerated the sympathies of French women for German soldiers, insulted the French general staff, and slandered the Foreign Legion. Referring to this slander, and Paramount's provocative *Beau Geste*, Ambassador Saint-Quentin suggested that the studio had engaged in "revolting" scenes crudely calculated to appeal to the viewer's "basest instincts"—an acerbic view, but arguably less so than the earlier complaint that Hollywood films "never required an ounce of intellectual effort."[53]

Habitual, too, was the employment of the print media, with varying

degrees of clandestinity. The energetic press agent Thérèse Bonney continued to secure contracts through the sympathetic offices of Oeuvres head Jean
Marx. And thus charged, she continued to place France-related text and photographs in American papers and magazines such as the *New York Times* and
the *Saturday Evening Post*, most if not all relating to the brilliance of French
art, film, and photography. Jean-Paul Freyss, director of the semiofficial Center for Documentary Information, with its New York office on Park Avenue,
was similarly engaged. Referring to Freyss's efforts to place officially endorsed articles in the American press, Ambassador Saint-Quentin engaged
the embassy in this enterprise but stressed the need for "the greatest discretion." Americans, he reminded his minister, were now accustomed to equat-
ing propaganda with subversion.[54] The same advice applied to Robert Valeur's
French Information Office, which not only responded to inquiries from the
American public but also used foreign ministry monies to sponsor such publications as *The French Say* and *French Opinion* and to distribute them to
subscribers.[55]

What was not habitual was occasional, although the scale of some
events was vast and time-consuming. Among the less demanding was the art
exhibition arranged in 1936 by Thérèse Bonney for the Maison Française at
the Rockefeller Center; the inauguration that year in Washington of a statue
of Jules Jusserand; in 1937, in Los Angeles, the installation of a statue of
Lafayette and, the same year, a display of French publications for an international book exhibition in New Orleans; in 1938, the official opening in the
Sloane Building of a "Salon du Louvre," a boutique specializing in replicated
objets d'art. Far more ambitious, and costly in money, materials, and personnel, were the plans for the construction and operation of a "thoroughly modern" French pavilion at the New York World's Fair of 1939, a structure
intended to associate France with the fair's forward-looking theme: "Building the World of Tomorrow." Although entrusted to the special offices of a
commissioner general, the planning for this imposing, six-thousand-square-
meter building and for the exhibitions mounted within certainly required
months of sustained support from diplomatic officers in both France and
America. And consistent with emphases from the past were those of the
present: France intellectual, across the humanities and sciences; France aesthetic and athletic, from art to sports; France luxurious, from interior design
to personal adornment; France powerful, past and present, on land and sea,
in air and empire.[56]

Just months before the New York fair opened its gates in the spring of
1939, the Quai d'Orsay received a comprehensive assessment of French pro-

paganda in America, one commissioned by the office of the premier and foreign minister. Its author was Jacques Kayser, director of the Paris-based information service Téléfrance. Given Téléfrance's America-targeted publication *Réalités françaises* and the author's personal familiarity with America, there was good reason for the ministry to pay heed to this thirty-five-page report.

Kayser made it clear that, within his government's campaign to cultivate American opinion, the word remained paramount, whether spoken or written. As for the former, of particular value was the debating forum on university campuses or in schools, clubs, and sundry associations. More effective than the set-piece lecture, an ably waged debate afforded rich opportunities to illuminate the French point of view—providing that accurate and timely information were at the participants' disposal. To extend these opportunities beyond the northeastern United States, Kayser added, to the more prominently isolationist Midwest, South, and Pacific Coast, would be of especial value to France. Sometimes the spoken word came from the stage, especially in New York, where the French Theatre, inspired by Gertrude Robinson Smith, regularly performed French productions and sponsored the visits of theater companies from France. More often the word was printed, either in the form of such French-language publications as *La semaine à New York*, *Le petit journal*, and his own *Réalités françaises* or in that of English publications such as *The French Say* or *French Opinion*, periodicals issued through the French Information Office, or the occasional pamphlets issued in English translation through the Paris-based Centre d'Informations Documentaires and its office in New York.[57] Or perhaps American exposure to things French came, instead, in the form of the French Book of the Month Club and Sequana, its sister association, which together enjoyed some six thousand American subscriptions.

The printed word was also the entrée to education in a more formal sense. Kayser applauded Oeuvres's purchase and distribution in 1936 of an American-published pamphlet entitled *Why Study French?* a document designed to resist school board efforts to cut back on the teaching of French.[58] Applause also went to ongoing French government purchases of another American-produced brochure, this one a handbook on French schools and universities. First published in 1926 under the auspices of the Institute of International Education, this Francophilic brochure by Dr. Horatio S. Krans was recognized as an asset worthy of indirect investment by the French Information Office, the French Line, the French Tourist Bureau, and the ministry of national education. More direct, because they were published through the French Information Office with costs defrayed by the French Line, were two other educational brochures, one called *Enjoy Your Studies: Summer Courses in France* and the other, *Schools in France*.[59]

Less happily, progress seemed slow, if perceptible, within the newer media of radio and film. As for the former, Kayser took heart from the fact that NBC and the Columbia Broadcasting System (CBS) were now capable of broadcasting direct from Europe and thus of alerting their audiences to periodic crises. But he was less sanguine about France's still technically troubled effort to broadcast regularly and well to the American market. Too often, French news broadcasts were either too late in the evening, too dated in content, or too weak in signal. As for the cinema, the situation was more mixed. Damage control was exceptionally difficult when a headstrong Hollywood regularly put entertainment before fact, a disposition that frequently led to embarrassing caricatures of France and its citizens, and embarrassing *contretemps* between its diplomats and the American film industry. More promising by far was the future of the French documentary film, an educational device in which American educators had expressed considerable interest. Thanks to a cooperative effort between the New York–based French Cinema Center and a consultative committee chaired by Professor James T. Shotwell that compiled a catalog of these French documentaries, by 1939 thousands of American schools and colleges had more reliable, low-cost access to quality French cinema productions.[60]

In all, therefore, the Kayser appraisal of France's propaganda work in America to 1939 combined praise and criticism. American opinion was turning away from the dictators; and, as a result of the June 1938 law that required State Department registration of any organization employed by a foreign government, the anxiety about *officially* acknowledged propaganda had actually diminished in contrast to an elevated concern about disguised and surreptitious attempts to manipulate American opinion. Much more work was needed on the development of French radio and film, on the speed with which French text and photographs could be transmitted and distributed in the United States, and on the provision of prominent and English-fluent speakers. But the emphasis on accuracy and candor, on education and culture generally, and on the enlistment of American agents remained as sensible as it had ever been. And above all else, the need for prudence.

Even with the sharper premonitions in August 1939 of a new war in Europe—this time Hitler-provoked—conventional wisdom remained unruffled. It was true that American press opinion had now swung strongly against Hitler's terror tactics at home and abroad, but shrewd observers understood that feelings against were hardly the same as feelings for. The vision of a new Anglo-French alliance against Germany only reminded some Americans of the last war, of the costs and the casualties, and of the suspicion that their president had been lured into war in 1917. The slowly intensifying national debate about the morality and the rationality of neutrality only meant that French propagandists had to "redouble their caution." As the consul in Boston put it, American "isolationist sentiment is particularly suspicious about anything or anyone critical of American neutrality." For that reason, Ambassador Saint-Quentin actually argued against using the outbreak of war in Europe to create a larger and more visible information service in America.[61]

CHAPTER 7

Words of War,
1939–1940

❧

$\mathcal{F}$or more than a half century, scholars have argued over the material and psychological condition of France upon the outbreak of war in September 1939. Given the early but brief and lackluster offensive against Germany that autumn, and given the equally brief and spectacularly unsuccessful effort to contain the German offensive the following spring, it was instantly apparent that France's defeat had been inevitable. Almost as instant were two, seemingly disparate diagnoses of the condition that had produced the defeat. Smug and complacent, overconfident about the superiority of its resources and its planning, France had fallen first to its own hubris and only second to the German army. Or, sedated by the fear of a new war, unnerved by the suspicion of Germany's military superiority, the country had entered the war halfheartedly, without conviction in the nation's cause or in its ability to prevail. In the past, I have tried to explain these contradictory diagnoses through an analysis rooted in the heterogeneity of any society within which contradictory perceptions have the luxury of self-expression. Together, the complacency and the fear produced an overarching ambivalence; and it was the latter that characterized France after 1918 and in 1940.[1]

Although virtually no one in 1939 anticipated the suddenness of a collapse but months removed, and although many continued to anticipate a distant Allied victory, there is no question but that the decade had been filled with premonitions. Principal among them was simply that of war reawakened after only twenty years. But that specter was fed not only by memories of the past but also by quite specific apprehensions about the future. Technicians, or rather some of them, worried about the comparative merits of French and German armored units—invoking statistics about steel plating, weapon caliber, fuel range, and maximum speed, to alert or alarm fellow experts.

Strategists, or some of them, worried about a failure to contain an initial German offensive, in the wake of which vital industries in northeastern France might be overrun as in 1914, thus compromising hopes of victory over the long term. Resource managers and economists, again some of them, worried about the pace of production as well as about the tension between spending in the present and husbanding financial resources for the future. The populace, much of it, worried about war in the skies, that fiery vision of incendiaries and poison gas delivered by the tons from undetected aircraft flying above their cities.[2]

Included on that list of apprehensions, swelling the ranks of French premonitions, was concern about the country's preparedness for a war of words. As André Malraux reminded an American audience early in 1939, some words were the equivalent of incendiary bombs, and ought to be wrapped "with a scarlet band on which one could read: 'High Explosives. Handle with care.'"[3] But here, too, in the eyes of some, France's record was as paltry as it was in the production of aircraft and tanks. With the advent of war in 1939 and, accordingly, with the stakes higher than in peacetime, one might have predicted a new wave of domestic criticism and a flurry of suggested reforms. Such a prophet would have been vindicated. The indictments, many of them perfectly well intentioned, were to pick up momentum within two months of war's return. While such complaints merit closer but later consideration, one might again predict their overall contour based on the pattern of the past. France needed to spend more, to coordinate its information services more effectively, to make better domestic and foreign use of radio and cinema as counteroffensive devices against Nazi propaganda, and to concentrate on those simple but true ideas and emotions with which ordinary citizens at home and abroad might relate. Before such complaints can be assayed, however, one has to be familiar with the French propaganda machine as assembled in the summer of 1939.

It was on 29 July that the government of Edouard Daladier set in place a Commissariat général à l'information. Not only was the body itself new, and thus suggestive of foresight, but it seemed to enter the world with some vigor. It was to operate under the direct authority of the premier's office. It would have as its head Jean Giraudoux, who beyond being an internationally renowned author and playwright, was a career diplomat with more than twenty years' experience in the field of cultural propaganda.[4] It was to have sweeping responsibilities across the scattered fields of information, including the censorship of inappropriate press, magazine, photographic, and cinematic materials destined for publication at home and abroad. Conversely, it was to gather, edit, translate where necessary, publish, and distribute appropriate materials in metropolitan France, the empire, and elsewhere. It had special offices to liaise with the military authorities, with the information services and censorship offices of other ministries, with the information centers operated by every *département*, and with sundry international organizations ranging from those involved with the press, medicine, and even electricity. Finally, it took under its administrative umbrella the most experienced propaganda agency in France, namely the Service des Oeuvres, a body devoted to the cultivation of opinion abroad.[5]

Invested with such responsibilities—and thus with the appearance of power—the commissariat soon boasted a star-studded cast from France's creative community, a wartime cast for which the majestic facilities of the Hotel Continental seemed well suited. Giraudoux's first choice was André Morize, an old school friend from the Ecole Normale Supérieure and in more recent years the director of the French-language school in Middlebury, Vermont, as well as frequent visiting professor at Harvard University. It was he who would direct Giraudoux's personal *cabinet*, as well as the two information agencies within the commissariat: one for metropolitan and imperial France, the other for the rest of the world. As for the latter, the Service de l'information à l'étranger had as its chief Paul Hazard, a professor at the Collège de France, a soon-to-be member of the Académie Française, and a scholar who, throughout the 1930s, regularly held appointments at Columbia University; and as successive heads of its North American desk, were André de Laboulaye, former ambassador to Washington, and Pierre de Lanux, former wartime director of information in New York. Further men of distinction included another former ambassador, Jules Laroche, who headed an office charged with the preparation of appropriate newspaper and magazine articles; Julien Cain, administrator-general of the National Library, who assumed responsibility for the preparation and distribution of suitable books; and René Huyghe, normally curator at the Louvre, now charged with literary-artistic programming for French national radio, a charge for which he received assistance from the prominent music critic Emile Vuillermoz, and from Gaston Rageot, the president of the Société des Gens de Lettres. On other fronts and for other occasions the commissariat recruited the talents of writers such as André Maurois and Philippe Hériat, the former glorified by the Académie Française, the latter by the Prix Goncourt. Henri Torrès, the high-profile lawyer, was another recruit, as was actor-director Louis Jouvet and cinematographer Louis Joxe, who was in fact a member of Giraudoux's personal staff. Referring to these sparkling components, Guillaume de Tarde, the commissariat's chief of information for France and the empire, once remarked to Giraudoux: "You've got a Rolls, but it's still in pieces."[6]

While the "Rolls" was subject to many complaints by the summer of 1940, complaints worthy of later review, it would be untrue to suggest that there was no ignition and no motion. Despite the fact that it was thrown together on the very eve of war, the commissariat did more than provide an administrative organigram for posterity.[7] Giraudoux or Morize did meet regularly with their heads of departments, including Paul Hazard, chief of foreign propaganda. His service, including its own North American desk and the affiliated Oeuvres, continued the old policy of drawing upon the ever reliable resources and cooperation of international organizations such as France-Amérique, Alliance Française, Amitiés catholiques, and French Chambres de Commerce. Consistent, too, with the past practice of recruiting volunteer agents, the commissariat developed lists of people to whom its information could be passed for subsequent circulation. Some thirty thousand were French "correspondents" living abroad; others were of foreign birth as well as location, most of them educators, politicians, industrialists and *commerçants* whose offices and skills amplified their voice among fellow citizens.

Others were even more obvious, among them the foreign journalists who flocked to the Hotel Continental in search of information and rumors. Received by commissariat officers responsible for the foreign press, these journalists fell into one of two categories. The first were reporters from neutral countries, for whom weekly press conferences were held at the commissariat and at the Quai d'Orsay. The second were the "Anglo-Americans," to whom were provided daily press conferences, a room of their own at the Continental, and direct phone lines to London. In America, America might be neutral. In Paris, America enjoyed the status of an associate power, a status that accorded well enough with the fact that most of the Paris-based journalists were either "intensely pro-French," or at least "anti-Nazi."[8]

That America was not really associated with the Anglo-French military coalition was, of course, self-evident. That America had come to have a special resonance in Paris is less so. It did not hurt, of course, to have André Laboulaye and, subsequently, Pierre de Lanux as head of the North American desk, especially the former, who as ambassador had developed very friendly relations with Franklin Roosevelt.[9] Nor did it hurt to have as their superiors Hazard, Morize, and Giraudoux, all with considerable experience in America. The commissioner himself had spent the better part of a year, in 1907–1908, at Harvard, from which he had returned thrilled by American clothing and electric razors. In 1917 he had been part of a wartime mission to the United States, in the course of which he not only developed "filial" affection for America; but also a strengthened conviction that educated Americans saw France as part of their own cultural patrimony. That he said so in 1917, in the middle of a war, is one thing. That he chose to say so again, in a new edition, a year before he was charged with coordinating all French propaganda, is another.[10] But there was more to his, and their, receptiveness of American culture, and more than a calculated desire to enlist American material resources for the fight against Hitler.

America, and the commissariat's perception of that country, may well have played a role of broader significance in France's wartime propaganda strategy. Certainly the latter's chosen themes were remarkably consistent with those long considered most appropriate for the American information market. The first principle was never to falsify information. A second was to stress Nazi repression and enslavement at home and abroad, and Nazi responsibility for pushing Europe over the brink of war. A third, as of late August 1939 and the pact between Germany and Russia, was to condemn both "brown and red bolshevism"—an indictment with which most Americans could feel comfortable. A fourth was to put an optimistic emphasis on the combined economic and financial superiority of Britain, France, and their respective empires. A fifth was to stress the inherent superiority of democratic regimes over the totalitarian.[11] And a sixth, unchanged since the 1920s, was to use educational and cultural exchange as a device for promoting mutual respect and—through it—peace among nations. If not "made in the USA," the themes developed by French wartime propagandists—many of whom had had a substantial peacetime experience in America—were especially suited to American sensibilities.

But it is true that no claim could be made for dramatic, America-targeted initiatives during the commissariat's brief existence. The combination of limited technical resources and a familiar reluctance to run the risk of offending Americans with too much and too obvious propaganda ensured a modest and prudent course. Although there were significant obstacles to overcome within the bureaucratic world of state broadcasting, and although France was far behind other European powers in shortwave transmissions, progress was made after September 1939 for programming directed at America. Equally important, cooperative arrangements were worked out between French state radio and CBS, which offered opportunities for French officials—including the prime minister—to speak directly to American audiences.[12] Similarly modest claims could be made for cinematic propaganda, the more so given the fact that the war had begun with France spending a million francs per year and Germany spending many hundreds of millions. Six months later, the commissariat had at its disposal five films that had been prepared for the New York World's Fair of 1939, with three more on the verge of release, and ten in production.[13]

Also under way from March 1940 was a new information center in New York, a successor to the French Information Office but still under the directorship of Robert Valeur. The new French News Service was to provide press clippings to the embassy and consulates and, in conjunction with British, Polish, and Czech diplomats, prepare and distribute materials "suitable for the American mentality." In short, to use Ambassador Saint-Quentin's private words, it was to set up "a propaganda network" and with funds officially earmarked as "crédit de propagande."[14] At the same time, older and more familiar devices were still in use: a few American intermediaries to distribute information packages to thousands of their fellow citizens, travel subventions for guest lecturers, subventions for the work of the Alliance Française and France-Amérique, subventions for right-minded publications such as the *French Digest* and *Facts against Fiction*, the latter being a bimonthly, explicitly designed corrective to the German-funded *Facts in Review*.[15]

Nevertheless, despite their efforts, practiced or more novel, these propagandists came under immediate fire. Many decades later, those early rebukes have given way to something worse, a silence inspired by the widely presumed incompetence and ineffectiveness of Giraudoux's commissariat. Predictably, the explanations for this condition have embraced both the systemic and the human; but together, they speak to the widespread conviction that French propagandists were hopelessly outclassed by their foreign competition. That conviction is not baseless. Whether it is more true than less remains to be seen.

One of the standing complaints against France as propagandist, leveled first by contemporaries, is its parsimony. And beneath that, to be sure, is the intended inference that it lacked both the will and the insight to invest seriously in the cultivation of opinion at home and abroad. Whether before, during, or after a world war, the Third Republic seemed hesitant to commit funds comparable to those being invested by its great power competitors, friends or foes. That complaint never seemed more true than it did during the brief history of Giraudoux's commissariat between the summer of 1939 and March 1940—at which time the status of the propaganda war rose with the creation of an actual ministry of information.[16] When Giraudoux became commissioner on the eve of war, he had neither paper budget nor liquid funds. For four months, his colleagues worked as volunteers, until December 1939 when the first installment of their modest salaries was at last dispensed. That is why there was something of substance behind his joke to a collaborator departing on a mission to Hungary. "Do you think," he is reported to have said, "that you could advance the government the cost of your trip?" Apocryphal or not, the anecdote does suggest that, compared to the financial resources of Joseph Goebbels, Germany's propaganda czar, Giraudoux's had him working on a shoestring. The Germans had been spending the equivalent of several billion francs per year since 1933. When Giraudoux finally got his budget for 1940, it was in the order of 2 hundred million.[17]

Money, however, was not the only obstacle to getting the Rolls into gear. There were at least two impediments of an administrative nature, one of them often familiar to students of administrations. From the beginning, it would seem, the commissariat's responsibilities were real but its powers illusory. Envisaged as a coordinating office for all forms of state propaganda, though one lacking in ministerial status, it never enjoyed a sense of being its own master. Although administratively, it looked as if it were going to function with the authority of the premier's office, in fact it was out-shouted by voices coming from the premier's other portfolio: the ministry of national defense. The end result was that, while responsible for coordinating the country's wartime censorship program, and its propaganda campaign by means of press, radio, cinema, and photographs, the commissariat was dependent upon the goodwill and cooperation of the army—an institution commonly criticized for its indifference to any war of words. Indeed, so the Chamber's foreign affairs commission concluded in late 1939, the army seemed to have "abandoned" the commissariat. So under the superficial brilliance cast by the literary stars of the Hotel Continental, beneath the aura of his "pleins pouvoirs," Giraudoux was restricted to "giving little speeches . . . when I am given permission."[18]

A related problem was what has been called "administrative promiscuity."[19] Because of the escalating sense of alarm in the summer of 1939, because of the lingering sense that France was desperately in need of a propaganda offensive, the newborn commissariat was hailed by many. Not only was it charged officially with coordinating the propaganda services within every ministry, but it was to do so from the elegant Hotel Continental, under the direction of the celebrated Jean Giraudoux and a growing number of talented collaborators. Thus within weeks, the playwright had some forty-five hundred written offers of help, and a *sur place* army of four hundred volunteers, some of whose services had been inherited, and some of whom had been foisted upon him by politicians trying to do favors. Given the two de-

cree laws of November 1939, which set the commissariat's personnel comple-
ment at a modest 250, the organization clearly began with an alarming surfeit of workers, far more than Giraudoux, an ill-disposed and ill-equipped
administrator, could handle. Conversely, there were experts in other ministries—again, especially in national defense—whose requested transfers to the
commissariat were met with months of bureaucratic inaction. And so the commissioner had to deal with people he could not use, in the absence of people
he wanted but could not get.[20]

Hastily assembled, charged with tasks it lacked the authority to fulfill,
constrained by uncertain and then modest funding, animated by men and
women whose backgrounds were in a range of different ministerial services,
the commissariat soon fell victim to a crescendo of criticisms about the way
it was, or was not, satisfying its mandate. Much of it, to be sure, was focused on Giraudoux, an intellectual seen by some as too set in his ways and
too rooted in old-fashioned notions of France. But before exploring these ad
hominem complaints, it may be useful to survey some of the other criticisms
that have been leveled against French wartime propaganda in 1939–1940.

One of those is censorship, an activity that is always subject to attack
from opposite directions: from those who find it a restriction on their liberties, and from those who find it insufficiently restrictive. As for the first,
people who make their living through the sale of information are seldom receptive to government attempts to control the market—unless, of course, they
are employed to say and write what the government wants heard and written. That is why Giraudoux's association with censors, who in fact were only
nominally under his control, incensed the artistic and libertarian circles with
which he was most familiar and comfortable. The libertarians, so the *Chicago Tribune* reported, "fear that dictatorial methods may become chronic"
given the near disappearance of civil rights and in light of the implementation of "absolute press censorship." That fear, ironically, was being fanned
by what was clearly a double standard, for while the French press was being
censored "severely," one Paris-based correspondent for the *Tribune* reported
that Americans were writing "pretty much as they please"; and several months
later, in February 1940, the *New York Times* claimed that the French censors
were "much more reasonable" than they had been in 1914. Furthermore, this
Paris resident observed that as yet, apart from the Communist press, there
had been no enforced closures of French newspapers.[21]

But that was the other side of the problem posed by censorship. Too
often, or so it was claimed, incorrect and misleading information was getting into the public sphere because the censorship was too lax, a condition

that then inspired a chorus of government denials. Too often what was censored was done so in such a clumsy manner that it was counterproductive. As one parliamentary committee observed: "Every blacked-out passage makes a reader curious. If too extensive, it creates anxiety and aggravation. If too silly, for example, when it is easy to guess the deleted detail, it becomes the subject of ridicule."[22] Thus, whatever the provenance of the criticism, whether it was from those who thought the censor's hand too light or those who said it was too heavy, the commissariat was certain to be found wanting.

Also found wanting was the ideological position it adopted before domestic and foreign audiences, a position that—like censorship—was certain to provoke outrage from opposing fronts. Under orders from their supreme boss, Premier Edouard Daladier, French propagandists tried to steer a course between the Scylla of Nazism and the Charybdis of Communism. Too much criticism of Hitler—his attack on Poland notwithstanding—ran the risk of alarming anticommunist patriots in France. Too much criticism of Joseph Stalin—his pact with Germany and autumn attack on Finland notwithstanding—ran the risk of alarming antifascist patriots in France. The government chose instead a bifocal approach, condemning a Soviet government with which it was not at war with the same intensity as it disparaged Nazi Germany, a country with which it was. Rephrased, not content with one enemy, the Third Republic had sought a second. By so doing, some have argued, by faulting the Soviet regime internationally and by waging a tough domestic campaign against the French communist movement, the government had blurred the focus of the war against Hitler and with it the French people's concentration on the German menace.[23]

Still another criticism of French propaganda in the period, this one with antecedents in previous decades, was directed at its underlying philosophy and, accordingly, its choice of methods. In a word, it was old-fashioned, too attached to the values and conventions of the past, too frequently animated by one elite for the sake of another, too reliant upon the book and the pen. What was needed in midcentury, some observed, was a propaganda calculated for mass consumption and waged by those more trained in psychology than the humanities. While it was true that "the popularizer was nothing without the intellectual," the latter was often "incomprehensible" without the former. This did not mean, the government was told early in 1940, that it had to emulate the cynical and deceitful ways with which the Nazis managed information. But it did need to know that some considered "our emphasis upon the noble and true to be worth nothing." More to the point, it needed to understand that modern propaganda was based not on any grasp of "Cartesian logic, absolute truth, or ideal beauty" but rather on how to reach the masses, whether by "belief, love, self-interest, altruism, pride, flattery, [or] envy," none of which had "anything to do with logic." That was why, according to the authors of this same report, intellectuals worldwide were chary about the very idea of propaganda—because it directed others how to think. And frankly, that was why those same intellectuals, with their "aristocratic" bearing and tastes, were judged ill suited to the task of modern propaganda.[24]

From this underlying condition there arose, according to the same critics, a related problem. No descendants of the masses, educated and conditioned to command as well as consume, France's propaganda agents lacked the language and psychology to deal effectively with ordinary citizens, just as they lacked an understanding of how to exploit the persuasive potential of the radio. Still too wedded to conventions and practices of the past, the commissariat personnel, it was said, did not fully appreciate the importance of monitoring domestic opinion via the services of the departmental information centers, of monitoring broadcasts beamed into France from foreign stations, or of tailoring their own transmissions to foreign claims and to fluctuating public moods. In the judgment of one parliamentary committee, the country was simply lagging behind its principal competitors. Citing the remarks of one expert, the committee recorded this stinging assessment: "Our radio monitoring system is half deaf and inattentive, our transmission system half mute and stuttering. Our equipment is to our adversary what the bow and the sling are to the machine gun and trench mortar. We lack experience. Authority is divided among several, and responsibilities among thousands."[25]

Even with allowances for such hyperbole, it is clear that many of the kinks in the French information system had not been worked out within the first six months of war. And given the fact that the commissariat was dependent on the army for its monitoring reports, on interior for departmental intelligence, and on the premier's office for broadcasting, that failure ought not come as a surprise.

There is one more criticism of the Third Republic's propaganda performance in 1939–1940, that which, perhaps more than any of the others, suggests a country that had no enthusiasm for war. Several scholars have observed that, when announcing the outbreak of war, Premier Daladier's remarks to parliament were far more pacifist in tone than bellicose. Others have employed the imagery of France entering the war like a timid bather, one toe at a time, ready to withdraw if the water got too cold or too deep.[26] Whatever the imagery, whoever the witness, there is a tradition of seeing France as reluctant and halfhearted, a country with no fire in its belly. That is, in part, what had disturbed the parliamentary critics for the better part of a decade. People like Ernest Pezet believed that war had returned in 1933 with the advent of Hitler, a cold war conducted not with guns but with ideas inflated by intolerance and circulated on currents of lies. But France, he believed, had not risen to the challenge, had not committed the human and financial resources to defend itself against Nazi charges, had not mustered the will and the energy to engage in this undeclared war of words. What there was, noble in the eyes of some and debilitating in those of others, was an underlying pacifism that had seeded itself many times over since the armistice of 1918.

It is this which takes us more directly to Jean Giraudoux, a man who, as commissioner, was much criticized for his work and who, as defendant, often offered splendid witness for the prosecution. For the fact is that, while hardly responsible for all the discerned deficiencies in the French propaganda effort, Giraudoux certainly did personify a fair number of them. He had no taste for administration and no patience for bureaucracy. He had more reservations about propaganda, rudely packaged, than he had about Germany and Germans. Official spokesman for a country engaged in a wartime cause, he detested war, disliked a good deal of what he had seen in prewar France, was temperamentally incapable of acting as a national tub thumper, and was not the least inclined to stir up the masses with cheap emotion and the argot of the street. Not a little reminiscent of the "elitist," "aristocratic," and the "academic," Jean Giraudoux exemplified the cast of official propagandists who were so targeted by certain parliamentary critics in 1939–1940 and whose "failures" have become the stuff of legend.

An obvious choice for the job in one respect, given his long diplomatic experience with cultural propaganda, Giraudoux's other credentials might have raised doubts about his suitability for the wartime post. Unlike some, he seems to have thought that France's low-key prewar propaganda efforts, which he described as an "exercise in seduction," had been entirely appropriate. To have created a prewar propaganda ministry, an oversight some were lamenting in April 1940, would have been like "putting the cart before the horse." But even with war returned, he rejected the notion of "spectacular publicity" campaigns designed to inflate "national egoism," just as he rejected proposals to control the numbers of private radio sets in France and to jam foreign news broadcasts beamed into the country. France would not become Germany, a "country of lies," and would not adopt German techniques.[27] Nazi techniques, more accurately phrased, because Giraudoux, culturally speaking, was a Germanophile. In his 1928 novel/play *Siegfried*, the work of a wounded war veteran, he had condemned both nationalist and racist solutions, as well as the lingering divide between French and German. "I refuse," he wrote, "to dig trenches inside my being." Indeed, a decade later, he was not even sure about the exploited dichotomy between democracy and tyranny. In fact, ideological difference could provide a healthy social stimulus, and it certainly need not preclude continued cultural interaction between such countries as France and Germany.[28]

What ruined everything, that which was irredeemable, was war. On this, he had suffered no second thoughts. In 1918 he had described his own emotional anguish on receiving yet one more letter detailing the death of yet one more friend, tearing the offending paper into pieces, erasing the name of the fallen from his address book, composing warnings in his mind: "Mères imprudentes, qui envoyez vos fils à la guerre!" Seven years later, when the names had been recaptured in bronze and granite, Giraudoux addressed war again—two of them, that of the specter in the future and that in the memory of a war before Troy. The woman Hecuba, mother of the warrior Hector, describes the face of war as ugly, "a monkey's ass, shiny, red, and scaly."[29] And four years later, as France's principal wartime propagandist, he coaxed French schoolchildren to think of themselves as a "generation of peace," urged listeners to think of a springtime armistice, identified war as a propitious time to plan for peace, and defended the government and high command against critics of military inaction, the so-called phony war. "We are not fighting for the sake of spectators," he told an American audience. "We would be untrue to ourselves if we were to sacrifice a single life unnecessarily to war's grand procession." And lest those before him failed to detect the intensity of this personal conviction, Giraudoux recalled his service, and his wounds, from World War I. "I had an intimate acquaintance with war. I met it in its youth, and in mine. . . . And now we meet again, when we are both old."[30]

Just how secure he was in his understanding of "true" France in 1939 is difficult to say; and that uncertainty does raise another question about his suitability to direct the verbal war. The truth is, he was not all that enamored with France of the 1920s and 1930s. Although he claimed that the country had found its true self the moment it had been confronted by the challenge of a new war, it had taken the lifting of a moral fog for it to have done so. Consistent with his belief that ideological differences among nations were not insuperable barriers to peace, Giraudoux argued that the real danger to France had come from within—from the manipulation of the state by a handful of business interests; from a society of too many "worn-out overcoats, soiled ties, and thin-soled shoes"; from a regime unsure of its principles; from a people who were having trouble reproducing themselves; and from a new generation of Frenchmen and women who lacked the manners and the honesty, as well as the commitment, industry, and stability of their forbears. Ironically, for a pacifist such as Giraudoux, it had taken a new war to snatch France from this "miserable" fog of self-indulgence. Or so he claimed in his last radio speech of May 1940.[31] Ominously, in the eyes of some, it was the disillusioned and unrepentant Giraudoux who went to work, briefly and apathetically, for the Vichy regime of Marshal Pétain that succeeded the Third Republic in June 1940.

Beside these, the disabused patriotism, the unconcealed pacifism, the self-administered constraints on the use and abuse of propaganda, Giraudoux's other perceived limitations were of lesser importance. Two of them come to mind: his casual approach to administration and his formal approach to propaganda. As for the first, it seems clear that Giraudoux displayed many of the qualities commonly attributed to artists. He spent a lot of time out of the office, and at least some of the time therein working on private occupations. He was a little casual about security issues and office decorum and sometimes indifferent to bureaucratic conventions and hierarchies. And he sometimes gave vent to a withering cynicism, of the sort that caused him in early 1940 to consider putting up this, typically erudite, announcement: "In view of recent events, the word 'impossible' is again a French word."[32]

Put together with an early administrative chaos that was not of his making, these qualities, this state of mind, certainly did not facilitate his career as commissioner. Neither, in one sense, did the erudition. If there was anything to what Ernest Pezet and other parliamentarians said about the need for a more dynamic and mass-based propaganda, Jean Giraudoux was an unlikely leadership candidate. Not only did he have misgivings about any form of propaganda beyond the purely cultural, not only did he believe more strongly in nuance and subtlety than in the unmissable and the crude, but he insisted on speaking as himself. For him, it was natural to draw upon Thermopylae and Valmy, Catherine of Alexandria and the emperor Maximian, Chaucer and Shakespeare, Gounod and Voltaire, for they were his currency, his lexicon. For him, it was natural to use a formal, tradition-honored French, free of argot and neologisms. Whether there was something of substance behind his critics, whether he was indeed too academic in content and style, was then, as it remains today, a matter of judgment. As for the commissioner himself, he retorted, fairly enough, that he could hardly tell the truth by pretending to be someone he was not.[33]

The complaints lodged against the commissariat in France found echoes in the United States—many of them deriving from a press that had scented criticism from within France, some of them deriving from local French agents unhappy with what they held to be an inadequate flow of information from Paris. While the American press proved accepting enough of the French censorship regime, especially in the early months of war when it enjoyed much greater freedom than the French newspapers, it did relate impressions of "chaotic disorganization" at the commissariat and reports of the premier's publicly expressed frustration over propagandists who ignored his instructions. So too did it draw attention to a system that depended on the caprice of individual censors, to the ensuing inconsistencies, and to situations in which Germany actually got substantially more coverage in America than did France. And by early 1940 there was more irritation being expressed over the growing time delays inflicted by the censorship system on the information flow to America.[34] French diplomats complained of the same thing, at least on occasion. If they were to do their job with the American media, they needed more photographic and broadcasting materials of a military nature—especially given the fact that the Germans were broadcasting seven times a day to the United States; and of a similar note was a plea for more photographs of German prisoners of war and damaged German planes to compete with the more readily available images of French prisoners and French planes that had been destroyed. Even worse was the situation by and through April 1940, in the wake of the restructuring in Paris that had seen the commissariat give way to the ministry. By then the consul general in New York was speaking openly of "the penury" of information from France.[35]

But notwithstanding the complaints provoked by the commissariat's perceived errors of omission and commission, there were moments when it appeared less inept and the Third Republic less uninspired—particularly in an America where an attentive elite had long appreciated propagandists of subtlety and refined taste and where opinion great and small had tired of Europe's several dictators. France's indigenous critics of the commissariat might have wished for more verbal pyrotechnics to capture the attention of the masses in Nîmes and Nebraska, but the argument for prudence and temperance remained as enduring in war as it had in peace. That is why Ambassador Saint-Quentin continued to stress the need for low-profile "discretion."[36] That is also why the Service des Oeuvres, whether under the umbrella of foreign ministry or Information Commissariat, continued to cultivate the fields of literature and music. In the words of one Oeuvres report from early 1940: "French Art, which has always been one of the most reliable conveyors of our prestige abroad, has never failed, even in wartime, to accomplish that mission. Never have our painters, sculptors, musicians, actors, lecturers, served more effectively and with greater distinction the cause of France's genius abroad."[37]

As befits the complex and layered agencies of modern states, the commissariat did much of its work behind the scenes, whether in France or abroad. The daily instances of interministerial communications, the weekly planning sessions, the preparation of texts destined for the printers, the distribution of such mass-produced materials, even the conduct of turf wars between competing bureaucracies—all were characteristic of the silent, quotidian life of the commissariat. Reminiscent of the proverbial iceberg, only a small fraction of its efforts was ever intended to be visible and unmistakable, the more so in a country like the United States where the fear of propaganda and the underlying fear of getting embroiled in a new war remained unbridled. In other words, in 1939 and 1940, as war approached and settled in, the need to say the right things to Americans was as deeply felt as ever by the French foreign ministry and the Commissariat for Information. And none could think of a better way of doing so than through the use of art.

Nadia Boulanger, the internationally renowned pianist, was one such instrument. Longtime faculty member of the Paris Conservatory and of the American Conservatory in Fontainebleau, this talented performer and teacher was a frequent, long-term visitor to the United States. Part of that traveling was made possible through the combined resources of Beaux Arts and Service des Oeuvres in Paris, through that time-tested program to promote the cultural genius of France; and part of it was made to glitter through gala dinners and receptions at the French embassy or various consulates. But in her case, the message was subtle, conveyed through her wizardry at the keyboard, through a fidelity less to country than to artistic ideal, and through her promotion of young American talent. Not from her, a once youthful pupil of Gabriel Fauré, would one detect the spore of national cultural conceit, the hint of superiority that had in the past offended too many Americans. Speaking of the teaching technique she employed for young composers in America, Boulanger said that she left them to themselves "when it comes to saying their say. What a composer has to express is his own affair, not mine. I view him in relation to his national culture. . . . He must be more, too, than a musician. He must be strong in the knowledge of his own country. . . . Otherwise, he will never be listened to."[38]

Here was the sort of thing, the sensitivity of expression, the praise for American musicians, the absence of chauvinism, that was so well calculated to appeal to American concertgoers in New York, Boston, Washington, Chicago, and San Francisco. And to appeal to readers of such papers as the *Times*, the *Monitor*, the *Post*, the *Tribune*, and the *Examiner*.[39]

A year later, with war well under way in Europe, French artists in America might have been expected to associate themselves with the country's struggle against Nazism. That was certainly the case of another celebrated pianist from Paris, Magda Tagliaferro. Like Boulanger, she was a proven "cultural missionary" in the United States and, again like her, at the behest and expense of the French government. Yet another likeness was the subtlety, which had her gently remarking in one New York interview on the difference between the French and German regimes. The latter, for reasons of race or ideology, had proscribed the music of Mendelssohn and Hindemith, the art of George Grosz, the literature of Thomas Mann. But in France, no "French artist would willingly submit to the elimination of German music from programs." Indeed, with the exception of a few contemporary composers too associated with the Nazi regime, all German music was still being included on musical programs in France. "We don't believe that music or thought should have any boundaries. . . . It is a pity that the totalitarian states are constituted so that their creative artists should be victimized by state decree."

So in defiance of this repression, it seemed fitting for an artist of the Paris Conservatory to include in her own programs in America, Schumann, Mozart, Bach, and Beethoven. Just as it seemed fitting to the editors of the *New York Times* and to a vast majority of those polled by George Gallup in December 1939.[40]

As might have been expected, given its practiced affinity for a France twice victim of German aggression, the *Times* also commented approvingly on the visits of the celebrated writer Eve Curie. Moreover, it did so without acknowledging that Mlle Curie—like Giraudoux—until recently had been a salaried officer of the foreign ministry's Service des Oeuvres.[41] It did, however, ensure that her message got out to its readers. Dictatorship, in any guise, was destructive and intolerable, including that of the Soviets. It was especially threatening to freedom of self-expression, the very latitude that artists anywhere required in order to create. Worse still, she told a large audience in April 1940, the dictators not only silenced those whose ideas did not concur with their own, but they enlisted the weak and the craven to do their bidding. "Some have been given full powers to create, by order of the dictator of the moment. . . . [But] having been ordered to speak, artists have nothing more to say." Not so in France, or in America, where "you are constantly adding . . . masterpieces of your national art." Lest the link be missed, Eve Curie ventured that Americans and French were "very much alike. . . . We all like the kind of life provided by democracy." On a yet more personal note, she added that she was returning to her homeland, "the most serene country in the world," but one that—so she assured a California audience—would never lay down its arms until Hitler's regime had been swept away.[42] Wherever she went in her transcontinental trip, this professional propagandist seemed to say the right thing, a conclusion drawn by a delighted ambassador who described the visit as a "triumphal success" and who reported on the particularly warm reception Curie had received from President and Mrs. Roosevelt.[43]

Other Americans proved equally receptive to the word and demeanor of wartime France, especially those of proven Francophilic credentials. James Wood Johnson, longtime resident of Paris, revived the American Volunteer Ambulance Corps. Professor Ellsworth Barnard of Williams College denounced the "equal guilt" thesis imbedded in the "revisionist" histories from the 1920s and exonerated the 1919 peace settlement from any responsibility for the rise of Hitler. Hamilton Fish Armstrong, editor of *Foreign Affairs*, publicly associated America's interests with those of the Anglo-French alliance, as did that much traveled banker Thomas W. Lamont, and the former secretary of state Henry L. Stimson, and the president of Swarthmore College, Frank Aydelotte. So did Nicolas Murray Butler, president of Columbia, who had no compunctions about branding Hitler a "mad and reactionary tyrant," any more than did Frederick R. Coudert, who associated the fate of France with the survival of American principles. And then there was Dorothy Thompson, who in December 1939 condemned the obsession with foreign propaganda and suggested that by failing to distinguish between the democracies and the dictators, those who had fueled that obsession had actually resisted the truth along with the lies.[44]

No less attuned to the perceptions of thoughtful women and men on both sides of the Atlantic was the commissioner himself, for here is the reverse side of one principal indictment against Giraudoux. If, in the eyes of some, he appeared to be too formal, erudite, and abstract for citizens of common station and education, he had exceptional appeal for those who savored language and were confident of his sincerity.[45] For the latter, there seemed every reason to agree that countries create their own "monster" when they subordinate truth to the interests of the state; and doubtless they enjoyed his mockery of French cultural propaganda taken too far—of the sort that had once hailed Paris as the "capital of thought" and France as the "dominion of intelligence."[46] There was an irreverence to the man that reading and theater audiences around the world continued to find refreshing. And a candor. In an October 1939 broadcast to the United States, entitled "The Democratic Front," Giraudoux did the unexpected. He told Americans that words they cherished, such as *liberty* and *democracy*, had been rendered commonplace by overuse. The French soldier, he observed, "does not fight democratically, fire his gun democratically, or sleep in the mud democratically." Yet not one of the 6 million who had been mobilized failed to understand why he was dug in on the frontier. It was, "très simple," to defend his home, family, and way of life: "Il est notre vie." In short, and in plain language, France was once again a victim of a war she had not planned and did not want.[47]

The aggressor, of course, was Germany; and Giraudoux's powers of intuition and expression allowed him to articulate brilliantly the difference between innocence and guilt, which is to say between the Third Republic and Hitler's regime. He did so, primarily, in a series of radio addresses that he delivered during his eight months as commissioner—some of them expressly intended for American audiences, all of them for alert and informed citizens worldwide. Which is to say, of course, that ideas were his principal means, and the educated elite his principal target, making for a strategy at odds with more commonplace notions of propaganda as emotionally couched, endlessly repeated phrases and images trained on mass opinion. Whether, therefore, Giraudoux was ahead or behind the times depends very much on one's own understanding of the relationship between elite and mass opinion, on one's own appraisal of the power of idea and language, and therefore doubtless on the personal background of every witness. Giraudoux's *formation* we are familiar with, as we are with that of the American elite to whom he appealed. What is needed now is exposure to the verbal imagery with which he hoped to inspire that elite and cultivate its sympathy.

War had returned, he said, simply because Germans were out to "take other people's land," the closer to Germany the better. What they wanted, as if by just entitlement, was "living space," which is to say, again, soil that did not belong to them. Such arrogance was completely consistent with a Germany fashioned in Hitler's image. This was a people who had been transfixed by a Führer now addled enough to associate himself with Providence. That was "the worst form of blasphemy," a practitioner of "black magic" pretending to be God. It was this "sorcerer's apprentice . . . who had set the destructive clockwork ticking, . . . [motion] that could not be stopped as long as he was around. The robots have been freed by him, and they are on the march." Already, according to Giraudoux, they had marched over what had been good in the old Germany, repressing or forcing into exile ideas and people. But there was worse: "The whole world is exiled from Germany. . . .

We who love Dürer, Goethe, we too are exiled from Germany. . . . All those who are repelled by blood, who are repelled by contempt for humanity, are exiled from Germany."

Compounding matters, the commissioner remarked, was the rank dishonesty with which the Nazi regime portrayed itself to the outside world—and portrayed itself so effectively with a barrage of radio broadcasts beamed to people too distant to have heard of Napoleon's death. To listen to their assurances, one would think that this was a country "where all citizens worship their government, where angels are in service to the police, where magnetic land mines come equipped with indicators pointing to peace, and where the single objective is to secure happiness for the world and for each of its citizens."[48]

Such they would have us believe, said Giraudoux. But the truth is that this is a Germany that is "pitiless, full of slaves, and soaked in its own crimes, one that has betrayed European culture and the cause of humanity." This is a country "where the family is the first refuge of the spy, where the public square is where one passes most quickly, where churches, temples, synagogues, and libraries are forbidden places where one only goes to steal. Eighty million people, and yet for freedom and for ideas, this is the largest desert the world has ever seen."

What a travesty, what an irony, that such a country, "where no one is allowed to know anything," should be so well equipped to spread its lies abroad.[49]

France, Giraudoux ventured, was a stunning contrast. Its schoolchildren were not fed lies; and theirs was "an innocent arithmetic" that required calculations based on train speeds or water flow rather than on numbers of bombs and the discharge of bullets. These children, whom he called a "generation of peace," found themselves in a state of conflict for one reason: to put an end to the silent, grasping war of nerves that Hitler had been conducting for years. That was why the French soldier had left for the front:

> to chase away from his foyer this third presence, this intruder who broke in three years ago, who has lived among us, who has been at the meal table, who has been present when the children are being dressed for school. This intruder who was always in the way between husband and wife, between mother and son. This Hitler. The soldier has gone to get rid of Hitler from the kitchen, the garden, the bedroom, the darkness. He will return when Hitler's shadow disappears from our hearths, when it no longer accompanies us to the theater,

no longer distracts us at our workplace, and is no longer the scare-crow in the middle of our fields.[50]

But as befitted France, this was to be no war of conquest. Not even one of revenge, although this was the third time Germany had initiated war with its neighbor, and although she became progressively less civilized on each occasion. Rather, he assured a group of assembled Americans, France's war objectives were precisely those of the Germans themselves.

> To give the German his legitimate living space, which is to say to strip him of his propensity for blind obedience; to give back to the German his true character, which is to say to forbid him from being either an active or passive accomplice to evil; to give to the German his true source of nourishment, which is to say to replace his book of hatred, lies, and arrogance with his classics from the past; to return his freedom, by freeing those he has enslaved in Austria, Czecho-slovakia, and Poland; . . . to return his conscience, by obliging him to see with his own eyes, . . . hear by his own voice, where his madness has taken the world. [51]

To do so, however, would require a military victory, an outcome about which the Daladier government could afford to leave no doubts. After a nearly two decades' effort to underplay France's defense expenditures—in the face of American resentment about defaulted war debts and suspicions about French imperialism—it was now time to uncover a more muscular France. Friendly neutrals, potential allies, even potential enemies had to be assured that the Anglo-French entente was unbeatable and that victory over time was assured. In mid-October 1939 Giraudoux's boss, the premier of France, broadcast such an assurance to his own citizens, remarking simply that Britain and France were "mistresses of the ocean," a status that always had assured victory in past conflicts.[52] Four months later, his finance minister and eventual successor, Paul Reynaud, publicly turned to his favorite map of the world to demonstrate the vast resources of the British and French empires and to repeat the optimistic and well-circulated slogan "We shall win, for we are stronger." In a speech broadcast to the United States in April 1940, the newly installed premier repeated that confident claim. The demographic, raw material, and fiscal resources controlled by London and Paris made victory inevitable. Controlled by, and with access to, he might have added; for there was a special message for America. To win this war, he said, in one reassuring interview, France did not actually need American military intervention, only American munitions and airplanes.[53] Indeed, Pierre de Lanux, as head of the commissariat's North American section, sharpened the point even further. "As a matter of fact," he remarked in California, "the Allies do not even want America in the war." So confident of victory were they, that Britain and France only needed material assistance—for which they had ample resources to pay.[54]

As for that other war, that of words, Jean Giraudoux was clear on a strategy worthy of France. Not even for victory, he affirmed, would France do what Germany had done, pretending to be gentle when in fact it was coarse. There would be no "second France"; and devices developed to communicate truth—namely the radio, cinema, and press—would not be used to camouflage it. Indeed, if anyone in the world needed reassurance on this score, if listeners needed to know that France would never try to inveigle their support for a war in which they, the citizens of a neutral country, did not believe, then here it is. "Sew the world with posts for spying, blackmail, corruption? Manipulate the neutral countries by undermining their institutions and their morale? That is something we have never considered doing."[55]

The point clearly bore repeating. Again, it was Reynaud who took it upon himself to stress to a group of Americans in Paris that their neutrality would never be "compromised by any act of France and her allies." And even as late as mid-June 1940, desperate for American aid, with the military front crumbling around him, he urged Roosevelt to make it clear that France was not looking for another expeditionary force.[56] The same message came from Pierre de Lanux, who seized upon another public occasion to stress that, because his government understood that the United States "is dead set against propaganda," it would never try to persuade America to join the war effort.[57]

We will never be sure how much of a presence America had when the battle lines were being drawn by the commissariat's propagandists in the early autumn of 1939. But it seems more than a coincidence that the Giraudoux-Morize-Hazard-Laboulaye-de Lanux combination had worked out a set of themes that corresponded so well to the things each of them knew Americans wanted, and did not want, to hear. They eschewed manipulation and distortion. They reiterated their commitment to an enduring peace, to civilized behavior and cultural exchange. They underlined the fact that war had been forced upon them by a Germany of insatiable appetite. They distanced themselves from Stalin, and stressed that the combination of Britain and France, together with their respective empires, was unbeatable. We will also never be sure to what extent their efforts, and those of their American network, contributed to the discernible shift in American opinion on the subject of war in Europe. But shift there was.

In August 1937 a Gallup study determined that the majority of those polled believed that another world war was in the offing, and 30 percent surmised that Germany would be most likely to start it. By April 1938, 46 percent of respondents anticipated that the United States would have to fight a war with Germany "in their lifetime"; and by July almost two-thirds said that they would "support" England and France in a war against Germany and Italy. In November 1938, a month after the Munich crisis, 92 percent said that they did not believe Hitler's latest assurance that his territorial demands had been satisfied. By March of the following year, less than 1 percent of respondents admitted to sympathies for Germany or Italy in the event of a new war; and by war's outbreak, 82 percent believed—along with President Roosevelt— that Germany was responsible for the collapse of peace, while only 3 percent held Britain and France responsible. One month later, in October 1939, 84 percent preferred an Allied victory, as opposed to 2 percent in favor of Germany; and as late as mid-May 1940, with the German attack on France well under way, 55 percent of respondents still believed that the war would end in an Allied victory. Amid all the statistics, however, there was only one finding that stood out. While almost two-thirds of Gallup's respondents believed that an Allied defeat eventually would lead to a German-American war, in September 1939, 84 percent were opposed to sending American army or navy forces to fight against Germany. And by the end of May 1940, with a German victory in the west all the more likely, 93 percent were still opposed to sending any American forces abroad.[58]

No victory this for French propagandists, perhaps not even in the shift of popular opinion away from Germany and toward the Allied cause. At least one surmises that the combination of Nazi foreign and domestic policies probably played a more important, adverse role than Allied propagandists were able to play a positive one. That said, if it is too much to suggest that French propagandists were responsible—even largely responsible—for the shift in American opinion, it is also too much to suggest that their efforts had been in vain and their impact negligible. For the fact is that the French propaganda machine appears to have done a creditable job with the American media, a job for which the foundation had been laid over two decades of careful construction and well-tempered prudence. By various means, through the carefully crafted speech, the documentary film, the telling photograph, the detailed press release, Giraudoux and his associates clearly succeeded in presenting via the American newspaper world the picture of a France that, while innocent of responsibility, was now relentless in its determination to crush this new German menace.

While it impossible to demonstrate a causal link between public opinion and press opinion, in either direction, there is no mistaking the fact that
the shift of the former—away from Germany and toward the Allies—was accompanied by a similar shift on the part of the press. Indeed, some of the
principal newspaper voices, from New York, Washington, and Boston, to Chicago and San Francisco, displayed a more and more explicit sympathy for
the Allied cause and for a France as the first line of defense against Hitler's
Wehrmacht. In those cities, where editors, journalists, and a collective reading public of several million sought to keep abreast of offshore events, the
evidence of German crimes and of French restraint seemed to mount week
by week.[59] It came as no surprise that the *New York Times* would say so, not
after years of perceptible sympathy for France. Nor did it surprise, upon the
outbreak of war, when the editors blamed Germany "for this reckless act"
and firmly associated America with the besieged democracies, "the outposts
of our own kind of civilization." More surprising, perhaps, was the *Washington Post*, a paper that had enjoyed a pro-German reputation in the 1920s and
an anti-Roosevelt reputation in the 1930s. But the editors had expressed alarm
about Hitler as early as 1933 and, encouraged by their owner, Eugene Meyer,
had no difficulty in distinguishing black from white in 1939. "Is there anyone . . . who can search his heart and really say it is of no concern to us who
wins? If so, he is truly neutral. But it may be doubted that he is truly an American."[60]

Robert McCormick's *Tribune* and Hearst's *Examiner* remained editori-
ally more circumspect, another nonsurprise, given their interwar history of
interpreting German complaints in the best possible light. Nonetheless, their
early wartime pages, like those of the *Monitor*, were filled with news and
headlines that spoke well of France. In the Chicago area, readers learned of
the calm with which French soldiers had responded to the mobilization call,
and yet of their eagerness to fight, get the job done, and return home; and
five days before the German attack in the west, the same readers were assured that France, already "mighty on land," was becoming strong on the sea.[61]
In Boston, the *Monitor*'s editors had characterized the French as "Freedom-
Wise," in contradistinction to the totalitarian states; and it ran many articles
praising the army's high command and extraordinary Maginot Line defenses,
celebrating the calm fortitude and high morale of French citizens, and—at
the end—assuring readers throughout New England that the "true" Paris could
never be conquered by force.[62] For its part, having limited its praise to France's
domestic offensive against communism—a wartime issue beyond which it
manifested little interest—the *Examiner* did one unusual thing. On 21 June

1940, shocked like its readers by the speed of the French collapse, the paper ran a large cartoon depicting France as female figure bound to an execution post, on top of which sat a vulture and below which were scattered skulls. The caption read: "The whole CIVILIZED world sorrows today over the fate of France, which led that world in beauty and charm—and is now crushed by barbarism!"[63]

More remarkable still was the repeated claim—circulated by French propagandists, by their own domestic critics, and by American Francophiles— that France had steered clear of propaganda activity in America. Mindful of American sensitivities about the word, never mind the deed, those with France's interests at heart had laboriously seeded the idea that that nation's agents had foresworn the temptations of propaganda in the United States. Recognizing since the days of Jusserand that to Americans, *propaganda* meant deception, the French—so the version went—simply had accepted the rules of the game and confined their work to information, education, and cultural exchange. What is more, as one lengthy Giraudoux report makes clear, one could even make a virtue out of necessity. Limited financial means and be- lated administrative status meant, as his critics helpfully pointed out, the ap- pearance of inaction in the field of propaganda. Paradoxically, however, this was an advantage in a country where even a touring nightclub singer or an academic lecturer for the Alliance Française was scrutinized by those suspi- cious of foreign intrigue and manipulation.[64] Thus the shortage of film pro- jectors, the weaker radio signals, the modest trickle of photographs and printed texts—all seemed to confirm the impression that France was either a hope- less neophyte in modern propaganda techniques or simply too fearful of play- ing games with Americans.

And the impression could only strengthen when distinguished academ- ics such as André Siegfried, a habitual visitor to America, disassociated the French Information Office in New York from "all" propaganda. Or when a prominent journalist for the *New York Times*, such as Percy Philip observed that so gun-shy had the French become about propaganda in America that they actually suppressed information beneficial to their cause.[65] Or when a writer as celebrated as Gertrude Stein could proclaim to her compatriots in 1940: "Propaganda is not French, it is not civilized to want other people to believe what you believe."[66] In short, and by inference, the information that actually made it through to America had to be the straight goods, delivered without artifice and free of any desire—never mind intent—to manipulate.

Perhaps this gradual suspension of disbelief is one of the reasons why there was such shock in America when France fell so quickly in June 1940.

Perhaps the surprise, and the sorrow, had something to do with the work done by French propagandists over two decades, work paradoxically amplified by critics who had long complained that nothing was being done. Whatever its intermittent economic woes, its instability of political regime, its moments of indecisiveness and self-indulgence, readers in America knew that France also indulged in the ballot box and in so many other freedoms of expression. It was a country associated with the creation and contemplation of beauty, and one that drew upon the impressive material and demographic resources of homeland and empire. Pushed in 1939 to the brink, its patience with Hitler exhausted, it had entered the war with one of the strongest armies and navies of the world, with an air force in full renaissance, and with a high command that had mastered the lessons of World War I. Familiar as we now are with the collapse of 1940, and therefore with the apparent inadequacies of precollapse forecasts, it is difficult for us to appreciate the shock experienced by all those in 1940 who had had every reason to expect another outcome. Until now, it has been equally difficult to entertain the possibility that subtle and effective French propaganda had played some part in that surprise—and certainly in that sorrow.[67]

Conclusion

❧

$\mathcal{B}$efore one could make even a tentative evaluation of French propaganda in America, it would be sensible to recall both the impediments and the opportunities that presented themselves to those propagandists. Accomplishment, in other words, should be measured by degree of difficulty. In this instance, the French certainly were not without important assets; however, the obstacles to their wooing of America would appear to have been more numerous and more substantial. The ensuing reprise begins with them, and with an opening distinction between American-based and French-based impediments.

Despite the best efforts of French propagandists and their sympathizers in the United States, many Americans entertained a range of apprehensions about France. And in a number of cases, these reservations were only reinforced, not created, by the events of World War I. One of them had to do with culture and two attendant resentments—the first of the latter being inspired by French claims of high-level artistic superiority, the second by their denials of low-level lascivious predilection. To self-seen American innocents, there was a galling range here of the smug, the lewd, and the hypocritical. From the Paris Exhibition of 1900 to the collapse of 1940, France never lost its capacity to conjure associations with dance halls, sexually suggestive postcards, alcohol, and excess in countless forms. From this perspective, the wartime experience only justified the decision not to have "allied" with the French. "Associating" with them had been close enough when one recalled the legends of "trench rent" and gouging restaurateurs or heard smutty jokes about the imagination of French whores.

Alarming, too, was an entirely different manifestation of French culture, though one that was similarly suggestive of corruption. That was the French penchant for decorations, especially decorations awarded to foreign sympathizers. Editorial writers for such papers as Chicago's *Tribune*, or those of the massive Hearst empire, did not like the fact that such rewards offended American egalitarianism. But their principal concern stemmed from a fear that the numerous American award holders of the French Legion of Honor somehow were left beholden to the state that had conferred the award. Of particular concern were the journalist recipients, fellow press people whose business it was to inform—or massage—opinion. Such decorations, these critics said, were but "trifles and trinkets," foreign ones at that, from a country "promiscuous in its awards"; and writers who accepted them ran the risk of being seen as frankly "anti-American . . . paid propagandists." It was time, the *San Francisco Examiner* suggested in 1928, for Congress to pass a law requiring future, peacetime recipients of foreign decorations to forfeit their American citizenship.[1]

A similar wariness put many Americans on edge about still other phenomena they preferred to associate with Europeans, namely, imperialism and militarism. To those of such perspective, France was typical of the European great powers that seemed always to have coveted the lands of other people—close at hand or distant—and that had an unhappy inclination to express that covetousness on the battlefield. French imperialism had at least two strikes against it. Not only was it grasping and exploitive in the finest of European traditions, but its colonial administrations tried to temper such qualities with more liberal, even integrationist approaches to race. For many Americans, certainly those preoccupied with racial tensions at home, such approaches were as disturbing as the former—as witnessed in the public furor over France's deployment of black troops among white German civilians during the occupation of the Ruhr in 1923. And closer to home, French diplomats in America acknowledged the caution that they had to observe when it came to offering prize donations to black schools. Creating resentments among America's white community seemed no way to strengthen Franco-American relations.[2]

Then there was the associated issue of French militarism. For many Americans of recent European origin, especially the generation that had arrived around the turn of the century, that continent's troubled history was one they would have preferred to forget. But neither the Great War nor the peace settlement had allowed them do so. The tensions seemed only to increase after 1918, competition in Europe and the empires only to intensify, the armaments race only to suffer a short retard. France, as a victor power with the largest army and air force in Europe, and as an imperial power strengthened with new mandate acquisitions in the Near East, was an obvious target for New World self-righteousness. Again, Hearst's many readers were regularly treated to editorials in the 1920s that fingered France as the "Real Militarist of Europe" and urged the American administration to express its "disgust."[3]

Some of that criticism, of course, had other inspirations. Germanophiles, for instance, many of whom were immigrants or descendants of immigrants from Germany, might resent French power not because it was power but because it was French. The Midwest, in particular, was reckoned to be a region where sympathy for the kaiser, then the Weimar Republic, and then the Führer, ran deepest, and where tolerance of France was at its lowest. Italophiles, especially since the advent to power of Mussolini in 1922, were regarded as a similar challenge by those charged with the advancement of France's cause. Once the Rome-Berlin Axis emerged in the mid–1930s, once the fascist propaganda machines were thrown into high gear, there was a growing concern among French observers—as well as a growing number of American sympathizers—that France was being vilified by Americans of divided loyalty. The same apprehension was directed at American Catholics, especially those of Irish descent. Within those communities, France was doubly tainted, first because of its prewar and wartime association with Britain—usurping and occupying power of Ireland—and second because of the French republic's prewar, anticlerical measures. Taken together, the latent animosities toward France of numerically significant ethnic and religious groups suggested that the United States could be vulnerable to internal hemorrhage.

Although many of these apprehensions about France predated World War I, the war years themselves did much to inflame them—and give birth to others. One of the latter was the tangled skein of capital: war debts, reparations, reconstruction costs, investments, and tariffs. As befits nations, France and America chose policies consistent with their respective visions of self-interest. The Americans said: pay your debts, collect your own reparations, let us bid on contracts to repair your wartime damages, but do not expect preferential tariffs that could endanger the interests of American producers. The French said: we'll pay as German reparations come in; reconstruction contracts with French suppliers are essential to our own economic recovery, as are tariffs designed to protect our most vulnerable producers. And that was that, understanding but little agreement. So it was, throughout the interwar period, that the French continued to resent what they regarded as American wartime profiteering, and the Americans—primed by the irascible William Randolf Hearst and his press empire—to resent the French failure to pay their debts in full.

To be sure, Franco-American financial issues were caught up in broader considerations of international order. Resolutely a nonparticipant in the war until mid–1917, America was quick to put its arms aside in late 1918 and to reestablish some of its previous equanimity toward Germany. That meant that the gulf that became apparent between President Wilson and Premier Clemenceau in 1919 only widened with their successors. In too many American eyes, France was the principal obstacle to a general European reconciliation, its position attributed to a destructive desire for revenge and for Continental hegemony. Worse, such blindness and ambition seemed especial folly at a time when communism, in the form of Soviet Russia, was now circulating in the European bloodstream. Such readings, combined with the rising, scholarly inspired skepticism about Germany's responsibility for war in 1914, assured American Francophiles of one huge challenge.

As if the task were not large enough, there was yet another agglomeration of problems, one that had to do with the manipulation of opinion. Between 1914 and 1918, American journalists and their readers often had been frustrated by the vagaries of French wartime censorship. Total news blackouts only fed rumors, selective editing fed ridicule, lengthy official communiqués fed disbelief. All this in a country where much of the press was dependent upon the services of the state-affiliated Agence Havas, where many newspapers were linked to prominent politicians, and where too many journalists were suspected of being for hire. Worse, from an American point of view, this press and this government were now and forever linked in some people's minds with a clandestine campaign to inveigle Wilson into war in 1917. In short, Americans had died because their president had been tricked by a covert propaganda campaign directed from London and Paris and implemented by foreigners in New York and Washington. Worse still, Americans had continued to die in France while their own government willfully fanned the jingoism of those at home. The postwar revelation of wartime work undertaken by the Committee on Public Information thus became a pivotal event in the growth of public skepticism about a news world too obviously subject to state direction. And the fact that France was one of the Allied countries thought to have maneuvered Wilson into war, and known to have collaborated with the committee in 1917–1918, meant that that nation would remain under suspicion for years to come.

This was further emphasized once the war had carried communism to power in Russia and the threat of contagion worldwide. By the 1930s, America's most attentive communist watchers had compiled a disturbing record of French misjudgments: the alliance with czarist Russia that had embroiled both France and Russia in world war; the new "alliance" of 1935, again to contain Germany but this time in concert with Stalin's treacherous regime; the advent of a communist-backed, Popular Front French government in 1936. Communism, Hearst's millions-strong readership was assured, "marches with giant strides in France"; and that readership was treated to a series of cartoons depicting a naive Marianne slowly falling prey to communist wiles. America, the *Examiner* trumpeted, was in enough trouble with its own subversive communist movement without extending the contagion by closer association with France.[4]

All the foregoing I have called American-based impediments to a successful French propaganda effort in the United States. Although not perhaps the most felicitous of phrases, it is intended to distinguish the obstacles associated with American attitudes toward France from those associated with problematic French attitudes toward the United States. It must be left to the reader to discern the interrelationships and continuous interplay among these sets of attitudes, the ways in which an American perception responded to a French perception, and vice versa.

Doubtless one of the principal obstacles to effective French propaganda work in America was broadly cultural in nature. Surface indications, symptoms of an underlying problem, included the difficulty of finding French citizens who could give lectures, make broadcasts, or produce films in English. Again and again France's agents in America complained that the country's image in the United States needed to be engraved in English. But of course that difficulty had deeper roots. Despite the constant presence of French observers who marveled at the United States and found its modernism not only compelling but even worthy of emulation in France, observers in the mainstream were more guarded. The belief in the unparalleled richness of French civilization—including its language—and the attendant conviction that drawing attention to this richness was a form of world service, slowed the acknowledgment that America had vaulted into world-power status, and set limits on the energies and resources that would be expended to court that country. France refused to produce English-market films with Hollywood-inspired plots, not because of technical or even financial impediments, but because of philosophical and psychological ones. In a word, the best of California products were banal, the worst, intellectually and aesthetically impoverished. France fell behind the Germans and Italians in shortwave broadcasting to America, not so much because of limited technical resources, but because the francophone minority in America was so small and because of a belief that the educated elite could and should function in French. Thus, the related phenomena of limited resources and unlimited cultural narcissism multiplied the challenges already abundant in American perceptions of France.

A final entry should be added to this already long list of obstacles. Every time French politicians or journalists complained about the inadequacies of France's propaganda effort abroad, they reminded hypersensitive American politicians and journalists that effort there was. Every time the government tried to defend itself against such charges, or promised that more resources were on the way, it alerted the same transatlantic auditors to anticipated interference in American affairs. Here the difference between admission and boast was minimal. As a result, the argument only strengthened within the Quai d'Orsay that America-targeted propaganda had to be accurate, moderate in volume, and centered on education and the fine arts.

All this is not to say that the foreign ministry lacked assets for its efforts in America. Although the obstacles were legion and, indeed, enduring, so too were the resources for the marketing of Marianne.

Two of these were actually liabilities metamorphosed. The first was the tiny Franco-American community, too small except in very local areas to be electorally significant, but accordingly too small to prompt concerns about a potential fifth column. Unlike the Germans, Irish, and Italians, whose numbers in the Midwest justified concerns about foreign-induced lobbying efforts, America's francophones were too small by number and too dispersed by geography to fan much of a flame over French meddling in America. The second was the side of the coin turned by Jules Henry and Jean Giraudoux. In one sense, too little money and too few cinematic and broadcasting resources minimized American concerns about French propaganda—at a time when disquiet about fascist and communist propaganda was escalating in the United States. Constrained and inconspicuous spending convinced Americans that the propaganda menace did not come from France, and this conviction made them, paradoxically, more susceptible to the words and images transmitted from Paris.

A second apparent liability, and even greater paradox, arose in the shape of Nazi Germany—without which the task of French propagandists would have been more difficult. Convinced from World War I that Allied propaganda had played a key role in the defeat of Germany, Adolf Hitler made propaganda a pillar of his regime. A prominent and floodlit one. Indeed, no single individual, including George Creel of the late Committee on Public Information, did more than Hitler to convince Americans that propaganda was an enormously powerful weapon. But because subtlety was cast aside in favor of the volatile and the endlessly repeated big lie, Nazi propaganda in America was too easy to spot and too outrageous to be believed. By contrast, French propaganda was almost subliminal in nature. Thus, and ultimately, the propaganda war in America was lost by the vaunted master and won by the self-effacing, self-professed novice.

There were, of course, assets that were unmistakable from the start. There were grounds for France's long association with freedom, notwithstanding the many moments when Americans found French society altogether too free, if not licentious. But France's assistance at the time of the American Revolution, and the ideals that were made the stuff of legend during its own, meant that France enjoyed an enduring association with the language of liberty, equality, and fraternity. Constitutions, like civil liberties, it had had in plenty, all of them ostensibly aimed at warding off the abuse of power; and by 1900, like America, it had a republican form of government and a parliamentary system based on manhood suffrage and free elections. Furthermore, and like America, it seemed committed to the publicly financed education of its citizens, an education that placed a certain emphasis upon appropriate civic deportment, upon the uplifting effect of the humanities, and upon France's contribution to world culture.

This last notion was also a part of the American school curriculum, at least in certain schools and at certain levels of instruction. This is an essential point, for it is a reminder of that educated elite whose length and quality of education had illuminated the ideas behind republicanism, constitutions, representative assemblies, and freedom of expression. Representing but a few percentage points of the national population, and assuredly not uniform in its Francophilia, this elite—concentrated in the eastern United States—nonetheless demonstrated an affinity for the combined historical cultures of Britain and France. More of its members knew more history than the average American; more of them had learned foreign languages and been exposed to the European "classics" in art and literature; more of them had studied, worked, and toured abroad; more of them dressed in fashions designed in Paris or London. And more of them read papers that covered news beyond the state capital, accordingly had opinions about world events, and were not only capable of but also accustomed to expressing those opinions to their fellow citizens. This was the leadership cadre upon which France relied, to whom the country's agents turned for assistance, and who often volunteered to help without waiting to be asked.

Money was sometimes involved, in the form of a contract with a press agency, or in that of a subvention for travel or for publishing. But for the most part the service was gratuitous and the rewards confined to embassy and consular functions or, often enough, to appointments to or promotion within the French Legion of Honor—awards that inevitably seemed less dangerous to the recipients than to their overlooked critics. Their métiers were diverse—public servants and postsecondary educators, journalists and publishers, artists and musicians, people of commerce and industry—but their collective profile featured affluence and education as well as accomplishment. And very often it included service in one of the numberless associations in America that had earned the gratitude of France: the Federation of the Alliance Française, the French Institutes, the French Maisons and Cercles Français, the France-America Society, the Chambers of Commerce, the Daughters of the American Revolution, the American Legion, the art institutes, the French-language newspapers, the French theaters, and . . . , and . . . , and. . . .

The backgrounds of this elite suggested the media to be employed and the message to be transmitted. France would use its scholarship, scientific as well as humanistic, to highlight its commitment and contribution to knowledge. It would use its canvases, sculpture, architecture, and musical scores to demonstrate its dedication to beauty. It would use its books in religion and philosophy and its literary classics to illustrate its ages-old quest for greater human understanding and for ways to tap the deepest wells of human emotion. It would use, wherever possible, its language as the universal currency with which one accessed these ideals. Hence the interest in American educators, publicists, leaders of the arts communities, and business circles affluent enough—and learned enough—to invest in and promote French culture.

But of what significance was this interest and this effort? The truth is that pre–1914 propaganda had not succeeded in bringing America into a French-sponsored coalition, had not caused the short-lived revocation of American neutrality in 1917, and had not been enough to secure a new revocation in 1939. Neither had it secured American ratification of the Versailles treaty, or much softened American views on war debts, tariffs, or disarmament. Apart from the initiative against war taken with respect to the Kellogg-Briand Pact—which briefly moved America because it was innocuous as well as idealistic—there is little sign that French policy-makers and opinion-shapers did much to make or shape American foreign policy. As for the shaping of American opinion, any claim to French success must also be modest. Mainly through the media of education and cultural exchange, they had managed to regain some of the initiative from Germany in pre–1914 America, a trend that slowly had escalated through the war years. However, that trend reversed itself in the postwar decade as the Franco-American relationship slowly soured over substantive policy differences—including mutual recriminations about who had caused the Depression—and as the Weimar Republic developed a more benign propaganda campaign to market German culture and German wartime innocence. Not until 1933 and Nazi repression at home was there any appreciable willingness among ordinary Americans to take a second look at France. And it was that willingness that slowly strengthened over the following half dozen years, partly, one might allow, because of the work of French agents and American Francophiles, and mainly because of Hitler's escalating curve of excesses.

That said, the experience of these propagandists is more illuminating and potentially more important than the preceding, simplistic calculation of cause and effect would allow. On the one hand, that experience invites a reconsideration of the meaning of propaganda itself. On the other, it invites a reconsideration of the record of France's Third Republic.

The kind of propaganda essential to this volume does not fit the definitional norm of the twentieth century, a norm commonly derived from totalitarian regimes. Such governments quickly dispense with free elections and a free press, then pummel their domestic audience with simple formulas that heighten emotions and dull the brain at one and the same time. Once they are in power, the task is easy, given sufficient financial and technological resources; it is less easy by far in countries that tolerate, indeed cherish, dissenting opinions. Here the overdrawn and the simplistic work less well, indeed can be counterproductive.

With the qualified exception of wartime, when censorship and tailored communiqués became common practice, the French state eschewed such ruthless measures. Whatever the efforts to centralize its news outlet in the Agence Havas, press opinion in France remained diverse, and much of it critical of the government. Abroad, at least in America, where the press was free and some sectors especially vigilant about foreign manipulation, the risks incurred by fraudulent statements were just as great. Dubious claims and simplistic formulas, made the more conspicuous by well-financed repetition and publicly identified paid agents, would only hurt the cause one was trying to advance. Instead, from Jusserand's day onward, the answer seemed to lie in the provision of information rather than misinformation, or rephrased, in the persuasion of free citizens through knowledge rather than in animation through anger or fear.

That approach was inspired as much by pragmatism as by principle, just as was its choice of agency. It was not merely because well-educated people were accustomed to communicating with well-educated people; another reason is that truth is often not only stranger but also more complex than fiction. Detailed information on boundary disputes in distant lands has no hold on people with limited geographical and historical knowledge. The same is true of tourist information for people who seldom travel, educational exchange information for those who no longer study, investment and currency exchange information for those with little to invest or exchange, and cultural information for those geographically or economically removed from museums, galleries, opera houses, and theaters. So it was that to familiarize Americans with the face of France, and to do so both broadly and in depth, French propagandists found it not only natural but also potentially more productive to concentrate on the American elite.

For that they received considerable criticism. Contemporaries complained that the foreign ministry was too elite-oriented in its thinking, that it was too interested in the few and too indifferent to the many. Its message, they said, was too stuffy for the ordinary citizen, and its emphasis on word, paper, and ink over image, celluloid, and airwaves was anachronistic. One ought not discard such criticisms outright, particularly in view of the fact that many French propagandists shared in some of those concerns, but more might be said about the inclination toward the elite and toward the emphasis upon education and cultural exchange.

While it is possible to give greater weight than I have to the impact of mass opinion on the thinking of the elite, in this volume I have opted for the reverse emphasis. To reiterate from Chapter 2, American public opinion about foreign issues is conditioned by the tiny ranks of an "attentive" public that diagnoses and discusses such news in the open, very often in the pages of what has been called the prestige press. In short, it is their views that acquire a public legitimacy, from which the less attentive are likely to take a lead. Hence, rather than persuade the masses to persuade their elites, the propagandist might well wish to persuade the elites—unelected as well as elected—to rally their masses. That, at any rate, is the strategy to which one recent author attributes the success of America's own propaganda campaign in World War II. Conducted, he writes, by "elite insiders in government, military, media, and political circles"—on whom "the ordinary citizen had little impact"—this campaign demonstrated the "enormous" power of press and radio journalists in shaping both government and public opinion.[5]

Thus vindicated in part from charges of misplaced confidence in the influence of national elites, the French propagandist may find solace in still other quarters. The emphasis upon culture, it seems, may have proved more insightful than critics once allowed. In 1935, fifteen years into the history of France's Service des Oeuvres, a British Foreign Office expert lamented the slow pace of his own government's adoption of cultural propaganda. The

French, he said, were already the "supreme" masters of this form of propaganda, a form that "benefits directly those who receive it and indirectly those who conduct it." Little more than a decade later that admiration found another form of expression: this time in the work of the United States Information Service, an agency committed to the distribution abroad of accurate if selective information on every aspect of American life and culture.[6] Yet even in the 1970s, it was being suggested to American students that the French approach remained visionary, the American still underdeveloped. Regrettably, they were told, cultural affairs continued to lag behind issues such as trade and monetary questions. What was needed in a cold war world was cultural exchange as a means of limiting the "misunderstandings, ignorance, and fears that carry the seeds of strife."[7] Intentionally designed for the long haul rather than to elicit a specific response at a predetermined moment, cultural propaganda does not have to resort to untruths and is only very distantly manipulative. That is, simultaneously, its weakness and its strength.

And as for the Third Republic, what conclusions might be drawn from its experience with propaganda in America? First, while it was not a regime that was ever prepared to commit heavy human and financial resources to the cultivation of opinion abroad, neither was it a novice. Indeed, if anything, the rather too frequent admission of its own backwardness in this regard should be taken for what it was: a subterfuge. Second, unlike the heavy-handed, unmissable propaganda in which the German empire had engaged during World War I, or Hitler in the 1930s, the French model adhered to the high road of education and culture, and to the enlistment of American volunteers as their primary agents. Third, these volunteers were of a particular caste, men and women whose personal *formation* included considerable exposure to the intellectual and aesthetic traditions of French civilization, this being so precisely because such agencies as the old Bureau des écoles and the newer Service des Oeuvres had prepared the soil for such seedlings. Fourth, because it had prepared this army of educated, elite recruits, refrained from exaggeration and vitriol, been comparatively stingy in the expenditure of its funds and ostentatiously fearful of offending propaganda-allergic Americans, the republic ultimately sold itself in America. By the outbreak of the second war, Americans, with Hitler's help, saw France as it wanted to be seen: innocent but well prepared, victim but strong, a republican sister in democracy who understood what *civilisation* meant in English. By 1940, Americans were not only pulling for France, but also were confident in its ultimate victory—partly out of sympathy, partly out of conviction that the Maginot

Line was impenetrable and the Anglo-French coalition invincible. If one were looking for a testimonial to the effectiveness of French propaganda, one need look no further than the "shock" of 1940. In the prescience we have generated over the past seven decades, we have lost sight of this, and in its blinding new light we have overlooked the patient and unspectacular efforts of French propagandists in America.

NOTES

List of Abbreviations

AP	Archives Privées
CT	*Chicago Tribune*
CSM	*Christian Science Monitor*
DDF	*Documents diplomatiques français*
FRUS	*Foreign Relations of the United States*
MAISON	Maison de la Presse
MAE	Ministère des affaires étrangères
NYT	*New York Times*
SDN	Société des nations
SF	*San Francisco Examiner*
SOE	Service des Oeuvres françaises à l'étranger
WP	*Washington Post*

Introduction

1. For a recent historiographical survey, see Robert J. Young, *France and the Origins of the Second World War* (London: Macmillan, 1996), 37–59.

2. Robert J. Young, *In Command of France: French Foreign Policy and Military Planning, 1933–1940* (Cambridge: Harvard University Press, 1978); *Power and Pleasure: Louis Barthou and the Third French Republic* (Montreal: McGill-Queen's University Press, 1992).

3. See Philippe Amaury, *De l'information et de la propagande d'Etat: Les deux premières expériences d'un "Ministère de l'information" en France ... juillet 1939–juin 1940, juillet 1940–août 1944* (Paris: Librairie Générale de Droit et de Jurisprudence, 1969); P. J. Floods, *France, 1914–1918: Public Opinion and the War Effort* (London: Macmillan, 1990); Jean-Claude Montant, *La propagande extérieure de la France pendant la première guerre mondiale* (Paris: Unpublished Doctorat d'Etat, Paris I, 1988); Denis Rolland, *Vichy et la France libre au*

Mexique: Guerre, cultures et propagandes pendant la Deuxième Guerre mondiale (Paris: Publications de la Sorbonne, 1990); Dominique Rossignol, *Histoire de la propagande en France de 1940 à 1944* (Paris: Presses Universitaires de France, 1991).

4. America claimed a neutral status for virtually the entire period under consideration. It renounced that status only in 1917–1918, and even then insisted that it was "associated" with, rather than "allied" to, the war effort against the Central Powers.

5. See Marjorie A. Beale, *The Modernist Enterprise: French Elites and the Threat of Modernity, 1900–1940* (Stanford: Stanford University Press, 1999), 11–47; Lisa Tiersten, *Marianne in the Market: Envisioning Consumer Society in Fin-de-Siècle France* (Berkeley and Los Angeles: University of California Press, 2001).

6. Young, *French Foreign Policy,* 10–11.

7. Thomas G. August, *The Selling of the Empire: British and French Imperialist Propaganda, 1890–1940* (Westport, Conn.: Greenwood Press, 1985); Tony Chafer and Amanda Sackur, eds., *Promoting the Colonial Idea: Propaganda and Visions of Empire in France* (New York: Palgrave, 2002).

8. Edward L. Bernays, *Propaganda* (New York: Liveright, 1928), 9–12; "Molding Public Opinion," in *Pressure Groups and Propaganda*, Annals of the American Academy of Political and Social Science 179, ed. Harwood L. Childs (Philadelphia, 1935), 82–87; Lester Markel, "Opinion: A Neglected Instrument," in *Public Opinion and Foreign Policy*, ed. Lester Markel (New York: Harper and Brothers, 1949), 12.

9. Jean-Marie Domenach, *La propagande politique* (Paris: Presses Universitaires de France, 1969), 63–69; Paul Rutherford, *Endless Propaganda: The Advertising of Public Goods* (Toronto: University of Toronto Press, 2000), 7–8.

10. Ernest R. May, *Strange Victory: Hitler's Conquest of France* (New York: Hill and Wang, 2000), 101–102.

11. Harold D. Lasswell, "Propaganda," *Encyclopedia of the Social Sciences*, vol. 12 (1934), 525.

12. J.A.C. Brown, *Techniques of Mass Persuasion* (Harmondsworth: Penguin, 1963), 21.

13. For a discussion of this complex subject, see the later pages of Chapter 2.

14. I mean no disrespect to the archivists who have been faced with extraordinary challenges when I recall the many cartons of undated, unpaginated, uninventoried, generally disheveled documents through which I have labored. They appreciate the historian's preference for having documents in that condition to not having them at all.

15. Thus we can have France-Amérique or France-America, the Association catholique or the Catholic Association, the Bureau de l'information française or the French Information Bureau, the French Chamber of Commerce of New York, or the Chambre de commerce française de New York. Etymologically speaking, it is often difficult to determine which language was the original; and certainly the French archival record supports the use of either or both.

CHAPTER 1 **From Peace to War, 1900–1914**

1. *New York Times* (henceforth *NYT*), 15 April 1900, 1.
2. *Chicago Tribune* (henceforth *CT*), 15 April 1900, 2. See also Richard D. Mandell, *Paris 1900: The Great World's Fair* (Toronto: University of Toronto Press, 1967).
3. *NYT*, 15 April 1900, 1.
4. *NYT*, 22 July 1900, 5; *CT*, 4, 11, 25 November 1900, page 7 in each case.
5. *NYT*, 14 July 1900, 47S. For treatment of the American artistic presence in Paris, see Diane P. Fischer, ed., *Paris 1900: The "American School" at the Universal Exposition* (New Brunswick: Rutgers University Press, 1999).
6. *NYT*, 12 August 1900, 7.
7. *NYT*, 5 July 1900, 7; *Tribune*, 4 July 1900, 13; 5 July 1900, 6.
8. *NYT*, 30 July 1900, 7.
9. *NYT*, 30 July 1900, 7.
10. *NYT*, 26 August 1900, 7.
11. *CT*, 28 October 1900, 32.
12. *Washington Post* (henceforth *WP*), 6 May 1900, 22; 2 July 1900, 6; 23 August 1900, 2. The Legion was created by Napoleon in 1802 as a device to recognize outstanding civil or military service to France by French nationals or by foreigners. There are five ascending ranks: *chevalier, officier, commandeur, grand officier,* and *grande croix*; and five grades of distinction: a red lapel ribbon, a red rosette, a red collar and cross; a star and collar, and a star and broad cordon. See *NYT*, 3 September 1900, 7.
13. *NYT*, 25 January 1900, 7; 7 May 1900, 6.
14. The *Tribune* of Chicago reported that the typical hotel price of $2.50 a night had been bumped up by a dollar or a dollar and a half. See editorial of 9 April 1900, 6.
15. See *NYT*, 14 July 1900, 6; 6 August 1900, 7; 3 September 1900, 7; *WP*, 22 April, 5.
16. *CT*, 26 September 1900, 16; *NYT*, 12 August 1900, 7.
17. *CT*, 19 June 1900, 10.
18. *CT*, editorial, 1 May 1900, 12.
19. *CT*, 10 September 1900, 6; 13 November 1900, 3.
20. *CT*, 5 May 1900, 10; *NYT*, 8 July 1900, 17.
21. *WP*, 20 May 1900, 4; *CT*, 4 June 1900, 6.
22. *NYT*, 8 July 1900, 7.
23. *NYT*, editorial, 29 January 1900, 6.
24. See, for instance, Charles W. Brooks, *America in France's Hopes and Fears, 1890–1920*, vol. 1 (New York: Garland, 1987), 124–141; and Yves-Henri Nouailhat, *France et Etats-Unis, Août 1914–Avril 1917* (Paris: Publications de la Sorbonne, 1979), 11–13.
25. Jusserand to Pichon, 4 February 1907, *Ministère des affaires étrangères* (henceforth *MAE*) AP\093\03, 25–28.
26. Henry Blumenthal, *France and the United States: Their Diplomatic Relations, 1789–1914* (Chapel Hill: University of North Carolina Press, 1970), 179–180. For more on the assets and liabilities of Franco-American trade between 1900 and 1914, see Nouailhat, *France et Etats-Unis*, 25–42.

27. See Allan Mitchell, *The German Influence in France after 1870* (Chapel Hill: University of North Carolina Press, 1979).

28. Sigmund Skard, *The American Myth and the European Mind: American Studies in Europe, 1776–1960* (New York: Perpetua, 1964), 44–46.

29. Donald Drew Egbert, "Foreign Influences in American Art," in *Foreign Influences in American Life*, ed. David F. Bowers (Princeton: Princeton University Press, 1944), 113–114. See also Thomas Hastings, "The Influence of the Ecole des Beaux-Arts upon American Architecture," *Architectural Record*, 10 (1901), 65–90.

30. Originally installed at 21 rue Cassette in Paris, in 1918 the *comité* moved its offices to 82 avenue des Champs-Elysées, "au coeur même du 'quartier américain.'" Gabriel Hanotaux, *Le Comité "France-Amérique"* (Paris: Comité "France-Amérique," 1920), 5, 11. J. B. Duroselle, *La France et les Etats-Unis des origines à nos jours* (Paris: Seuil, 1976), 81. Note that in the United States, the organization was called the France-America Society.

31. Editorial, *Christian Science Monitor* (henceforth *CSM*) 20 June 1911, 16.

32. Jusserand to Poincaré, 10 February 1912, *MAE*, AP\093\05, 126–128.

33. See Jusserand to Pichon, 15 February 1910, *MAE*, AP\093\04, 120–122; Jusserand to Cruppi, 23 May 1911, *MAE*, AP\093\05, 38.

34. Jacques Portes, *Une fascination réticente: Les Etats-Unis dans l'opinion française, 1870–1914* (Nancy: Presses Universitaires de Nancy, 1990), 215–218.

35. Jusserand to Pichon, 14 April 1907, *MAE*, AP\093\03, 89. For Carnegie's faith in the German kaiser, see Joseph Frazier Wall, *Andrew Carnegie* (New York: Oxford University Press, 1970), 924–926.

36. In fact, a total of three new *sous-sections* were added to the *direction*, including one for South America and one for the Far East. See Young, *French Foreign Policy*, 6.

37. Young, *French Foreign Policy*, 9–11.

38. Young, *French Foreign Policy*, 11–12.

39. Originally created, by ministerial decree of 4 April 1909, as a *service* within the ministry, the office was upgraded to a *bureau* by a decree of 13 August 1910. Its Western Section was mainly addressed to western and northern Europe. The Eastern included countries in the Balkans, the Near East, and northern Africa. See unsigned report of 10 October 1910, *MAE*, Service des Oeuvres (henceforth Oeuvres), 01.

40. Report of 10 October 1910, *MAE*, Oeuvres, 01.

41. Jusserand to Pichon, 4 January 1911, *MAE*, AP\093\04, 190; to de Selves, 7 November 1911, ibid., 05, 59; to Poincaré, 10 February 1912, ibid., 05, 126–128; to Jonnart, 11 March 1913, ibid., 06, 169–171; to Pichon, 17 June 1913, 07, 56.

42. Jusserand to Cruppi, 28 March 1922, *MAE*, AP\094\04, 222–225; to Poincaré, 7 April 1912, ibid., 05, 177; to Jonnart, 11 March 1913, ibid., 06, 171.

43. Jusserand to Cruppi, 23 May 1911, *MAE*, AP\093\05, 37–38; to Poincaré, 29 January 1912, ibid., 117; to Poincaré, 4 December 1912, ibid., 06, 70.

44. Report of 10 October 1910, *MAE*, Oeuvres, 01; Jusserand to Pichon, 27 November 1913, *MAE*, AP\093\07, 144–146. From its inception in 1912, and installation on West 177 Street, near Columbia University, the Comité de New York assumed the name of France-America Society. By 1920, however, there were

chapters of the society in New Orleans, Los Angeles, San Diego, San Francisco, Seattle, and Salt Lake City. See Hanotaux, *Le Comité "France-Amérique,"* 17, 19. Following contemporary practice, I use interchangeably the names France-America Society, France-America, Comité France-Amérique, and France-Amérique.

45. Jusserand to Pichon, 1 November 1910, *MAE*, AP\093\04, 153.

46. In 1907, for example, the most contentious diplomatic issue between France and America was, in fact, that of satisfying each other's standards for agricultural imports—principally meat. See the series of exchanges between January and October in *Foreign Relations of the United States* (henceforth *FRUS*) 1907, Reel no. 23, vol. 1.

47. Blumenthal, *France and the United States*, 234–239. J. B. Duroselle observes that while the United States had become the fourth-largest importer of French goods by 1913, behind Britain, Germany, and Belgium, its investment capital in France remained very slight. See Duroselle, *La France et les Etats-Unis*, 66–67.

48. See *Le Temps*, 7 July 1913, 1.

49. Paul Gerbod, "L'enseignement de la langue française aux Etats-Unis au xxe siècle," *Revue Historique* 576 (October–December 1990): 388–390.

50. See Portes, *Une fascination réticente*, 365–377.

CHAPTER 2   *Senders and Receivers, 1900–1940*

1. Louis-Bernard Robitaille, *Et Dieu créa les Français* (Montreal: Editions Robert Davies, 1995), 11–13.

2. Preface to Pierre Frédérix, *Un siècle de chasse aux nouvelles: De l'Agence d'Information Havas à l'Agence France-Presse, 1835–1957* (Paris: Flammarion, 1959), i.

3. Theodore Zeldin, *France, 1848–1945*, vol. 2, *Intellect, Taste, and Anxiety* (Oxford: Clarendon Press, 1977), 127–129.

4. For the mixed reaction to German culture in France, see Claude Digeon, *La crise allemande de la pensée français, 1870–1914* (Paris: Presses Universitaires de France, 1992).

5. Priscilla P. Clark, *Literary France: The Making of a Culture* (Berkeley and Los Angeles: University of California Press, 1987), 111; Jean-Pierre Rioux and Jean-François Sirinelli, *Le temps des masses*, vol 4. of *Histoire culturelle de la France* (Paris: Editions du Seuil, 1998), 154.

6. Eugen Weber, *Peasants into Frenchmen: The Modernization of Rural France, 1870–1914* (Stanford: Stanford University Press, 1976), 493–494; Barnett Singer, "From Patriots to Pacifists: The French Primary School Teachers, 1880–1940," *Journal of Contemporary History* xxi, no. 3 (1977): 413–414; Maurice Crubellier, *L'école républicaine, 1870–1940* (Paris: Editions Christian, 1993), 41–44.

7. Crubellier, *L'école*, 77–87.

8. There was one notable exception to this fanciful architectural plan, the level called the *écoles primaires supérieurs*, highly selective schools whose candidates, before 1900, were actually fewer in number than those of the *écoles secondaires*. It was from the former that the Republic selected the very best graduates for

subsequent instruction in the nation's teacher-training schools, the *écoles normales*. See Rioux and Sirinelli, *Le temps des masses*, 29.

9. Ibid., 29. Antoine Prost's calculations are less sanguine—one scholarship for every eight boys enrolled in secondary school, and only 110,000 total secondary enrolments, including girls, by 1930. See his *Histoire de l'enseignement en France, 1800–1967* (Paris: Colin, 1968), 327–328.

10. Rioux and Sirinelli, *Le temps des masses*, 29–31.

11. Ezra N. Suleiman, *Elites in French Society: The Politics of Survival* (Princeton: Princeton University Press, 1978), 49; Rioux and Sirinelli, *Le temps des masses*, 148; Christophe Charle, *Naissance des "Intellectuels," 1880–1900* (Paris: Editions de Minuit, 1990), 67–81. For the constraints on university education for women, see Martha Hanna, "French Women and American Men: 'Foreign' Students at the University of Paris, 1915–1925," *French Historical Studies*, 22, no. 1 (1999): 87–112.

12. Roger Magraw, *France, 1815–1914: The Bourgeois Century* (Oxford: Oxford University Press, 1986), 364–366. See also G. Chaussinand-Nogaret, J. M. Constant, C. Durandin, and A. Jouanna, *Histoire des élites en France du xvie au xxe siècle* (Paris: Tallandier, 1991), 431.

13. Young, *Power and Pleasure*, 29–30.

14. Jean Estèbe, *Les ministres de la République, 1871–1914* (Paris: Presses de la Fondation Nationale des Sciences Politiques, 1982), 21–22, 40–41, 104, 122, 152–153, 186–188; J. Gilbert Heinberg, "The Personnel of French Cabinets, 1871–1930," *American Political Science Review* 25 (1931): 389–396.

15. See Young, *French Foreign Policy*, 23–25; Henry Kittredge Norton, "Foreign Office Organization: A Comparison of the Organization of the British, French, German, and Italian Foreign Office with That of the Department of State of the U.S.A," in Annals of the American Academy of Political and Social Science 143, supplement (Philadelphia, 1929), 32–33.

16. Marc Martin, *Médias et journalistes de la République* (Paris: Editions Odile Jacob, 1997), 123–126; Pierre Albert, "La presse française de 1871 à 1940," in *Histoire générale de la presse française*, ed. Claude Bellanger et al. (Paris: Presses Universitaires de France, 1972), 249.

17. David Strauss, *Menace in the West: The Rise of French Anti-Americanism in Modern Times* (Westport, Conn.: Greenwood Press, 1978), 19; Skard, *The American Myth*, 44–45; Portes, *Une fascination réticente*, 215–218.

18. Elizabeth Fordham, "From Whitman to Wilson: French Attitudes toward America around the Time of the Great War," in *Across the Atlantic, Cultural Exchanges between Europe and the United States*, ed. Louisa Passerini (Brussels: Peter Lang, 2000), 119; Zeldin, *Ambition, Love, and Politics*, 128–135.

19. August, *Selling of the Empire*; William H. Schneider, *An Empire for the Masses: The French Popular Image of Africa, 1870-1900* (Westport, Conn.: Greenwood Press, 1982).

20. The following biographical data is taken from a range of sources, including: *Current Biography*; *Dictionnaire des parlementaires français, 1889–1940*, 8 vols.; *Dictionnaire de biographie française*; *New York Times Obituaries*; *Who's Who in*

France; David Bell, et al., eds., *Biographical Dictionary of French Political Leaders since 1870* (New York: Simon and Schuster, 1990); Serge Berstein and Giselle Berstein, *La Troisième République* (Paris: MA Editions, 1987); Henry Coston, ed., *Dictionnaire de la politique française*, 2 vols. (Paris: Publications Henry Coston, 1972); Patrick J. Hutton, ed., *Historical Dictionary of the Third French Republic, 1870–1940*, 2 vols. (Westport: Greenwood Press, 1986).

21. Lawrence W. Levine, *Highbrow/Lowbrow: The Emergence of Cultural Hierarchy in America* (Cambridge: Harvard University Press, 1988), 214–218; Henry Blumenthal, *American and French Culture, 1800–1900: Interchange in Art, Science, Literature, and Society* (Baton Rouge: Louisiana State University Press, 1975), 477–479; Nelson W. Aldrich, *Old Money: The Mythology of America's Upper Class* (New York: Knopf, 1988), 63.

22. For a brief and general introduction to elites in America, see Harold D. Lasswell et al., "The Elite Concept," in *Political Elites in a Democracy*, ed. Peter Bachrach (New York: Atherton, 1971), 13–26. For a more current examination of these elites, see Robert Lerner, Althea K. Nagai, and Stanley Rothman, *American Elites* (New Haven: Yale University Press, 1996).

23. Martin Kriesberg uses a figure of 73,691,000 Americans over the age of twenty-five in 1940. His calculation that 25 percent of the electorate could be considered knowledgeable about foreign problems in 1940 seems somewhat optimistic—given the fact that only 19 percent had a grade-eight certificate or more. See his "Dark Areas of Ignorance," in *Public Opinion and Foreign Policy*, ed. Lester Markel (New York: Harper and Brothers, 1949), 49–52. See also Catherine Gillot, "La France au miroir de l'Amérique dans les années 1920: Morand, Duhamel" (Ph.D. diss., New York University 1998), 61.

24. André Kaspi, *La vie quotidienne aux Etats-Unis au temps de la prospérité, 1919–1929* (Paris: Hachette, 1980), 82.

25. Gerbod, "L'enseignement," 387–406. Gerbod also reports the gradual decline of this interest in French throughout the course of the 1930s, and subsequently. See also Bertram Gordon, "The Decline of a Cultural Icon: France in American Perspective," *French Historical Studies* 22, no. 4 (1999): 634; and Paul Finkelman, "The War on German Language and Culture, 1917–1925," in *Confrontation and Cooperation: Germany and the United States in the Era of World War I, 1900–1924*, ed. Hans-Jurgen Shroder (Providence: Berg, 1993), 177–205.

26. Part of this increase is to be explained by the return of demobilized American soldiers who had developed an interest in France as well as some familiarity with the French language. Gerbod, "L'enseignement," 393. For the decline in German, see Willis Rudy, *Total War and Twentieth-Century Higher Learning: Universities of the Western World in the First and Second World Wars* (Rutherford, N.J.: Farleigh Dickinson University Press, 1991), 30.

27. Jeremy Popkin, "'Made in U.S.A.': Les historiens français d'outre-Atlantique et leur histoire," *Revue d'Histoire Moderne et Contemporaine* 40, no. 2 (1993), 310.

28. Although the proportion of private to public secondary schools dropped from about 40 percent in 1890 to 13 percent in 1918, the actual numbers of private schools increased from some sixteen hundred to two thousand, and the

enrollments from 95,000 to almost 160,000. See R. Freeman Butts and Lawrence A. Cremin, *A History of Education in American Culture* (New York: Holt, Rinehart and Winston, 1953), 421.

29. See James McLachlan, *American Boarding Schools: A Historical Study* (New York: Schribner's, 1970); C. Wright Mills, *The Power Elite* (New York: Oxford, 1956), 63-64.

30. Gerbod, "L'enseignement," 394–395; Emile Lauvrière, "La France dans le développement des Etats-Unis," *La Grande Revue*, 148 (August 1935), 285. In 1918, more than two-thirds of the private schools were under denominational control, of which the same proportion were Roman Catholic. By the first decade of the twentieth century, there were about 1,250,000 students in Catholic schools at the primary level, and more than 16,000 at the secondary level. See R. Freeman Butts and Lawrence A. Cremin, *A History of Education in American Culture* (New York: Holt, Rinehart and Winston, 1953), 417, 421.

31. For the claim that anti-French sentiment was "weakest among those who possess the cosmopolitan spirit," see Howard M. Jones, *American and French Culture, 1750–1848* (Chapel Hill: University of North Carolina Press, 1927), 570.

32. For an insight into the American elite's ambivalent response to different European cultures, see Mary Cable, *Top Drawer: American High Society from the Gilded Age to the Roaring Twenties* (New York: Atheneum, 1984), 116–124.

33. The principal and indispensable source for the career profiles that follow is Philip J. Burch Jr., *Elites in American History*, 3 vols.; vol. 2, *The Civil War to the New Deal*; vol. 3, *The New Deal to the Carter Administration* (New York: Holmes and Meier, 1980–81).

34. I reiterate my indebtedness to the work of Philip Burch and draw attention as well to Donald R. Matthews, *The Social Background of Political Decision-Makers* (New York: Random House, 1954), 25–33.

35. Clayton D. Laurie, *The Propaganda Warriors: America's Crusade against Nazi Germany* (Lawrence: University Press of Kansas, 1996), 19–20.

36. The biographical elements that appear in the section that follows have been taken from various editions of *American Authors and Books*, *Contemporary Authors*, *Current Biography Yearbook*, *Dictionary of North American Authors*, *Dictionary of Literary Biography*, *International Who's Who*, *New York Times Obituaries*, *Who Was Who in America*, and *Who Was Who among North American Authors*.

37. See Linda Lumsden, "'You're a Tough Guy, Mary—and a First-Rate Newspaperman': Gender and Women Journalists in the 1920s and 1930s," *Journalism and Mass Communication Quarterly* 72, no. 4 (1995): 913–921.

38. Oscar W. Riegel once suggested how difficult it was for foreign correspondents "to insulate themselves against the desire to cultivate friendly relations" with officials in the countries with which they are accredited. *Mobilizing for Chaos: The Story of the New Propaganda* (1934; reprint, New York: Arno Press, 1972), 145–147.

39. William L. Shirer, *Twentieth Century Journey: A Memoir of a Life and the Times*, vol. 1 (New York: Simon and Schuster, 1976), 259.

40. Edward L. Bernays, *Crystallizing Public Opinion* (1923; reprint, New York: Liveright Publishing, 1961), xxxiii.

41. Markel, "Opinion," 9–10; Ralph B. Levering, *The Public and American Foreign Policy, 1918–1978* (New York: William Morrow, 1978), 19–21, 21–31; Melvin Small, "Historians Look at Public Opinion," in *Public Opinion and Historians: Interdisciplinary Perspectives*, ed. Small (Detroit: Wayne State University Press, 1970), 18.

42. Differences in educational level are said to be much more significant than differences in wealth. See Gabriel A. Almond, *The American People and Foreign Policy* (New York: Praeger, 1960), 126.

43. Levering, *Public*, 123.

44. Lippmann estimated that there were twelve hundred press agents operating in New York by 1914, and Michael Schudson reports that by the 1920s, any large newspaper could have been receiving as many as 150,000 words daily from sundry public relations offices. See Lippmann, *Public Opinion* (New York: Macmillan, 1922), 324–325, 345; and Schudson, *Discovering the News: A Social History of the American Newspaper* (New York: Basic Books, 1978), 129.

45. William O. Chittick, *State Department, Press, and Pressure Groups: A Role Analysis* (New York: Wiley-Interscience, 1970), 182. For Franklin Roosevelt's careful monitoring of the press, see Richard W. Steele, "The Pulse of the People: Franklin D. Roosevelt and the Gauging of American Public Opinion," *Journal of Contemporary History* 9, no. 4 (1974): 195–216.

46. William O. Domhoff, *The Higher Circles: The Governing Class in America* (New York: Random House, 1970), 149–150. One 1949 survey of press readers determined that only 6 percent read international news "very carefully," as opposed to 47 percent who read only the headlines of both national and international news. Bernard C. Cohen, *The Press and Foreign Policy* (Princeton: Princeton University Press, 1963), 257.

47. This and subsequent figures do not include the sales of what Bernard C. Cohen called other "prestige papers," such as the *New York Herald Tribune, Wall Street Journal, Baltimore Sun, Washington Evening Star, St. Louis Post-Dispatch, Louisville Courier-Journal, Milwaukee Journal*, or *Minneapolis Tribune*, all papers that provide significant foreign news coverage. See *Press and Foreign Policy*, 138–139.

48. Robert J. Young, "Forgotten Words and Faded Images: American Journalists before the Fall of France, 1940," *Historical Reflections* 24, no. 2 (1998): 208.

49. Ian Mugridge, *The View from Xanadu: William Randolph Hearst and United States Foreign Policy* (Montreal: McGill-Queen's University Press, 1995), 19; Domhoff, *Higher Circles*, 116–119; Levering, *Public*, 39–40.

CHAPTER 3   *Words as Weapons, 1914–1919*

1. Col. Thomas B. Mott, *Myron T. Herrick: Friend of France* (New York: Doubleday, Doran, 1929); "France Pays Highest Honor," *SF*, 10 December 1914, 3; "Gertrude Atherton Sees Paris," *NYT*, 2 July 1916, v, 8.

2. See Jean-Claude Montant, "L'organisation centrale des Services d'informations et de propagande du Quai d'Orsay pendant la Grande Guerre," in *Les sociétés européennes et la guerre de 1914–1918*, ed. J. J. Becker and Stéphane Audoin-

Rouzeau (Paris: Université de Paris X, Nanterre, 1990), 136–137; Ross F. Collins, "The Development of Censorship in World War I France," *Journalism Monographs*, no. 131 (1992): 5.

3. Collins, "Development of Censorship," 13–14, 21. He reports that the last directive to censors was dated 15 October 1919, long after the Armistice and the conclusion of the Peace Conference.

4. Jean-Louis Maurin, "Les missions de presse près de l'armée française pendant la première guerre mondiale," *Guerres mondiales et conflits contemporains* 164 (October 1991): 29–30.

5. Maurin, "Les missions," 31–32, 43. The two American journalists in late 1916 were Robert Berry of the Associated Press with its eighteen hundred newspapers, and Henry Wood of United Press, with its eight hundred newspapers. Maurin, "Les missions," 32.

6. The Bureau Ponsot was located at the Quai d'Orsay and included principals such as Alexis Léger, Henri Hoppenot, and Louis Massignon. See Montant, "L'organisation centrale," 137. For information on wartime collaboration between the French government and Agence Havas, see Albert, "La press française," 409–427; Frédérix, *Un siècle*, 328; Clifford F. Weigle, "The Rise and Fall of the Havas News Agency," *Journalism Quarterly* 19 (September 1942): 277–286.

7. Collins, "Development of Censorship," 19; Daniel Langlois-Berthelot, "Philippe Berthelot (1886–1934)," *Nouvelle Revue des Deux Mondes* 6 (1976): 574–582; Jean-Claude Montant, "Propagande et guerre psychologique: La Maison de la Presse," in *Les affaires étrangères et le corps diplomatique français*, vol. 2, ed. Jean Baillou (Paris: CNRS, 1984), 334–345.

8. Montant, "L'organisation centrale," 137–141.

9. "La propagande pendant la guerre," unpaginated, located in the inventory for the Maison de la Presse, 1914–1928, MAE.

10. "La Maison de la Presse," anonymous article from 1916. See inventory for the Maison, MAE. See also Riegel, *Mobilizing*, 39–46, 91–92.

11. In keeping with this work's focus on French propaganda in America, this chapter contains only passing reference to French efforts in enemy or allied (excepting the United States) countries.

12. "La Maison de la Presse," MAE; Montant, "L'organisation centrale," 138–139.

13. The best account of the atrocity debate is provided by John Horne and Alan Kramer in "German 'Atrocities' and Franco-German Opinion, 1914: The Evidence of German Soldiers' Diaries," *Journal of Modern History* 66 (March 1994): 1–33; and their *German Atrocities, 1914* (New York: Yale University Press, 2000). See also Phillip Knightley, *The First Casualty. From the Crimea to Vietnam: The War Correspondent as Hero, Propagandist, and Myth Maker* (New York: Harcourt Brace Jovanovich, 1975), 83–107.

14. Collins, "Development of Censorship," 9.

15. Jusserand to Berthelot, 1 January 1916, MAE, AP\010\18\Berthelot, 26–30; "Note sur la propagande française aux Etats-Unis," 27 February 1916, ibid., 69–73. See also Stéphane Audoin-Rouzeau's "'Bourrage de Crâne' et information en France en 1914–1918," in *Les sociétés européennes*, ed. Audoin-Rouzeau and Jean-Jacques Becker, 163–174.

16. Gilbert Chinard to Berthelot, 1 February 1916, MAE, AP\010\18 Berthelot, 40–41; Instruction publique to Ernest Guy (Maison), 7 December 1916, MAE, Maison, vol. 20.

17. Jusserand to MAE, 7 January 1916, MAE, AP\010\18\Berthelot, 32.

18. Whitney Warren to Premier Aristide Briand, 19 November 1915, MAE, AP\010\18\Berthelot, 1–2. James Hazen Hyde to Berthelot, 14 November 1915, MAE, AP\010\20\Berthelot, 6–24. See also articles by Warren and Mrs. Whitney Warren in *NYT*, 5 December 1915, iv, 16–17, and 16 July 1916, v, 7–8.

19. Davis to Jusserand, 3 February 1916, MAE, AP\093\99\Davis, 68–69; "Note sur Edward Marshall," 28 December 1916, MAE, AP\010\20\Marshall, 60–65. Alan Price, *The End of the Age of Innocence: Edith Wharton and the First World War* (New York: St. Martin's Griffin, 1996), 150.

20. James Hazen Hyde to Berthelot, 14 November 1915, MAE, AP\010\20\Berthelot, 7–24.

21. G. Heslouin (New York Consulate) to Berthelot, 4 March 1916, MAE, AP\010\18\Berthelot, 80–81; and 5 June 1916, ibid., 127–132.

22. Bracq's *The Provocation of France* was published in 1916. See *NYT*, 14 January 1917, vi, 10. A review of his reprinted *France under the Republic* appeared on 9 September 1917, vii, 33. For samples of Francophilic pieces submitted by Butler, see *NYT*, 25 October 1914, v, 5; 3 January 1915, v, 5; 9 May 1915, v, 8. For a useful article on Butler's service to France, see an article by Baron d'Etournelles de Constant in *NYT*, 8 June 1919, iv, 8. See also McClellan's article on brave France, *NYT*, 19 September 1915, iv, 9–10.

23. Kahn, a British citizen, was a partner in Kuhn, Loeb and Company. It was he who convinced the prominent lawyer Paul Cravath to chair the committee, one that included the New York lawyer Frederic R. Coudert and James M. Beck. See Casenave (New York) to MAE, 15 December 1916, AP\010\19\Berthelot, 93–104; M. de Sillac to Jusserand, MAE, 15 December 1916, ibid., 114–118; Polignac (New York) to Ernest Guy (Paris), MAE, 30 December 1916, AP\010\20\Polignac, 163. For the more pronounced Anglophilia of Morgan and Lamont, see Martin A. Horn, "A Private Bank at War: J. P. Morgan and Co. and France, 1914–1918," *Business History Review* 74 (spring 2000): 85–112.

24. Jusserand (DC) to Lauzanne (NY), MAE, 30 October 1916, AP\093\88\Lauzanne, 14–15.

25. "Note sur la propagande par le cinématographe aux Etats-Unis," 1916, MAE, Maison\20; "Note sur la propagande française," 27 February 1916, MAE AP\010\18, 69–73; Casenave (New York) to MAE, 30 January 1917, MAE, AP\010\19, 152–153; Polignac to Tardieu, 10 March 1917, MAE, AP\166\84\Tardieu, 11–27.

26. Jusserand to Lauzanne, 13 March 1917, MAE, AP\093\88\Lauzanne, 57–58. See also MAE to Consulate (New York), 22 February 1917, MAE, AP\010\18\Berthelot, 66. For his great admiration of America, see his *With Americans of Past and Present Days* (New York: Scribner's, 1916). In any event, the ambassador claimed in August 1915 that he had no budget for propaganda, "pas un seul dollar." See Nouailhat, *France et Etats-Unis*, 151.

27. Heslouin (New York) to Berthelot, 4 March 1916, MAE, AP\010\18\Berthelot, 80–81; Heslouin report on propaganda, 5 June 1916, MAE, Maison, vol.20.

28. Casenave (New York) to MAE, 15 December 1916, MAE AP\010\19\Berthelot, 93–104. Kahn was also chairman of the French American Association for Musical Art. For his public remarks on "sinister . . . Prussianism," and his stunning claim that France had "never tried to propagandize her national art," see *NYT*, 16 October 1918, 13.

29. See Briand (Paris) to Jusserand, 2 October 1916, MAE, AP\093\88\Lauzanne, 6. As late as May 1917, Lauzanne was still being identified by the *New York Times* simply as former editor of *Le Matin*.

30. Lauzanne to MAE, 2 December 1916, MAE, AP\093\88\Lauzanne, 32–33; Lauzanne to Laboulaye (DC), 25 September 1917, ibid., 94. Lauzanne's principal assistant in New York, and eventual successor in the postwar Bureau of Information, was Marcel Knecht, an early recruit to the Maison de la Presse in Paris. See Casenave (New York) to Jusserand, 1 November 1916, MAE, AP\093\88\Lauzanne, 17–18.

31. Lauzanne to Berthelot, 16 December 1916, MAE, AP\010\19\Berthelot, 106–111. For samples of major press articles by Lauzanne see *NYT*, 17 December 1916, v, 1; 6 May 1917, viii, 1; 10 March 1918, vi, 93; 28 July 1918, vi, 5;17 November 1918, iv, 9.

32. Lauzanne to Jusserand, 12 March 1917, MAE, AP\093\88\Lauzanne, 55–56. See the interview with Lauzanne, the review of his *Fighting France*, and his article urging a tough American position on German reparations, all in *NYT*, 28 July 1918, vi, 5; 18 August, v, 358; 17 November 1918, iv, 9.

33. "Mission du Marquis," 6 May 1916, MAE, AP\010\20\Polignac, 87–88; Polignac to Berthelot, 7 July 1916, ibid., 128–130; Polignac to Berthelot, 23 December 1916, ibid., 160. Polignac had in mind a man like his adversary Count Bernstorff, but one "with a French manner." See Polignac to Guy, 30 December 1916, ibid., 163. See also Reinhard Doerries, *Imperial Challenge: Ambassador Count Bernstorff and German-American Relations, 1908–1917* (Chapel Hill: University of North Carolina Press, 1989).

34. Pierre de Lanux to Polignac, June 1917, MAE, Guerre, vol. 513, 239–243; Godfrey Hodgson, *The Colonel: The Life and Wars of Henry Stimson, 1867–1950* (Boston: Northeastern University Press, 1990), 176–178.

35. French National Committee (New York) to Henri Ponsot (Maison), 26 March 1917, MAE, Maison, vol. 21.

36. "Note sur l'action en Amérique," 3 April 1916, MAE, AP\010\18\Berthelot, 82–85; Pierre de Margerie (MAE) to Jusserand, 24 July 1916, MAE, AP\010\19\Berthelot, 31; Résumé de l'activité, 1917, MAE, AP\166\84\Tardieu, 30; Jusserand to MAE, 6 March 1917, Maison, vol.21.

37. Berthelot to Polignac, 19 September 1916, MAE, AP\010\20\Polignac, 138–139; Circular to Agents, 13 December 1916, MAE, AP\010\19\Berthelot, 91; Polignac to Guy, 17 Janaury 1917, MAE, AP\010\20\Polignac, 168–171; Pechkoff file, 1916, MAE, AP\010\20\Pechkoff, 66–77. After the war, Périgord became an American citizen and a professor in California. See Harold L. Ickes, *The Autobiography of a Curmudgeon* (1943; reprint, Chicago: Quadrangle Paperbacks, 1969), 191; and Robert K. Hanks, "Culture versus Diplomacy: Clemenceau and

Anglo-American Relations during the First World War" (Ph.D. diss., University of Toronto, 2001), 194.

38. For a major work on the recruitment of intellectuals for the war of words, see Martha Hanna, *The Mobilization of Intellect: French Scholars and Writers during the Great War* (Cambridge: Harvard University Press, 1996).

39. See untitled document of February 1916, file no. 5, MAE, AP\010\3\Berthelot, 72–89; Alfred Baudrillart, "Notre propagande," *Revue Hebdomadaire* 25 (8 April 1916): 141–184.

40. See "Résumé de l'activité du service de la propagande aux Etats-Unis," 1917, MAE, AP\166\84\Tardieu, 28–37. "La propagande pendant la guerre," 1920, and "La Maison de la Presse," MAE, Maison Inventory; Montant, "L'organisation centrale des services d'information," 140–141; Maurice Mégret, "Les origines de la propagande de guerre française: Du Service général de l'information au Commissariat général à l'information," *Revue d'Histoire de la Deuxième Guerre Mondiale*, no. 41 (January 1961): 5. While "technically" the Maison disappeared, references to its work abound after the spring of 1917; and the archival holdings under its name extend to 1920. The commissariat, it should be said, was primarily responsible for propaganda in allied and neutral countries, while an associated Centre d'action de propagande contre l'ennemie concentrated on France's foes. See Mégret, "Les origines de la propagande," 5–6.

41. The *New York Times* introduced its readers to the "Brilliant Record" of Tardieu by publishing a long, translated article on the commissioner from the Paris *Le Temps*. See *NYT*, 20 May 1917, vi, 11. See also François Monnet, *Refaire la République: André Tardieu, une dérive réactionnaire, 1876–1945* (Paris: Fayard, 1993) 53, 82–85.

42. André Tardieu, *France and America: Some Experiences in Cooperation* (New York: Houghton Mifflin, 1927), 215–234. Underscoring the need for coordination of effort in May 1917, Tardieu recalls the artillery, engineering, aviation, naval, and railroad missions, which operated in "joyful independence" and "competed against each other," 236.

43. By October 1918 this study and information department also relied on the services of Professors Vatar and Schoelle of Bryn-Mawr University in Pennsylvania. The High Commission also included a Service des missions artistiques et expositions, headed by A. M. Guiffrey and his deputy, Lieutenant Dumeret, as well as a New York office for photographic and cinematic material headed by Edmond Ratisbonne. See report of 2 October 1918, MAE, Series B, vol. 22, 103–116; and De Billy to J. P. Jones, 29 January 1919, MAE, AP\166\83\Tardieu, 369–374.

44. For information on the Committee on Public Information, including its relationship with the French, see George Creel, *Rebel at Large: Recollections of Fifty Crowded Years* (New York: Putnam, 1947); Robert C. Hilderbrand, *Power and the People: Executive Management of Public Opinion in Foreign Affairs, 1897–1921* (Chapel Hill: University of North Carolina Press, 1981); James B. Mock and Cedric Lawson, *Words That Won the War: The Story of the Committee on Public Information, 1917–1919* (Princeton: Princeton University Press, 1939);

Stephen Vaughn, *Holding Fast the Inner Lines: Democracy, Nationalism, and the Committee on Public Information* (Chapel Hill: University of North Carolina Press, 1980).

45. Mission Tardieu, March–May 1917, MAE, Guerre, vol. 512; High Commission to MAE, 31 January 1918, MAE, Maison, vol. 21; report by Gabriel Puaux, 20 July 1918, MAE, AP\166\83\Tardieu, 508–512; Note of Commissariat Général, 1–15 September 1918, MAE, Y, vol. 1, 198–218; Report of 2 October 1918, MAE, B, vol. 22, 103–116; and of 6 November 1918, ibid., 138–156.

46. Text of Tardieu's statement to the *New York Times*, 18 September 1917, MAE, AP\166\83\Tardieu, 487–499; Commission to MAE, 17 June 1918, MAE, AP\166\85\Tardieu, 252–253. Commission to MAE, 20 June 1918, MAE, B, vol. 22, 26–29.

47. Tardieu to MAE, 22 December 1917, MAE, AP\166\85\Tardieu, 22–23; Tardieu to Pichon, 24 January 1918, ibid., 48; Tardieu to Klotz, 19 February 1918, ibid., 70–73; Tardieu to MAE, 22 March 1918, ibid., 99–101; Tardieu to MAE, 25 May 1918, ibid., 229.

48. Unidentified to Tardieu, 1 June 1918, MAE, AP\166\85\Tardieu, 247–248; Casenave to Tardieu, 9 August 1918, MAE, B, vol. 22, 186–188; Tardieu to Clemenceau, 26 July 1917, MAE, Guerre, vol. 513, 178–179. See also chapters 5 and 6 of Peter Buitenhuis, *The Great War of Words: British, American, and Canadian Propaganda and Fiction, 1914–1933* (Vancouver: University of British Columbia Press, 1987).

49. Lauzanne to Jusserand, 31 October 1918, MAE, AP\093\88\Lauzanne, 165–170; Casenave to Tardieu, 9 August 1918, MAE, B, vol. 22, 191. See Monnet, *Refaire la République*, 53. On Tardieu's departure for France, Edouard de Billy became the acting high commissioner.

50. Monod was Tardieu's *chef de cabinet*. Monod to C. B. Slemp (House Committee on Appropriations) 16 March 1918, MAE, AP\166\65\Tardieu, 90–92.

51. Commission to MAE, 17 June 1918, MAE, AP\166\85\Tardieu, 252–253; Casenave to Tardieu, 9 August 1918, MAE, B, vol. 22, 183–185. See Stéphane Lauzanne, "Resources of France," *NYT*, 25 August 1918, viii, 4. Alsace and Lorraine were incorporated into Germany in 1871 following the Franco-Prussian War, but remained a contentious issue between the two countries until their return to France in 1918–1919.

52. Report of the Commissariat Général (Paris), September 1918, MAE, B, vol. 22, 81–101; report from High Commission, 2 October 1918, ibid., 103–116.

53. MAE to Joseph Reinach, 11 June 1918, MAE, Maison, vol. 1.

54. For example, Tardieu wanted to use an article by Jean Dupuy of *Le Petit Parisien*, an article that financially linked the Russian Bolsheviks with the German government. Pichon to Tardieu, 18 January 1918, MAE, AP\166\85\Tardieu, 41; High Commission to MAE, 31 January 1918, MAE, Maison, vol. 21; report of Commissariat Général, September 1918, MAE, B, vol. 22, 81–101; report of October 1918, MAE, Maison, vol. 74/7.

55. High Commission to MAE, 12 July 1918, MAE, AP\166\85\Tardieu, 290–291; 16 July, ibid., 296–298; 7 August, ibid., 326–327.

56. Marcel Rouffie (French Information Bureau) to Pichon, 22 March 1919, MAE,

AP\166\85\Tardieu, 534–535. These were delivered by a corps of some thirty military and civilian speakers, and included lectures delivered under the auspices of the American Committee for Public Information.

57. "Propagande," 30 January 1918, MAE, Y, vol. 1; Pichon to Tardieu, 2 April 1918, MAE, AP\166\85\Tardieu, 131–132; Tardieu to Paul Brunet (Pathé), 25 May 1918, ibid., 228; report of 1–15 July 1918, MAE, Maison, vol. 73/3.

58. Tardieu to MAE, 12 January 1918, AP\166\83\Tardieu, 64; report from Commissariat Général, 15–30 June 1918, MAE, Y, vol. 1, 130; High Commission report, 2 October 1918, MAE, B, vol. 22, 113.

59. Harold Lavine and James Wechsler, *War Propaganda and the United States* (New Haven: Yale University Press, 1940), 16–20. By June 1919 the American desk at the Information Commission in Paris reported that it had seven thousand correspondents in America, which is to say individuals associated with a wide range of pro-Allied or expressly Francophilic organizations. MAE to the Direction Générale des Services Français (successor to the High Commission) in New York, 18 June 1919, MAE, Maison, vol. 21.

60. See Meyer Berger, *The Story of the "New York Times," 1851–1951* (New York: Simon and Schuster, 1951); Elmer H. Davis, *History of the "New York Times," 1851–1921* (1969; reprint, New York: Scholarly Press, 1971); Gay Talese, *The Kingdom and the Power* (New York: World, 1969); Waverley Root, *The Paris Edition: The Autobiography of Waverley Root, 1927–1934* (San Francisco: North Point Press, 1987).

61. Willis Rudy, *Total War*, 57. See also Carol S. Gruber, *Mars and Minerva: World War I and the Uses of Higher Learning in America* (Baton Rouge: Louisiana State University Press, 1975), 56–65. For Thomas W. Lamont's view of "Prussians . . . for generations bred for armed aggression," see his *Across World Frontiers* (New York: Harcourt Brace, 1951), 128; and for Myron Herrick's "France no more started the war than America did," see Mott, *Myron T. Herrick*, 277.

62. France-Amérique (Paris) to Ponsot, 31 October 1916, MAE, Maison, vol. 1.

63. See, for example, the account of an article on Kaiser Wilhelm II, prepared by the Information Commission's Service de l'information à l'étranger, and published by the morning paper *Oui*. Service to Commission, 19 June 1918, MAE, Maison, vol. 1.

64. Information Commissariat to High Commission, 12 August 1918, MAE, B, vol. 22, 51; Tardieu to Monseigneur Touchet, 5 September 1918, MAE, AP\166\86\ Tardieu, 7. See also Baudrillart, "Notre propagande," 141–184, and *Les Carnets du Cardinal Alfred Baudrillart, 1914–1918*, ed. Paul Christophe (Paris: Les Editions du Cerf, 1994).

65. Comité du Livre (rue du Bac) to MAE, 26 June 1917, MAE, Maison, vol. 1.

66. Pichon to Tardieu, 14 March 1918, MAE, AP\166\85\Tardieu, 82; Commissariat . . . Franco-Américaines, September 1918, MAE, B, vol. 22; Maison report, October 1918, MAE, Maison, vol. 74/7. For a report on the government-sponsored "Mission of French Scholars to the United States," see *NYT*, 11 November 1918, 13.

67. Pichon to Tardieu, 27 March 1918, MAE, B, vol. 22, 11; Public Instruction to MAE, 2 July 1918, ibid., 34; report of October 1918, MAE, Maison, vol. 74/7.

68. Klobukowski to Clemenceau, 20 June 1918, MAE, AP\095\61\Klobukowski.
69. Casenave (New York) to High Commission, 9 August 1918, MAE, B, vol. 22, 181.
70. Ibid., Lauzanne to Jusserand, 31 October 1918, MAE, AP\093\88\Lauzanne, 165–170. To illustrate his optimism, Lauzanne provided a sheaf of clippings from papers that had most vocally resisted American participation in the war, including the *Philadelphia Enquirer*, the *Chicago Tribune*, the *Nebraska State Journal*, and the *Nashville Citizen*. See report of 6 November 1918, MAE, B, vol. 22, 157–159.
71. The New York–based Committee on Allied Tribute to France included Alliance Française, France-America Society, Italy-America Society, Jewish Welfare Board, League to Enforce Peace, League of Foreign-Born Citizens, National Civic Federation, National Committee of Patriotic Societies, National League for Women's Service, National Security League, National War Work Council of the Young Men's Christian Association, Pilgrims Society, Polish Citizens Committee, and the War Committee of the Knights of Columbus. See High Commission report, 6 November 1918, MAE, B, vol. 22, 152–153.
72. See Casenave's report of 8 August 1918, MAE, B, vol. 22, 190–191; High Commission reports of 2 October 1918, ibid., 103–116 and 6 November, ibid. 147; Lauzanne to Jusserand, 31 October 1918, MAE, AP\093\88\Lauzanne, 169–170.
73. See Reinhard R. Doerries, "Promoting *Kaiser* and *Reich*: Imperial German Propaganda in the United States during World War I," in *Confrontation and Cooperation: Germany and the United States in the Era of World War I, 1900–1924*, ed. Hans-Jurgen Schroder, 135–165 (Providence: Berg, 1993); and Frank Trommler, "Inventing the Enemy: German-American Cultural Relations, 1900–1917," in *Confrontation and Cooperation*, ed. Schroder, 99–126.
74. Rapport de Presse, 28–29 November 1918, MAE, AP\166\83\Tardieu, 28–29. For complaints from the Information Commissariat about American press coverage of events leading up to the convening of the peace conference, see also the unsigned "Note pour le Ministre," 19 December 1918, MAE, AP\095\61\ Klobukowski.
75. Interministerial Conference on . . . Propaganda, 9 November 1918, MAE, Y, vol. 1, 268; Klobukowski to Pichon, 7 February 1919, Y, vol. 2, 16; De Billy to Tardieu, 11 March 1919, MAE, AP\166\82\Tardieu, 255. The offending article appeared on 16 March 1919 in Hearst's *New York American*. High Commission to MAE, 27 March 1919, MAE, AP\166\85\Tardieu, 547–548. On the rise of anti-French sentiment, see Byron Farwell, *Over There: The United States in the Great War, 1917–1918* (New York: Norton, 1999), 143–145.
76. Tardieu to Pichon, 26 January 1918, MAE, AP\166\85\Tardieu, 54–55; François Monod to Tardieu, 20 February 1919, MAE, AP\166\82\Tardieu, 108–124.
77. "Notice sur les correspondants," 10 August 1919, MAE, AP\166\83\Tardieu, 637–658.
78. Tardieu to High Commission, 20 December 1918, MAE, AP\166\83\Tardieu, 335; 23 December, ibid., 337–338. Klobukowski to Pichon, 16 February 1919, MAE, Y, vol. 2, 21.
79. Those charged with photographic and cinematic propaganda in America were

especially frustrated by the lean budgets accorded to them. By one reckoning, although France was spending more in North America than anywhere else in the world, on a per capita basis the expenditure was actually less than it was for Spain and Switzerland. See "Note sur les besoins," 30 January 1918, MAE, Y, vol. 1, 35–36.

80. De Billy to Firmin Roz, 20 February 1919, MAE, Maison, vol. 21; Casenave to Tardieu, 23 May 1919, MAE, AP\166\83\Tardieu, 448. For Bédier's early propaganda role, see Horne and Kramer, "German 'Atrocities,'" 4–14.

81. Information Commission, Résumé des opérations, 27 February to 15 March 1919, MAE, AP\95\Klobukowski; Commission to MAE, 7 April 1919, MAE, B, vol. 22, 231.

82. De Billy to Tardieu, 13 March 1919, MAE, AP\166\86\Tardieu; Tardieu to French Commission, 4 August 1919, MAE, ibid., 159–160.

83. *WP*, 4 August 1918, ii, 1. The paper had made the same "no French propaganda in America" claim in May 1915, as had, that summer, the *Boston Herald* and the *New York World*. See Nouailhat, *France et Etats-unis*, 159–160. Interestingly, the British ambassador's letters contain substantial material on British and German wartime propaganda in America, but none on France. See Sir Cecil Spring Rice, *The Letters and Friendships of Sir Cecil Spring Rice*, ed. Stephen Gwynn, 2 vols. (1929; Westport, Conn.: Greenwood Press, 1971), 368.

84. Chambrun to Pichon, 5 March 1919, MAE, B, vol.1, 33; De Billy to Tardieu, 29 March, MAE, AP\166\82\Tardieu, 266; Casenave to Tardieu, 8 May, ibid., 288–289. A forerunner of the United Nations, the League was intended to be the postwar world's principal device for averting another armed struggle.

85. Senate opposition concentrated on Article X of the League Covenant, wherein lay the potential for future American commitment to the security of other powers. For his part, Wilson refused to separate the article from the covenant, or the covenant from the peace treaty with Germany. See Thomas J. Knock, *To End All Wars: Woodrow Wilson and the Quest for a New World Order* (Princeton: Princeton University Press, 1992), 252.

86. Jusserand to MAE, 17 November 1919, MAE, B, vol. 23, 94. See also Erika G. King, "Exposing the 'Age of Lies': The Propaganda Menace as Portrayed in American Magazines in the Aftermath of World War I," *Journal of American Culture*, 12, no. 1 (1989): 35–40.

87. President to MAE, 19 December 1919, MAE, B, vol. 38, 141.

88. In 1914 Britain "possessed nothing that could even remotely be described as an official propaganda department." See Philip M. Taylor, "Propaganda in International Politics, 1919–1939," in *The Origins of the Second World War*, ed. Patrick Finney (London: Arnold, 1997), 354.

89. It has been judged by some scholars "an object lesson in futility," by others a case study of "every kind of blunder which it was possible to make." See Lavine and Wechsler, *War Propaganda*, 32, and James Duane Squires, *British Propaganda at Home and in the United States from 1914 to 1917* (Cambridge: Harvard University Press, 1935), 45.

90. This undertaking was instrumental in Clemenceau's decision not to insist on a more punitive peace. His domestic critics rightly underscored the risks of tying

that guarantee to American ratification of the Versailles treaty. By the end of 1919 it seemed clear that the treaty had failed in America, and probable that the assurances to France were now inoperative. See William R. Keylor, "France's Futile Quest for American Military Protection, 1919–1922," in *Une occasion manquée? 1922: La reconstruction de l'Europe*, ed. Marta Petricioli (Bern: Peter Lang, 1995), 71.

91. This long-term, low-key strategy has been called both "subpropaganda" and "facilitative communication," which is to say "communication designed to render a positive attitude toward a potential propagandist." See Garth S. Jowett and Victoria O'Donnell, *Propaganda and Persuasion* (London: Sage, 1986), 20.

CHAPTER 4   *From War to Peace, 1920–1929*

1. Interministerial Conference, 9 November 1918, MAE, AP\095\61\Klobukowski, 14.
2. François Monod to Tardieu, 20 February 1919, MAE, AP\166\82\Tardieu, 114.
3. Embassy to MAE, 8 May 1923, MAE, Oeuvres, 40; and 14 February 1924, MAE, B, vol. 5, 167–170. The latter refers to the German government's initial decision not to show the German flag during the obsequies for President Wilson.
4. By the 1930s, Hearst newspapers included the *Journal*, the *Mirror*, and the *American* in New York City; two Syracuse papers, the *Journal* and the *Sunday American*; the Albany *Times-Union* and the Rochester *Journal*; the Washington *Herald* and the *Times*; the Boston *Record* and *Sunday Advertiser*; the Baltimore *News, Post,* and *Sunday American*; the Atlanta *Georgian*; the Pittsburgh *Sun-Telegraph* and the *Post-Gazette*; the Milwaukee *Wisconsin News* and the *Sentinel*; the Chicago *American* and the *Herald Examiner*; the Nebraska *Bee-News*; the Los Angeles *Examiner* and the *Herald Express*; the San Francisco *Call-Bulletin* and *Examiner*; the Oakland *Post-Inquirer*; and the Seattle *Post-Intelligence*. His magazine holdings included *Cosmopolitan, Good Housekeeping, Harper's Bazaar, Town and Country, Home and Field*, and the *American Weekly*, this last accompanying his Sunday papers. See Ferdinand Lundberg, *America's Sixty Families* (New York: Halycon House, 1937), 267–269; and Kaspi, *La vie quotidienne aux Etats-Unis*, 147.
5. Jusserand to Briand, 15 March 1921, MAE, Y, vol. 410, 161; Jusserand to MAE, 25 November 1923, MAE, B, vol. 62, 148–149; Claudel to MAE, 21 April 1927, MAE, B, vol. 27, 146; Claudel to MAE, 16 November 1928, MAE, B, vol. 7, 114. See Paulette Enjalran, "Paul Claudel: Son itinéraire de consul et d'ambassadeur, 1890–1934," *Claudel Studies* 11 (1984): 4–23, and Mugridge, *View from Xanadu*, 108–125.
6. Liebert (Consul) to MAE, 15 January 1924, MAE, Maison, vol. 3; Claudel to MAE, 6 April 1928, MAE, B, vol. 67, 141–144; 6 July 1928, B, vol. 69, 41; Claudel to MAE, B, vol. 69, 42.
7. Jusserand to Poincaré, 29 November 1922, MAE, B, vol. 65, 38–47; 10 March 1924, vol. 6, 5–6; *NYT*, 3 October 1922, 1–2.
8. Jusserand to MAE, 2 March 1930, MAE, B, vol. 23, 133–141.
9. Jusserand to MAE, 28 Janaury 1922, MAE, B, vol. 62, 10–11; 2 February, vol.

65, 3; 29 March, vol. 4, 96–97; 9 December, vol. 65, 69; 16 March 1923, vol. 4, 187–188.

10. Embassy to MAE, 11 May 1924, MAE, B, vol. 6, 43–49; Claudel to MAE, 15 May 1928, MAE, B, vol. 28, 110; Claudel to MAE, 23 September 1929, MAE, B, vol. 7, 160. For New York Francophile suspicion that German money had gone into the publicity for this book, see Jarray to Alphand, 11 August 1932, MAE, B, vol. 348, 159.

11. Jusserand to Millerand, 17 February 1920, MAE, B, vol. 2, 117; MAE to Embassy, 24 February, B, vol. 39, 12; Jusserand to MAE, 26 February, ibid., 14–15.

12. Jusserand to MAE, 19 December 1920, MAE, B, vol. 61, 5; Millerand to Jusserand, 17 February, MAE, B, vol. 2, 112. The French press often drove Jusserand to distraction, partly by its gratuitous sniping at America, and partly by its failure to praise the France-sympathetic works of American writers and journalists. Positive reviews of American work, he believed, were one of the most effective propaganda techniques France could employ. See Nouailhat, *France et Etats-Unis*, 157–158.

13. Jusserand to MAE, 19 May 1920, MAE, B, vol. 23, 174; 19 May 1924, B, vol. 63, 56. For further evidence of French anti-Americanism in the 1920s, see Harvey Levenstein, *Seductive Journey. American Tourists in France from Jefferson to the Jazz Age* (Berkeley and Los Angeles, University of California Press, 1998), 257–275.

14. Maurois's first two visits to America were in 1927 and 1931. See his *En Amérique* (New York: American Book, 1933), 58, 67–68; and *Memoirs, 1885–1967* (1942; reprint, New York: Harper and Row, 1970), 174–175.

15. See André Siegfried's *Les Etats-Unis d'aujourd'hui* (Paris: Colin, 1928) and Skard's appraisal of the work in Strauss, *Menace in the West*, 204.

16. See Portes, *Une fascination réticente*, 365–369; Bernadette Galloux-Fournier, "Un regard sur l'Amérique: Voyageurs français aux Etats-Unis (1919–1939)," *Revue d'Histoire Moderne et Contemporaine* 37 (April–June 1990), 314–319; Baudrillart, *Les carnets*, 954, 963–964. For information on escalating American investment and technology in postwar France, particularly in oil, electricity, automobiles, telephones, and cinema, see Strauss, *Menace in the West*, 140–149.

17. See Melvyn P. Leffler, *The Elusive Quest: America's Pursuit of European Stability and French Security, 1919–1933* (Chapel Hill: University of North Carolina Press, 1979), 362–364.

18. William R. Keylor, "'How They Advertised France': The French Propaganda Campaign in the United States during the Breakup of the Franco-American Entente, 1918–1923," *Diplomatic History* 17, no. 3 (1993), 354; Strauss, *Menace in the West*, 124.

19. Strauss, *Menace in the West*, 126–128; Henry Blumenthal, *Illusion and Reality in Franco-American Diplomacy, 1914–1945* (Baton Rouge: Louisiana State University Press, 1986), 145–147.

20. Tardieu, *France and America*, 282–301. Exacerbating French resentment over reparations and war debts was the fact that roughly half of Germany's reparation payments was made possible by borrowed money from America. See Blumenthal, *Illusion and Reality*, 123.

21. Strauss, *Menace in the West*, 111–116; Keylor, "Futile Quest," 77–78; Joel Blatt, "France and the Washington Conference," in *The Washington Conference, 1921–22: Naval Rivalry, East Asian Stability, and the Road to Pearl Harbor,* ed. Erik Goldstein and John Maurer (London: Cass, 1994), 192–219.
22. Buitenhuis, *Great War of Words*, 150–151, 170–171.
23. There is early evidence that liaison between *Oeuvres* and Information was, in fact, not very close. See Charles Daniélou, *Les affaires étrangères* (Paris: Figuière 1927), 19.
24. The Service d'information, with a staff of eighty by 1921, was responsible for preparing, and circulating within the ministry, daily and weekly bulletins on the foreign press. It offered telegraph, radio, and translation services, as well as a press-clipping service for journalists interested in following foreign press coverage. Note of March 1920, MAE, Oeuvres, carton 1; and Young, *French Foreign Policy*, 15.
25. Milhaud (January 1920–October 1921); Giraudoux (October 1921–April 1924); Naggiar (October 1924–June 1926); Pila (June 1926–July 1933). See Decree of 15 January 1920, MAE, Oeuvres, 1; Note of March 1920, ibid; Antoine Marès, "Puissance et présence culturelle de la France: L'exemple du Service des Oeuvres françaises à l'étranger dans les années 30," *Relations Internationales*, no. 33 (spring 1983), 66.
26. See note "Action . . . dans le domaine de la propagande," undated but located in the Inventory for the Maison de la Presse, 1914–1928, MAE.
27. See budget samples for 1925, 1929–1930, MAE, Oeuvres, 1, 2; and Jean-Claude Allain and Marc Auffret, "Le Ministère français des affaires étrangères. Crédits et effectifs pendant la IIIe République," *Relations Internationales*, no. 32 (winter 1982), 415–416.
28. See Monseigneur Baudrillart's report to the foreign ministry, on behalf of the Comité catholique de propagande française à l'étranger, 31 March 1920, MAE, B, 23, 160–169; and that of Abbé André Monod, 19 October, MAE, Oeuvres, vol. 59. The Catholic organization, which circulated a monthly called *Les amitiés catholiques françaises*, had its office on the rue Garancière and, as of June 1928, on the rue des Fossées Saint-Jacques. The Protestant office was on the rue de la Victoire and subsequently on the rue de Clichy.
29. Keylor, "'How They Advertised France,'" 358–359.
30. Jusserand to MAE, 6 April 1920, MAE, B, vol. 2, 156–158; Abbé Lugan to MAE, 31 December 1921, ibid., vol. 24, 221–224; Jusserand to Coudert, 21 March 1922, MAE, AP\093\98\Coudert, 324–325.
31. Jusserand to MAE, 29 November 1921, MAE, vol. 24, 210–213; 19 December 1923, ibid., 126–127.
32. Jusserand to MAE, 6 April 1920, MAE, B, vol. 2, 158; 13 May 1920, ibid., vol. 39, 89; 10 January 1921, ibid., 186–187; 24 February 1921, ibid., vol. 3, 150.
33. Jusserand to MAE, 19 December 1920, MAE, B, vol. 61, 5.
34. Jusserand to MAE, 21 June 1922, MAE, B, vol. 4, 121–122; 16 March 1923, ibid., 187–188; 30 March 1923, ibid., 191–192; ibid., vol. 5, 8–10.
35. Liebert to Jusserand, 25 March 1921, MAE, AP\093\93\Liebert, 80–81; 20 February 1922, 108–109.

36. Jusserand to MAE, 8 January 1923, MAE, B, vol. 62, 84–86.
37. Liebert to MAE, 24 March 1922, MAE, B, vol. 25, 30; 1 May 1922, ibid., 76. For a campaign to rid Chicago-area schools of "pernicious British influence," in the 1920s, see Lloyd Wendt, *"Chicago Tribune": The Rise of a Great American Newspaper* (Chicago: Rand McNally, 1979), 517.
38. Liebert to MAE, 19 April 1923, MAE, Maison, vol. 23. See also the editorial in *NYT*, 1 March 1923, 14.
39. See Liebert letter (unaddressed), 4 June 1923, MAE, Maison, vol. 23.
40. Recent scholarship tends to confirm the French case. For a succinct summary, and references to the work of Sally Marks, Stephen A. Schuker, and Marc Trachtenberg, see William R. Keylor, "France and the Illusion of American Support, 1919–1940," in *The French Defeat of 1940: Reassessments*, ed. Joel Blatt (Providence: Berghahn Books, 1998), 219.
41. See Bulletin no. 4, 25 June 1923, MAE, Maison, vol. 23.
42. Liebert to MAE, 4 January 1924, MAE, Maison, vol. 23; 25 January 1924, ibid; 1 February 1924, ibid; 16 June 1924, ibid., vol. 25.
43. Liebert to MAE, 16 June 1924, MAE, Maison, vol. 25; 21 August 1924, ibid.
44. Author (indecipherable) to Jusserand, 9 May 1921, MAE, AP\093\93\Liebert, 144; Unsigned note to MAE, 17 April 1924, MAE, Maison, vol. 24.
45. The figures comes from Paul Claudel, *Claudel aux Etats-Unis, 1927–1933,* Cahiers Paul Claudel, vol. 11 (Paris: Gallimard, 1982), 68–69.
46. Liebert to MAE, 3 June 1924, MAE, Maison, vol. 25, dossier 25; Pavey to Liebert, 4 June 1924, ibid; Liebert to MAE, 6 June 1924, ibid.
47. For a portrait of Daeschner, see *NYT*, 14 December 1924, ix, 12. The Paris office of the *comité* was located at 82 Champs Elysées. Its president was Gabriel Hanotaux; its director-general, Gabriel-Louis Jaray; its secretary-general, Georges Chabaud.
48. Maurice Léon to MAE, 3 February 1925, MAE, B, vol. 26, 80; Cunliffe-Owen to Embassy, 3 June 1925, ibid., 144–148. See the praise-filled piece on French leaders at the Genoa conference by Cunliffe-Owen in *NYT*, 9 April 1922, ii, 7. He was married to a French woman who wrote a syndicated, Francophilic column for papers such as the *New York Sun* and *Chicago Tribune* under the pseudonym La Marquise de Fontenoy.
49. MAE to Embassy (DC), 7 July 1925, MAE, B, vol. 27, 11–15; note of 24 October 1926, with extract from *New York Herald*, MAE, ibid., 129. Patenôtre had been born in the United States, where his father, Jules, had served as French ambassador in the 1890s.
50. For Wood's efforts, see note of 28 September 1925, MAE, Oeuvres, vol. 41. For that of Gompers, see Jusserand to MAE, 16 January 1924, B, vol. 63, 14–21. For Bache, see Keylor, "'How They Advertised,'" 361.
51. Jusserand to MAE, 9 January 1924, MAE, Series B, vol. 63, 10.
52. Claudel to MAE, 12 April 1927, MAE, B, vol. 27, 142.
53. See untitled note of December 1920, and a clipping from *France-Etats-Unis*, MAE, B, vol. 24, 52; "French Institute'" *NYT*, 20 April 1924, viii, 10. The monthly bulletin was called *Le Moniteur Franco-Américain* and offered articles on French literature, art, and science. See contents of dossier 2, MAE, B, vol. 29C.

54. "Proposition pour l'organisation d'un service," 1920, MAE, Oeuvres, 91.
55. Paul Fichet (SOE) to Premier Briand, 21 October 1921, MAE, Oeuvres, 91; "Note," 12 November 1921, ibid.
56. See, for example, the collection of documents addressed to commerical competition and distribution issues in the film industry in *FRUS*, 1928, vol. 2, 844–849, and 1929, vol. 2, 1006–1023; and Gerben Bakker, "America's Master: The Decline and Fall of the European Film Industry (1907–1920)," in *Across the Atlantic: Cultural Exchanges between Europe and the United States,* ed. Luisa Passerini (Brussels: Peter Lang, 2000), 213–240.
57. Sartiges to Hays, 25 October 1926, MAE, Oeuvres, vol. 84; *NYT*, 16 November 1927, 9; Claudel to MAE, 18 November 1927, MAE, B, vol. 28, 28–30. So upset were Oeuvres personnel over this film, and its perceived insult to the French army, that they warned the protocol division of the ministry against requests by the producers for French decorations. See SOE to Protocol, 7 January 1927, MAE, Oeuvres, vol. 84.
58. In May 1927 the embassy described a release called "Barbed Wires," in which there occurred a succession of escalating horrors: attempted rape by a French sergeant, a resulting beating of the same by a German prisoner of war, and an instance of fraternization between French and German soldiers. See Chargè to Paris, 31 May 1927, MAE, Oeuvres, vol. 84.
59. "Note," 8 April 1921, MAE, B, vol. 24, 157–158; MAE to Embassy, 2 May 1923, MAE, Oeuvres 39; Claudel to MAE, 7 May 1928, B, vol. 28, 108.
60. See note dated January 1927, on stationery of the Direction politique et commerciale, MAE, B, vol. 27, 136–139.
61. Charles de Fontnouvelle to MAE, 18 January 1927, MAE, B, vol. 296, 2. See also Alice Felicitas Carse, "The Reception of German Literature in America as Exemplified by the *New York Times*, 1914–1944" (Ph.D. diss., New York University, 1973), 320–323.
62. Claudel to MAE, 18 November 1927, MAE, B, vol. 28, 28–30. See also Roger P. Gilbert, "Paul Claudel, diplomate," *Claudel Studies*, vol. 11 (1984), 69–84; Emmanuel Monick, "Paul Claudel, Diplomate et Economiste," in Cahiers Paul Claudel 4 (Paris: Gallimard, 1962), 347–349.
63. See Jean Baptiste Duroselle, *La France et les Etats-Unis*, 144. Ultimately, fifteen countries signed the multilateral declaration against resort to war.
64. Claudel to Briand, 23 January 1928, MAE, B, vol. 66, 128–134; 31 January, ibid., 152.
65. Claudel to Briand, 2 May 1928, MAE, B, vol. 64, 60; 7 May, ibid., vol. 28, 108.
66. Claudel to Briand, 25 June 1928, MAE, B, vol. 69, 23–29; 14 November, ibid., vol. 7, 109–110.
67. Claudel to Briand, 16 November 1928, MAE, B, vol. 7, 114–116.
68. Claudel to MAE, 11 December 1928, MAE, B, vol. 70, 7–14; 17 January 1929, ibid., 58–60, 62–70.
69. Claudel to MAE, 25 February 1929, MAE, B, vol. 7, 139. See also Paul Claudel, *Journal*, vol. 1 (1904–1932), ed. F. Varillon and J. Petit (Paris: Gallimard, 1968), 765.

CHAPTER 5   *The End of the Postwar Period, 1930–1935*

1. For the most comprehensive study on the war debts issue, see Kathy Calhoun Weir, "Franco-American Relations, 1931–1933; The War Debts" (Ph.D. diss., Washington State University, 1987). For a recent, succinct account, see Keylor, "France and the Illusion," 218–221.
2. See John M. Carroll, "Owen D. Young and German Reparations: The Diplomacy of an Enlightened Businessman," in *U.S. Diplomats in Europe, 1919–1941*, ed. Kenneth Paul Jones (Santa Barbara: ABC Clio, 1983), 43–60; Michael J. Hogan, "Thomas W. Lamont and European Recovery: The Diplomacy of Privatism in a Corporatist Age," ibid., 5–22.
3. Blumenthal, *Illusion and Reality*, 123.
4. Claudel to Paris, 25 November 1932, *Documents diplomatiques français* (henceforth *DDF*), 1st Series, ii, no. 35, 73.
5. For an explanation of the French refusal to ratify this accord, concluded between Ambassador Henry Bérenger and the American secretary of the Treasury, Andrew W. Mellon, see Strauss, *Menace in the West*, 131.
6. This, despite Claudel's reservations about his own government's reactions and his efforts to represent Hoover as far more understanding than Congress. See Claudel, *Claudel aux Etats-Unis*, 279–280.
7. State to Strauss (Paris), 31 July 1933, *FRUS*, 1st Series, ii, 210, 158.
8. Strauss, *Menace in the West*, 145–147. The co-sponsors of the act were Senators Reed Smoot, Republican from Utah, and Willis Chatman Hawley, Republican from Oregon.
9. Strauss, *Menace in the West*, 99.
10. Henry to Paris, 15 August 1932, *DDF*, 1st Series, i, 104, 185.
11. *Le Temps* editorials of 17 May 1930, 1; 29 October 1930, 1; 14 October 1931, 1; 3 July 1932, 1; and Hanotaux's review of 20 February 1932, 2.
12. André Géraud (Pertinax), "A French Diagnosis of America," *NYT*, 17 August 1930, v, 1.
13. See account of public remarks by Paul Morand and Henri Matisse in New York. Comité national des conseillers du commerce extérieur (New York) to Paris, 25 March 1930, MAE, Oeuvres, 43; Consulate to Paris, 23 September 1930, MAE, Oeuvres, 43.
14. *CT* editorials, 24 February 1930, 14; 20 June 1932, 10; 24 July 1932, 10; 20 December 1932, 8; 6 March 1933, 6. For the widespread tendency to blame Versailles for German behavior, and France for Versailles, see Arnold A. Offner, "The United States and National Socialist Germany," in *The Origins of the Second World War*, ed. Patrick Finney (London: Arnold, 1997), 245–247.
15. Claudel to MAE, 16 April 1930, MAE, Series B, 358, 59–60; Laboulaye to MAE, 11 July 1933, ibid., 341, 207–209. See also report on a series of hostile articles in 1931, Claudel to MAE, Series B, 349, 50.
16. See Claudel to MAE, 3 May 1932, MAE, B, 349, 92–93; MAE to Laboulaye, 30 December 1933, ibid., 350, 45; Collective letter to Mme Doumergue (the premier's wife), 6 June 1934, ibid., 343, 94–95. This last, written by a number

of French teachers in Philadelphia, said that the *Fortune* article had created a "veritable storm of hatred against France."

17. Claudel to Paris, 20 August 1932, MAE, B, 359, 194–196.

18. See Jules Henry to MAE, 2 May 1930, MAE, B, 349, 1; also of 5 September, 358, 204; also Rodney Carlisle, "The Foreign Policy Views of an Isolationist Press Lord: W. R. Hearst and the International Crisis, 1936–1941," *Journal of Contemporary History* 9, no. 3 (1974): 217–227.

19. *SF* editorials and cartoons, 12 November 1930, 34; 23 October 1931, 18; 17 January 1932, 1; 12 April 1932, 10; 29 November 1932, 8; 22 December 1932, 6.

20. Claudel to Paris, 28 November 1932, MAE, B, 349, 160.

21. Comité France-Amérique (Paris) to Alphand, 11 August 1932, MAE, B, 348, 156–160.

22. See report of January 1931, MAE, Oeuvres, 2. See also the key article by Antoine Marès, "Puissance et présence culturelle de la France: L'exemple du Service des Oeuvres française à l'étranger dans les années 30," *Relations Internationales*, no. 33 (spring 1983), 65–80.

23. Report on Oeuvres for 1930, January 1931, MAE, Oeuvres, 2.

24. Lebel's organization was the Centre d'informations documentaires. Philip's committee, the Comité français pour le développement des rapports intellectuels et économiques avec l'étranger, was constituted in October 1930. It was an umbrella organization comprising representatives from le Comité national des conseillers du commerce extérieur; la Fédération thermale et climatique française; la Chambre syndicale de la cinématographie; la Société des gens de lettres de France; la Société des artistes françaises; la Société nationale des beaux-arts; and l'Association de la presse médicale française. See note of 4 June 1932, MAE, Oeuvres, vol. 126.

25. For description and illustration of the French Line's fleet of luxury liners, showpieces of French art, fashion, and interior design, see John Malcolm Brinnin and Kenneth Gaulin, *Grand Luxe: The Transatlantic Style* (New York: Henry Holt, 1988).

26. Société des amis de l'université. See Bargeton to André Honnorat, 23 March 1935, MAE, B, 344, 127; Ralph Schor, *L'opinion française et les étrangers, 1919–1939* (Paris: Publications de la Sorbonne, 1985), 366.

27. See the report of A. Declos to the National Office of Universities, 20 January 1932, MAE, B, 340, 51–65. Germany, he pointed out, had a total of sixty-five scholarship students in the United States, all of them better funded and better prepared for propaganda purposes than their French counterparts. Indeed, the consul general in New York described the German students as well-trained "apostles of the German cause." See Fontnouvelle to Paris, 30 March 1932, MAE, B, 340, 70–71.

28. In 1931, for example, the Maisons at Harvard, Chicago, and Columbia were among those to receive subventions.

29. January 1930, MAE, Oeuvres, Carton 43; 28 January 1931, ibid. In one imprecisely dated memorandum, the head of Oeuvres's literary section said there were two ways to provide lectures for service abroad. The Quai could wait until appropriate, independent bodies invited French lecturers, in which case planning

was difficult. Or it could initiate the lecture tours, and thus open itself to charges of propaganda. See Jean du Sault, 1933, MAE, Oeuvres, vol. 486.

30. Marx to Chinard, 22 January 1930, MAE, Oeuvres, 126; Chinard to Marx, 16 November 1931, ibid.

31. Pila to Consulate (NY) 3 February 1930, MAE, B, 358, 14; Meric de Bellefon (consul, San Francisco) to MAE, B, 340, 99; 4 February 1934, MAE, B, 342, 165–169.

32. Canada was added to the title and the federation's activities in 1905. See the historical account provided by the *Courrier des Etats-Unis*, 4 February 1934, MAE, B, 342, 165–169.

33. While consistency of names and titles was not a French forte in the period, it would appear that from 1932 on this was the name that replaced the original Association française d'expansion et d'échanges artistiques. It was created jointly by the foreign and education ministries to "facilitate" the work of the latter's fine arts branch. See undated (likely 1932) note, "Notice sur l'Association française d'expansion et d'échanges artistiques," MAE, Oeuvres, 485; and Marie-Claude Genet-Delacroix, *Art et Etat sous la IIIe République* (Paris: Publications de la Sorbonne, 1992), 253–255.

34. For assistance in distinguishing between *association, conseil*, and *comité*, see Maurice Pezet, *Defense et illustration de la France: Sous les yeux du monde* (Paris: Spès, 1935), 224–226; and Genet-Delacroix, *Art et Etat*, 244–250.

35. Mardrus enjoyed subsidized trips in 1926, 1931, and 1932. See spring 1931, MAE, Oeuvres, 43, and the note by Oeuvres's Fernand Pila to the Association, 29 December 1932, MAE, Oeuvres, 576; 11 July 1933 Agenda for the Administrative Council, MAE, Oeuvres, 485; Action Artistique to Embassy\Consulates, 10 January 1933, MAE, Oeuvres, 485; Robert Brussel (Action Artistique) to Jean Marx, 31 October 1933, MAE, Oeuvres, 576.

36. See, for example, *CT*, 18 March 1932, 4; 7 July 1933, 7; 14 July 1933, 5.

37. See his letter of 27 February, under cover of 14 March 1933, to MAE, B, 341, 91; Laboulaye to Paris, 12 February 1934, MAE, B, 342, 173. For glimpses of Finley and the others, see Arthur Krock, *Memoirs: Sixty Years on the Firing Line* (New York: Funk and Wagnalls, 1968), 81–91.

38. Berthelot to Claudel, 1 March 1932, MAE, B, 349, 74; Claudel to Paris, 29 November 1932, ibid., 340, 245–246; Claudel to Paris, 12 January 1933, ibid., 349, 185; Laboulaye to Paris, 3 May 1933, ibid., 341, 150.

39. Laboulaye to Paris, 7 June 1934, MAE, B, 343, 79; Comert to Embassy, 19 June, ibid., 96.

40. Meric de Bellefon to Paris, 17 January 1933, MAE, B, 341, 22–23; Bellefon to Laboulaye, 19 October, ibid., 342, 22–24; Comert to Bellefon, 5 July 1935, ibid., 344, 236.

41. For the most useful report on the paper's connections with the foreign ministry, and its "constante collaboration" with the Press and Information Service, see 19 November 1935, MAE, B, 350, 247–252. The service was inclined to accept claims of a circulation of twenty thousand, which Laboulaye pared down to twelve thousand. See Laboulaye to Paris, 21 December 1935, MAE, B, 350, 263–265.

42. See Note pour le Cabinet du Ministre, 25 October 1930, MAE, B, 348, 1–6; Jules Henry to Laboulaye, 3 March 1932, ibid., 39.

43. See Pierre Comert to Consulate (NY) 10 May 1933, MAE, B, 341, 153; Bonney to Comert, 7 June 1933, MAE, Oeuvres, 569; Pila to Association, 13 July 1933, ibid., notes from Jean Marx (SOE), 19 August 1933, ibid.; Paul Bargeton (Oeuvres) to Beaux-Arts, 16 October 1934, MAE, B, 343, 177–178; SOE to Laboulaye, 3 December 1934, ibid., 228–229. Thérèse Bonney (1894–1978) became a celebrated photojournalist during World War II and was the author of two wartime photoessay books.

44. See Claudel to Senator Peytral, president of the proposed "Palais de France" in New York, 24 April 1931, MAE, Oeuvres, 41; "Note sur la Maison," 4 June 1932, MAE, Oeuvres, 126; Premier Herriot to commerce, June 1932, ibid.; Herriot to Jean Philip, 5 July 1932, ibid.; Alexis Léger to Commerce, 18 July 1932, ibid.; Hervé Alphand to Jean Philip, 14 November 1932, ibid.; note by Jean Marx (SOE), 22 January 1934, Oeuvres, 478.

45. Paul Bargeton to Laboulaye, 16 October 1934, MAE, B, 179–180; and to education, ibid., 177–178.

46. Claudel to Paris, 6 March 1930, MAE, B, 358, 27; and 26 April 1932, 340, 108.

47. Laboulaye to Paris, 29 January 1935, MAE, B, 343, 317–322.

48. See Claudel to Paris, 14 February 1930, MAE, B, 358, 23; Mandelstamm's report of 17 March, under cover of 4 April 1930, ibid., 50–56; Laboulaye to Paris, 13 March 1935, ibid., 344, 104–109.

49. Foreign Minister Herriot to Claudel, 8 July 1932, MAE, B, 340, 152; Laboulaye to Paris, 3 October 1933, ibid., 342, 29; Bargeton to Laboulaye, 12 February 1934, ibid., 171.

50. Guthrie to Jules Henry, 8 February 1932, MAE, AP\093\91\Guthrie, 280. Guthrie, who had attended school in Paris between 1862 and 1873, and taught law at Columbia between 1911 and 1921, was a founder of the France-America Society in New York in 1912 and its president since 1923. See press clipping, 6 November 1932, MAE, AP\093\91\Guthrie, 467, also the tribute to Guthrie in *Le Temps*, 23 April 1932, 2.

51. "La charrue avant les boeufs." Henry to Henry Cosme, sous-directeur d'Amérique, 25 April 1932, MAE, B, 348, 122–125.

52. Claudel to Paris, 12 May 1932, MAE, B, 340, 116–126; and his cover of 15 April for Fontnouvelle's report, ibid., 348, 78–86.

53. Note of 31 July 1932, MAE, B, 348, 152–153. Comert's criticism should be seen not as a denial of ministerial influence on Havas, but rather as confirmation. One unsigned report of 20 December 1938 acknowledged the "front-unique Havas-Orsay," which Comert had controlled between 1932 and 1938. See the four-page, unsigned memorandum, 13 April 1933, and that of December 1938, in Dossier Comert, MAE/Havas.

54. Herriot (premier and foreign minister) to Embassies and Consulates, 12 December 1932, MAE, Maison, 81; note by Comert, January 1933, MAE, B, 348, 208–220.

55. Meric de Bellefon (Los Angeles) to Paris, 17 January 1933, MAE, B, 341, 18; for the report of Peretti della Rocca, see the cover note of 15 February 1933, ibid., 69.

56. See *CT*, 11 April 1933, 11; *WP*, 21 April 1933, 2; *NYT*, 9 May 1933, 16.

57. Laboulaye to Paris, 22 February 1934, *DDF*, 1st Series, iv, no. 423, 797; Fontnouvelle to Paris, 1 March 1933, MAE, B, 341, 81; Laboulaye to Paris, 18 April 1933, MAE, B, 349, 230–233. The papers were the *New York Times*, the *New York Evening Post*, and the *Washington Star*. See also Ronald Brownstein, "The *New York Times* on Naziism (1933–1939)," *Midstream*, 26, no. 4 (1980), 14–19.

58. Louis Wiley to Mme Jusserand, 29 August 1933, MAE, AP\093\92\Wiley; cover of 5 December 1933, MAE, B, 339, 8–9.

59. See Brett Gary, *The Nervous Liberals: Propaganda Anxieties from World War I to the Cold War* (New York: Columbia University Press, 1999).

60. See "Suggestions pour l'organisation," 20 November 1932, MAE, Maison, 81; and Laboulaye to Paris, 1 June 1933, *DDF*, 1st Series, iii, no. 347, 621.

61. Laboulaye to Paris, 30 June 1933, MAE, B, 341, 200–210; 18 January 1934, MAE, SOE, 569; 26 December 1934, MAE, B, 348, 228–229. For an opposing view, namely that France's official role be as imperceptible as possible, see the report of 1933, "Enquête sur la Conférence," MAE, Oeuvres, dossier 2, 486.

62. See Comert to Laboulaye, 24 December 1934, MAE, B, 348, 225; Laboulaye to Paris, 26 December 1934, ibid., 226–227; "Note pour Monsieur Rochat," 28 December 1934, ibid., 230–232; and Robert J. Young, "A Douce and Dextrous Persuasion: French Propaganda and Franco-American Relations in the 1930s," in *French Foreign and Defence Policy, 1918–1940*, ed. Robert Boyce (London: LSE/ Routledge, 1998), 206.

63. Claudel to Paris, 3 February 1932, MAE, B, 348, 12–15; see his dispatch of 28 March 1932, in Claudel, *Claudel aux Etats-Unis*, 290.

64. Laboulaye to Paris, 2 March 1935, Mae, B, 344, 3–12.

65. Pezet, *Sous les yeux du monde*.

66. Pezet provides a list of nearly fifty different, France-based propaganda agencies, both official and private, including all the ones previously identified in this volume. See his *Sous les yeux du monde*, 458–461. On the systematic use of ministerial "fonds secrets," see Albert, "La presse française," 487–499.

CHAPTER 6   *From Peace to War, 1936–1939*

1. Laboulaye to Paris, 10 July 1933, MAE, B, 349, 281–286; Delage (New Orleans) to Paris, 18 December 1934, B, 343, 245.

2. See American press clippings in the *bordereau* of 5 December 1933, MAE, B, 339, 9–10, and the anonymous, but privately sponsored, pamphlet entitled *The German Reich and Americans of German Origin* (New York: Oxford University Press, 1938); also Sander A. Diamond, *The Nazi Movement and the United States, 1924–1941* (Ithaca: Cornell University Press, 1974); Deborah E. Lipstadt, *Beyond Belief: The American Press and the Coming of the Holocaust, 1933–1945* (New York: Free Press, 1986).

3. Bonnet to Paris, 15 June 1937, MAE, B, 346, 39–46; Saint-Quentin to Paris, 31 August 1939, B, 351, 274–275.

4. Report by *missionnaire* Serge Youriévitch for the education ministry, 20 August 1930, MAE, B, 350, 15.

5. For this, I have relied on Mario Rossi, *Roosevelt and the French* (Westport, Conn.: Praeger, 1993). Frederick W. Marks III, however, portrays an FDR more jaded about France and surrounded by like-minded colleagues, among them Frances Perkins, his labor secretary, and Henry J. Morgenthau, his Treasury secretary. See *Wind over Sand: The Diplomacy of Franklin Roosevelt* (Athens: University of Georgia Press, 1988), 124–126.

6. Rossi, *Roosevelt and the French*, xix, 2–11, 15, 17, 20; Blumenthal, *Illusion and Reality*, 243; Painlevé's applause for FDR was reprinted from *Le Petit Parisien* by San Francisco's *Examiner*, 1 April 1933, 3; Ickes, *Autobiography*, 193, 210, 322–323, 341. Hoover, by contrast, is said to have been "strongly anti-French." See Robert H. Ferrell, *American Diplomacy in the Great Depression* (New York: Norton, 1970), 200.

7. Saint-Quentin to Paris, 26 March 1938, *DDF*, 2d Series, ix, no. 58, 113; Rossi, *Roosevelt and the French*, 13–15, 29. Press conference, 7 September 1934, in Edgar B. Nixon, ed., *Franklin D. Roosevelt and Foreign Affairs*, 3 vols. (Cambridge: Belknap Press, 1969), ii, 209.

8. See Chapter 5 (note 21) in the present volume, ministry of interior to MAE, 5 June 1934, MAE, B, 343, n.p. Much of the invective was addressed to French disarmament policy, which had been targeted by one article in *Fortune* and a series of articles in Philadelphia's *Public Ledger*. See letter addressed to Mme Doumergue, the premier's wife, 6 June 1934, MAE, B, 343, 94–95.

9. Fontnouvelle to Paris, 7 May 1936, MAE, B, 345, 138–140; and 9 September 1937, ibid., 346, 117–123.

10. "L'esprit de propagande." For the Quai d'Orsay's reading of the German propaganda machine, see the "Note" prepared by the Service d'information et de presse, of 19 May 1938, MAE, Maison, 81, 1–18. For the suggestion that German cultural propaganda was waning by the late 1930s, see Saint-Quentin to Paris, 28 March 1939, MAE, Oeuvres, 577.

11. J. B. Duroselle, *La France et les Etats-Unis*, 146.

12. Henry to Paris, 18 August 1936, *DDF*, 2d Series, iii, no. 170, 243. William Bullitt to FDR, 10 January 1937, in Orville H. Bullitt, ed., *For the President, Personal and Secret: Correspondence between Franklin D. Roosevelt and William C. Bullitt* (London: Andre Deutsch, 1973), 207.

13. Laboulaye to Paris, 19 March 1935, *DDF*, 1st Series, ix, no. 452, 647. See also the undated (1936) report by Jean-Paul Freyss, of the Paris-based, semiofficial Centre d'Informations Documentaires, MAE, B, 348, 268–277; and Bonnet to Paris, 15 June 1937, ibid., 346, 43.

14. Joseph Goebbels actually tried to constrain the propaganda efforts of American nationals, for fear of further damaging German-American relations. See Laurie, *Propaganda Warriors*, 21–23.

15. Jules Henry to Paris, 14 August 1936, MAE, B, 345, 201; Kayser report, February 1939, ibid., 347, 79–80. The British ambassador, Lord Lothian, reported that any whisper of foreign propaganda sent Americans into a "cold fury." See Todd Bennett, "The Celluloid War: State and Studio in Anglo-American Propaganda Film-Making, 1939–1941," *International History Review* 24, no. 1 (2002): 68.

16. Between 1929 and 1934, American exports to France had dropped from $265

million to $115 million, and French exports to American from $171 million to $57 million. See Blumenthal, *Illusion and Reality*, 189.

17. For the impact of the gold standard on national currencies, and thus on international relations, see Kenneth Mouré, "The Gold Standard Illusion: France and the Gold Standard in the Era of Currency Instability, 1914–1939," in *Crisis and Renewal in France, 1918–1962*, ed. Mouré and Martin S. Alexander (New York: Berghahn Books, 2002), 66–85. See also Rossi, *Roosevelt and the French*, 16–17, and Eric Mechouland, "L'incompréhension diplomatique franco-américaine, 1932–1933," *Revue d'Histoire Moderne et Contemporaine* 42–44 (October–December 1995): 577–592.

18. Vice Consul (Los Angeles) to Paris, 15 February 1934, MAE, B, 342, 209–210; Consulate General to Paris, 1 March 1935, MAE, B, 344, 1–2.

19. Press clipping of 5 April 1936, forwarded from Laboulaye to Paris, 6 April, MAE, B, 351, 21–22.

20. Jules Henry to Paris, 16 July, 6 August 1936, MAE, B, 351, 48–49, 57–67.

21. "French Journalists," 21 April 1933, *WP*, 2; editorial, 21 May 1933, ibid., 6. Three years later, in a self-confessed "distribe," Ambassador Jesse Strauss repeated the criticism to President Roosevelt. See Strauss to Roosevelt, 20 January 1936, in Nixon, *Franklin D. Roosevelt and Foreign Affairs*, iii, 166–170.

22. "France Plunged in Gloom," 1 January 1937, *Chicago Tribune*, 5; editorial, 19 June 1937, ibid., 10.

23. A. Vulliet to Marx, 30 March 1936, MAE, Oeuvres, 571; 31 March 1936, ibid., 573.

24. Graham J. White, *FDR and the Press* (Chicago: University of Chicago Press, 1979), 60–61; Krock, *Memoirs*, 144, 150, 181, 191. For a long report on the rearmament effort, and on the dissent it caused in America, see Saint-Quentin to Paris, 9 December 1938, *DDF*, 2d Series, xiii, no. 79, 151–158.

25. "Proposition de loi," 6 June 1936, MAE, Maison, 80, 7. For evidence of British close-mindedness on the subject of propaganda abroad, and an attendant parsimony throughout most of the interwar years, see the second chapter of Philip M. Taylor, *The Projection of Britain: British Overseas Publicity and Propaganda, 1919–1939* (Cambridge: Cambridge University Press, 1981), 44–82.

26. "Proposition de loi," 9.

27. "Première Conférence," 8 September 1936, MAE, Maison, 81.

28. Senate. Foreign Affairs Commission, 19 February 1937, MAE, Y, 04, 249–279.

29. Note. Service d'information et de presse, 19 May 1938, MAE, Maison, 81, 17.

30. "Proposition de résolution," 9 February 1939, MAE, Maison, 80, 12, 14.

31. See "Radio," 14 October 1938, *Monitor*, 4; "Propaganda Law." 25 April 1939, ibid., 4.

32. *Presse Publicité: Journal Technique de Toute la France* is described as an "organe corporatif" of the French media world. Capturing its interest in publicity abroad, the journal carried on its masthead Bishop Bossuet's "La voix de la vérité doit se faire entendre au monde." See issue of August 1939, MAE, Maison, 82.

33. Daladier to Lebrun, 29 July 1939, MAE, Maison, 82; Edmond Taylor, "French Cabinet Sets Up Office of Propaganda," 30 July 1939, *Chicago Tribune*, 10.

34. Laboulaye to Paris, 5 February 1937, MAE, B, 351, 106–108; Bonnet to Paris, 15 June 1937, ibid., 346, 45.

35. Henry to Paris, 14 August 1936, MAE, B, 345, 201.
36. André Honnorat to Marx, 10 March 1938, MAE, Oeuvres, 570; N. Bankowsky (architect) to Bonnet, 15 July 1938, MAE, B, 347, 4–5.
37. Bonnet to Paris, 27 May 1937, MAE, B, 346, 19–24.
38. Henry to Paris, 14 January 1938, MAE, B, 351, 176–181. He claimed that Raoul Roussy de Sales was now the only regular French correspondent in Washington, excluding two reporters from Agence Havas. The British had more than thirty between Washington and New York, and the Germans more than a dozen.
39. Henry to Paris, 29 July 1936, MAE, B, 345, 183–187; 14 August 1936, ibid., 200–219. Regarding a proposal to create a science library at the French Institute in Washington, the ministry urged its chargé to find a way of concealing its participation through some form of indirect contribution. See Henry to Paris, 26 July 1937, MAE, B, 346, 77–78; Paris to Henry, 28 July, ibid., 83–84.
40. Henry to Paris, 2 September 1937, MAE, B, 346, 106–113. Note that by the end of the year, the commercial attaché in Washington had created a coordinating committee of representatives from the tourist office, the French Line, and the National Railway Office, with a view to promoting tourism in France. See Henry to Paris, 3 January 1938, ibid., 199–201.
41. Henry to Paris, 2 September 1937, MAE, B, 346, 106–113. It is here that Henry laments the disappearance of such long-standing, prominent Francophiles as William Guthrie, Nicolas Murray Butler, Georges Wickersham, Elihu Root, and Frederick Coudert. The French Institute of New York was located at 20 East Fiftieth Street and had approximately one thousand members.
42. Quoting Lippmann, who was made an officer in the Legion of Honor in July 1938, the embassy recorded: "A la seule exception de la France, il n'est pas de grande puissance sur le continent qui n'ait établi une stricte censure gouvernmentale. Pas une ligne n'est pas imprimé, pas un mot n'est prononcé à la radio, qui aille à l'encontre des désirs du Gouvernement." Laboulaye to Paris, 15 September 1936, MAE, B, 351, 82.
43. Headed by the pianist Henri Casadeus, a familiar figure on the American concert stage, this group was expressly engaged in "propagande artistique." See Saint-Quentin to Paris, 15 December 1938, MAE, SOE, 577.
44. See in particular Jules Henry to Paris, 8 December 1937, B, 346, 168–173.
45. The secretary-general of education's fine arts division in the mid-to-late 1930s was Georges Huisman. See Chapter 5, note 33, in the present volume for more information. Sometime between 1935 and 1939, the name Association française d'expansion et d'exchanges artistique was changed to Association française d'action artistique. Its headquarters were in the Palais Royal, and its long-serving director was Robert Brussel.
46. One example of the perplexing overlaps between ostensibly official and ostensibly private participants in the decision-making process was Yves Chataigneau. He was a diplomat within Oeuvres, a key source of arts funding; a member of the nominally private association; a member of the association's subcommittee on cinema, which advised an executive council, which was co-chaired by Jean Marx, head of the foreign ministry's Ouevres, and by Philippe Erlanger, head of the education ministry's action artistique.

47. Prince de Beauvau-Craon and Aymé Bernard were president and secretary of the center respectively. By 1939 Jean-Paul Freyss had become the principal figure in the center's New York office at 301 Park Avenue. André Vulliet directed the Office français de renseignements in Paris.

48. M. Gaucheron, first secretary in the Washington embassy, was responsible for facilitating the work of intellectual groups such as the Gens de lettres. See Marx to Mme Marbo, 30 April 1937, MAE, Oeuvres, 491.

49. See *NYT*, 22 February 1937, 16; 14 December 1937, 33; 2 January 1938, 2; 25 January 1938, 24; 8 February 1938, 17; 29 November 1938, 26; 24 January 1939, 17; and annual report of Quatre Saisons, 20 December 1937, 1 April 1938, 17 May 2938, 29 June 1938, 4 April 1939, MAE, Oeuvres, 577.

50. *SF*, 19 March 1939, 11; 25 March 1939, 5; *NYT*, 21 January 1940, 36; 19 March 1940, 8.

51. Laboulaye to Paris, 3 March 1936, MAE, Oeuvres, 570; April 1937, ibid., 477; Saint-Quentin to Paris, 10 March 1938, ibid., 570; *WP*, 21 July 1939, 21.

52. Viala to Embassy, 21 March 1939, MAE, B, 347, 160; Consul (NY) to Paris, 8 December 1937, MAE, Oeuvres, 570. One major difficulty was the disparity between the numbers of French films shown annually in America, and those of Germany and England. In 1935, for instance, there were fifty-nine German films and nineteen French. See Fontnouvelle to Paris, AME, B, 345, 128–140. See also Rémy Pithon, "Opinions publiques et représentations culturelles face aux problèmes de la puissance: Le témoignage du cinéma français (1938–1939)," *Relations internationales*, no. 33 (spring 1983): 91–102.

53. Paramount did modify some of the scenes. See Saint-Quentin to Paris, 2, 10 August 1939, MAE, B, 351, 268–170, 173. My three other references are to 1937 films entitled *Stolen Holiday*, *The Road Back*, and *The Life of Emile Zola*. Viala to William H. Hays, 3 May 1937, MAE, B, 346, 2–4; 16 July 1937, ibid., 73–74; Meric de Bellefon to Paris, early 1936, MAE, B, 345, 88. Predictably, Hearst's *Examiner* equated French complaints with censorship. See 18 March 1939, 8.

54. In Bonney's case, the work for the *NYT* was done on that paper's request. The circumstances surrounding Freyss's work are less clear. Bonney to Marx, 3 February 1936, MAE, Oeuvres, 573; Saint-Quentin to consul (Philadelphia), 9 and 10 March 1939, MAE, B, 347, 142, 145.

55. André Vulliet (Office Français . . . Paris) to Comert, 3 February 1937, MAE, B, 348, 296–299; letter signed Pierre de Lanux, 15 March 1937, MAE, Oeuvres, 570; Marx to Saint-Quentin, 4 November 1938, ibid.; Vulliet to Comert, 17 Janaury 1938, MAE, B, 348, 300–301; *NYT*, 10 January 1937, 10; 24 February 1939, 7. For a report on the Center of Information Concerning France, at Boston University, established in 1937 and publisher of the monthly *La Gazette Française*, see *CSM*, 21 February 1939, 7.

56. See *CSM*, 5 July 1938, 6; 25 May 1939, 6; 22 August 1939, 6; *NYT*, 9 June 1939, 18; Notes of 1 May and 3 June 1939, MAE, SOE, 573, Pascal Ory, "Plus dure sera la chute: Les pavillons français aux Expositions internationales de 1939," *Relations internationales*, no. 33 (spring 1983), 81–90.

57. *La Semaine* ran one thousand copies weekly, *Le Petit Journal* some twenty-five thousand copies. The latter, published by André Humbert, a naturalized American,

became the natural successor to the *Courrier des Etats-Unis*, which folded in January 1938 after 110 years of operation. See Kayser to Paris, 11 February 1939, MAE, B, 347, 81–84.

58. The author was Professor Michael S. Pargment of the University of Michigan. Kayser report, 11 February 1939, MAE, B, 347, 97–98.

59. Kayser, 98–100.

60. Some ten thousand catalogs were produced by the center, almost half of which were distributed to schools equipped with 16-mm projectors. The center was in contact with school boards in every state, and it advertised its film collection in many scholarly magazines. Rental fees were nominally five dollars, although the center was prepared to take less. Kayser, 90, 93–95.

61. Saint-Quentin, 31 August, 15 September, 1939, MAE, B, 351, 274–275, 277–278; Brière to Paris, 11 September 1939, MAE, B, 347, 215.

CHAPTER 7   *Words of War, 1939–1940*

1. Young, *France and the Origins.*

2. See, for instance, Robert J. Young, "The Use and Abuse of Fear: France and the Air Menace in the 1930s," *Intelligence and National Security* 2, no. 4 (1987), 88–109.

3. Maurois, *Memoirs, 1885–1967,* 204.

4. Giraudoux had worked in the Quai's press office before 1914, had directed Oeuvres and subsequently the ministry's Service d'information et de presse in the 1920s, and as of 1934 had propaganda responsibilities associated with his office as inspector general of Diplomatic and Consular Posts. See Jean Baillou, "Giraudoux et la diplomatie: De l'école normale au Quai d'Orsay," Cahiers Jean Giraudoux 13 (Paris: Grasset, 1983), 13; Maurice Barthélemy, "Giraudoux et la diplomatie: La 'Carrière' de Jean Giraudoux," ibid., 15–41; Jean Joire, "Giraudoux et la diplomatie: Jean Giraudoux et le Service des Oeuvres françaises à l'étranger," ibid., 42–52; Brett Dawson, "Giraudoux et la diplomatie: Jean Giraudoux et Philippe Berthelot," ibid., 67–91.

5. The most informative treatments of commissariat activity include Mégret, "Les origines de la propagande," 3–27; Jean-Louis Crémieux-Brilhac, *Ouvriers et soldats,* vol. 1 of *Les Français de l'an 40* (Paris: Gallimard, 1990), 278–296; Maurice Barthélemy's introduction to Jean Giraudoux's *Messages du Continental: Allocutions radiodiffusées du Commissaire général à l'information, 1939–1940,* Cahiers Jean Giraudoux 16 (Paris: Grasset, 1987), 14–27. For a more scathing contemporary account, written by a member of the censorship service, see R. Cardinne-Petit, *Les soirées du Continental: Ce que j'ai vu à la censure, 1939–1940* (Paris: Editions Jean-Renard, 1942).

6. Crémieux-Brilhac, *Ouvriers et soldats,* 281; Maurois, *Memoirs,* 225.

7. For such an organizational chart, see Jean Giraudoux, *Messages du Continental,* Cahiers Jean Giraudoux 16 (1987), 30.

8. Much of the foregoing and succeeding information about the commissariat is drawn from a nearly two-hundred-page "Rapport sur le Commissariat général à l'information," of February 1940, by Maurice Pezet, chair of the Chamber's for-

eign affairs commission. See Dossier 23, *Commission des affaires étrangères*, 1940, *Archives de l'Assemblée Nationale*. See also Lavine and Wechsler, *War Propaganda*, 168.

9. William Bullitt to Roosevelt, 8 November 1936, in Nixon, *Franklin D. Roosevelt and Foreign Affairs*, iii, 475–476.

10. See Paul Morand, *Giraudoux: Souvenirs de notre jeunesse* (Geneva: La Palatine, 1948), 34; Jean Giraudoux, *Amica America* (1918; reprint, Paris: Grasset, 1938), 10, 51.

11. Pezet report, February 1940, Commission des affaires étrangères, Dossier 23, *Ass.Nat.*, 32–33.

12. Giraudoux's undated report to parliament, *Archives Nationales*, Commissariat à l'information, Series F41/20, 44–47; Crémieux-Brilhac, *Ouvriers et soldats*, 298. See also André-Jean Tudesq, "L'utilisation gouvernementale de la radio," in *Edouard Daladier, chef de gouvernement* (Paris: Fondation Nationale des Sciences Politiques, 1977), 255–265; and "French War Director of Radio," *NYT*, 11 December 1939, 5.

13. Giraudoux's undated report uses a figure of four hundred thousand francs for 1939. See *Archives Nationale*, Commissariat à l'Information, Series F41/20, 49; Crémieux-Brilhac, *Les Français*, 292, uses a 10,000,000 figure for the 1940 budget. For Giraudoux's own advocacy of cinema as art and informational form, see an interview of 16 March 1930, *NYT*, ix, 6.

14. Saint-Quentin to Paris, 6 April 1940, MAE, B, 347, 271–275; see undated document, headlined "Washington" in Series F41/32, sous-dossier "Amérique du Nord," *Archives Nationales*.

15. Note from Section Amérique du Nord, 31 October 1939, *Archives Nationales*, Series F41, 28, Dossier v; assorted documents, 1939–1941, ibid., 32, dossier "Etats-Unis, 1940"; Saint-Quentin to Paris, 6 April 1940, MAE, B, 347, 271–275.

16. L. O. Frossard was named minister by the new premier, Paul Reynaud. Giraudoux became chair of a new Conseil supérieur de l'information, and retained his office at the Continental.

17. See footnote 7 to the text of a Giraudoux speech delivered in December 1939, in his *Messages du Continental*, 118; Crémieux-Brilhac, *Ouvriers et soldats*, 286.

18. Pezet report, February 1940, Commission des affaires étrangères, Dossier 23, *Ass.Nat.*, 141. See also Jacques Body, *Jean Giraudoux: The Legend and the Secret*, trans. James Norwood (Rutherford: Fairleigh Dickinson University Press, 1991), 117, and Jean Giraudoux, *Pleins pouvoirs* (Paris: Gallimard, 1939).

19. André Beucler, *Les instants de Giraudoux* (Paris: Milieu de Monde, 1948), 151.

20. Maurice Barthélemy's introduction to Giraudoux, *Messages du Continental*, 21; Pezet report, February 1940, Commission des affaires étrangères, Dossier 23, *Ass.Nat.*, 143–145.

21. "French Give Up Liberties," 22 September 1939, *CT*, 3; "France Lenient," 2 October 1938, ibid., 4; "The Talk of Paris: 'Anastasie,'" 25 February 1940, *NYT*, vii, 11. Examples of French press criticism of the censorship regime, excerpted from *Cyrano* and *Gringoire*, can be found in MAE, 22 and 28 September 1939, Maison, 82.

22. Louis Deschizeau (deputé de l'Indre) to Quai d'Orsay, 28 November 1939, *Maison*, vol. 82, 5; Pezet report, February 1940, Commission des affaires étrangères, Dossier 23, *Ass.Nat.*, 174–176.

23. Crémieux-Brilhac, *Ouvriers et soldats*, 277. It is worth noting, however, that the parliamentary appraisal of the French propaganda system, critical as it often was, did not object to the government's two-front offensive. See Pezet report, February 1940, Commission des affaires étrangères, Dossier 23, *Ass.Nat.*, 32. For one who does, see Michael Jabara Carley, *1939. The Alliance that Never Was and the Coming of World War II* (Chicago: Ivan R. Dee, 1999).

24. Pezet report, February 1940, Commission des affaires étrangères, Dossier 23, *Ass.Nat.*, 129–137.

25. Pezet report, February 1940, Commission des affaires étrangères, Dossier 23, *Ass.Nat.*, 168.

26. Alfred Sauvy, *De Paul Reynaud à Charles de Gaulle* (Paris: Casterman, 1972), 97; Guy Rossi-Landi, *La drôle de guerre: La vie politique en France, 2 septembre 1929–10 mai 1940* (Paris: Colin, 1971), 17.

27. Giraudoux speeches of 10 September, 26 November, and 24 December 1939, and April 1940, *Messages du Continental*, 51–52, 97, 116, 150.

28. Body, *Jean Giraudoux*, 11; Giraudoux, *Pleins pouvoirs*, 18.

29. Giraudoux, *Amica America*, 75, 151; *La Guerre de Troie n'aura pas lieu* (Paris: Librairie Générale Française, 1991), 162.

30. Giraudoux speeches of 8 October, 11 November, 14 December 1939, 11 February 1940, *Messages du Continental*, 64, 87, 107, 134. Daladier himself pointed out to parliament that only 2,000 French servicemen had lost their lives in the first three months of war, compared with the 450,000 mortalities between August and December 1914. See Rossi-Landi, *La drôle de guerre*, 171.

31. Giraudoux, *Pleins pouvoirs*, 177–178; Giraudoux, *Messages du Continental*, 116, 154–155; Body, *Jean Giraudoux*, 110–111.

32. Beucler, *Les instants de Giraudoux*, 155.

33. Giraudoux, *Messages du Continental*, 131–132.

34. See *CSM*, 26 October 1939, 5; ibid., 28 February 1940, 4; *WP*, 25 February 1940, iii, 4.

35. Saint-Quentin to Paris, 16 September 1939, MAE, B, 347, 216; ibid., 7 November 1939, 236; Fontnouvelle to Paris, 8 May 1940, ibid., 293–294.

36. Saint-Quentin to Paris, 15 September 1939, MAE, B, 351, 277.

37. Note entitled "Depuis la guerre: L'art français," early 1940, MAE, Oeuvres, 481.

38. Interview by Winthrop P. Tryon, *CSM*, 27 February 1939, 7. See also William Wiser, *The Crazy Years: Paris in the Twenties* (New York: Atheneum, 1983), 126–127.

39. See also the *WP*, 19 February 1939, vi, 5; 26 February, iv, 1; *NYT*, 2 April 1939, x, 7; *CT*, 3 April 1939, 23; *SF*, 12 June 1939, 16.

40. *NYT*, 17 March 1940, x, 8; 91 percent of those polled believed that German music should not be banned in America. See George Gallup and Claude Robinson, "Gallup and Fortune Polls," *Political Science Quarterly* 4, no. 1 (March 1940): 96.

41. Curie was the daughter of the distinguished scientists Pierre and Marie Curie

and was the author of a best-selling book on her parents' lives. Shortly after the outbreak of war in September 1939, she was made director of Women's War Activities in France, a new office within the commissariat.

42. See *NYT*, 20 January 1940, 13; 10 April 1940, 23; *CSM*, 12 April, 3.
43. Consul (San Francisco) to Paris, 14 March 1940, MAE, Oeuvres, 571; Saint-Quentin to Paris, 3 May 1940, ibid.
44. Lavine and Wechsler, *War Propaganda*, 72–79, 85–86, 102, 108.
45. One German propagandist is reported to have told Giraudoux that his radio addresses had been surprisingly effective, having a strong influence on German radio audiences, indeed on "elites around the world, especially in America." See Amaury, *De l'information et de la propagande d'état*, 45.
46. Jean Giraudoux, *De pleins pouvoirs à sans pouvoirs* (Paris: Gallimard, 1950), 211; "Pour attirer le touriste," republished from a 1935 article of *Le Journal,* in Cahiers Jean Giraudoux 13 (Paris: Grasset, 1984), 162.
47. Giraudoux, *Messages du Continental*, 76–80. This speech of 27 October 1939 was broadcast as part of a three-day forum for American intellectuals, organized by Ogden Reid and the *New York Herald Tribune* around the theme of "The Challenge to Civilization." See also "Pourquoi nous faisons la guerre," of 14 December 1939, in *Messages du Continental*, 104.
48. Giraudoux, *Messages du Continental*, 89, 109–110, 138. Like Giraudoux, with whom he worked in the commissariat, Paul Claudel detected blasphemy in Hitler's Germany. In a radio address of October 1939, the former ambassador observed: "Germany has excommunicated herself from the Christian world, from the civilized world . . . . You have literally sold your soul to Satan." See "Addresse au peuple allemand," in *Claudel diplomate*, Cahiers Paul Claudel 4 (Paris: Gallimard, 1962), 279.
49. Giraudoux, *Messages du Continental*, 63, 95–96.
50. Ibid., 68, 99.
51. Ibid., 110.
52. *WP*, 8 October 1939, 4.
53. *WP*, 10 November 1939, 11; the text of his radio broadcast is reproduced in *Le Temps*, 5 April 1940, 3.
54. *CSM*, 5 March 1940, 1.
55. Giraudoux, *Messages du Continental*, 97.
56. *WP*, 10 November 1939, 11; *Le Temps*, 15 June 1940, 1.
57. *CSM*, 5 March 1940, 1.
58. George H. Gallup, *The Gallup Poll: Public Opinion, 1935–1972.*, 3 vols., vol. 1, 1935–1948 (New York: Random House, 1972), 65, 96, 125, 145, 175, 182, 226; *Public Opinion Quarterly* 4, no. 3 (September 1940): 550. For the president's views, see Robert Dallek, *Franklin D. Roosevelt and American Foreign Policy, 1932–1945* (New York: Oxford University Press, 1979), 197.
59. The *Tribune* had a daily circulation of about 1,000,000; the *Times*, about 500,000 and as many as 800,000 on the weekend. The *Post* and the *Monitor* were each running more than 100,000 daily; and the *Examiner* was part of an interlocking Hearst newspaper and magazine empire that, in total, appears to have had a circulation of upward of 7,000,000 by the late 1930s.

60. *NYT*, 4 September 1939, iv, 8; Robert J. Young, "In the Eye of the Beholder: The Cultural Representation of France and Germany by *The New York Times*, 1939–40," in *The French Defeat of 1940*, ed. Joel Blatt, 245–268; Chalmers M. Roberts, *The "Washington Post": The First 100 Years* (Boston: Houghton Mifflin, 1977), 229; Tom Kelley, *The Imperial Post: The Meyers, the Grahams, and the Paper That Rules Washington* (New York: William Morrow, 1983).

61. *CT*, 27 August 1939, 5; 15 March 1940, 13; 24 March, 6; 13 April, 7; 5 May, 4; 12 June, 2. "The *Tribune* took it for granted that its readers were anti-German. They did not have to be reminded . . . that Hitler was a totalitarian dictator." Jerome Edwards, *The Foreign Policy of Col. McCormick's "Tribune," 1929–1941* (Reno: University of Nevada Press, 1971), 148.

62. *CSM*, 17 June 1939, 18; 2 September, 6; Magazine, 11 November, 5; Magazine, 2 March 1940, 5; 14 June 1940, 22; 24 June, 24. See also Erwin D. Canham, *Commitment to Freedom: The Story of the "Christian Science Monitor"* (Boston: Houghton Mifflin, 1958), 290–295.

63. *SF*, 21 June 1940, 11.

64. Undated, fifty-two-page report to the Chamber of Deputies. Commissariat général à l'information, *Archives Nationales*, Series F41, 20.

65. *NYT*, 24 February 1939, 7; 7 April 1940, 5.

66. Gertrude Stein, *Paris France: Personal Recollections* (1940; reprint, London: Peter Owen, 1971), 56.

67. This interpretation was first advanced in my "Forgotten Words and Faded Images," 205–229.

Conclusion

1. *CT*, 11 January 1919, 8; *SF*, 8 February 1928, 26, and 2 April 1928, 26.

2. Sally Marks, "Black Watch on the Rhine: A Study in Propaganda, Prejudice and Prurience," *European Studies Review* 13 (1983), 297–334; Levenstein, *Seductive Journey*, 263–266; Saint-Quentin to Paris, 16 March 1939, MAE, B, 347, 151.

3. *SF*, 2 April 1923, 28; 9 April 1923, 24.

4. *SF*, editorial, 14 July 1936, 12; cartoons of 17 July, 10; 27 July, 10; 31 July, 12; 10 August, 1; 22 August, 1.

5. Laurie, *Propaganda Warriors*, 2, 19–20. For the philosophical and ideological concerns about underplaying the capacities and the role of the masses in democratic societies, see Gary, *Nervous Liberals*.

6. W. Phillips Davison, "Voices of America," in *Public Opinion and Foreign Policy*, ed. Lester Markel (New York: Harper and Brothers, 1949), 156–179. See also Martha E. Bernstein, "The French Dilemma: Reaction to U.S. Cultural Policy, 1950–1954," in *Proceedings of the Western Society for French History (1999)* 27 (2001): 182–189.

7. Rex A. Leeper, "British Culture Abroad," *Contemporary Review* 148 (August 1935), 203; Kenneth W. Thompson and Soedjatmoko Thomson, "Cultural Diplomacy," in James N. Rosenau, Kenneth W. Thompson, and Gavin Boyd, eds., *World Politics: An Introduction* (New York: Free Press, 1976), 405.

BIBLIOGRAPHY

Primary Documents

Archives Nationales

Série F 41. Information

14   Rôle et attribution des services, 1939
               Textes officiels, 1939
               Organisation de service, 1939
20   Discours de Giraudoux, 16 April 1940
               Rapport de Giraudoux à la Chambre, 1940
21   Radiodiffusion: Textes officiels, 1938–1939
               Affaires étrangères, 1939–1940
28   Subventions à revues et journaux étrangers, 1940
               Informations: Section Amérique du Nord, 1939
29   Correspondance . . . sujet des subventions, 1940
               Instruction . . . aux services financiers aux E-U, 1940
32   Etats-Unis, 1940

Assemblée Nationale

Commission des affaires étrangéres, 1939–1940

Auditions de Georges Bonnet, Edouard Daladier, Georges Pernot, Jean Giraudoux (June 1939–February 1940)
Rapport sur le Commissariat général à l'information, by Ernest Pezet, February 1940

Ministère des affaires étrangères (Paris)

Série Maison de la Presse

01   Dossier général, 1914–1924
02   Commissariat général de la propagande, 1917–1921
04   Service radio-télégraphique, 1916–1923

20   Etats-Unis. Dossier général, 1914–1917
21   Etats-Unis, 1917–1923
23–25   Etats-Unis. Bureau français de renseignements, 1923–1925
74   Rapports généraux du Commissariat général . . . 1918

*Série Information-Presse-Propagande, 1914–1940 (Reorganized and
supplemented materials from the old Série Maison de la Presse)*

80   Rapports de Pezet et Dariac, 1932–1939
81   Service des Oeuvres, 1930–1939
82   Création du Commissariat général . . . 1939–1940

Série B. Amérique

01–7   Affaires politiques, 1919–1929
22–29C   Propagande de la France, 1918–1929
37   Télégraphie sans fil, 1919–1920
38–39   Etats-Unis et Versailles, 1919–1929
61–70   Etats-Unis, Correspondance politique, 1919–1929
295   Ambassade de France, 1922–1939
296   Consulats de France, 1927–1939
339   Propagande des Alliés, 1932–1939
340–347   Propagande de la France, 1930–1940
348   Bureau d'Information, 1930–1938
349–351   Etats-Unis, Presse, 1930–1940
352   Correspondance politique (Radios) 1936–1938
352   Correspondance: Haut Commissariat, 1930
358–363   Etats-Unis-France, 1930–1937

Série guerre, 1914–18

512–514   Etats-Unis. Mission Tardieu, 1917–1918

Série SDN. Société des nations

1904   Presse: Dossier général, 1921–1939
1916–1918   Associations françaises de propagande, 1929–1940

Série Y. Internationale

01–4   Propagande de la France, dossier général, 1918–1937
06   Instructions aux agents diplomatiques, 1933
132   Comité interallié de propagande, 1918–1922
410   Etats-Unis (1920–1921)

Série papiers d'agents

            095 Klobukowski

61   Dossier Commissariat général, 1918–1921
            010 Berthelot
01–2   Dossier général, 1915–1916
03   Propagande. Comités, 1916–1917
18   Propagande, 1915–1916
19   Propagande, 1916–1917
20   Personal dossiers. Polignac et al.
            166 Tardieu
82–86   Missions aux Etats-Unis, 1918–1919
            095 Jusserand
03–8   Chrono, 1907–1914
88   Stéphane Lauzanne, 1908–1922
91   William D. Guthrie, 1914–1935
92   Louis Wiley, 1925–1935
93   Gaston Liebert, 1916–1924
96   Dr. John Finley, 1917–1930
98   Frederick Coudert, 1919–1922
99   Richard Harding Davis, 1914–1916

Dossier: Agence Havas. Rapports avec le Ministère des Affaires Etrangères, 1931–1940

Ministère des affaires étrangères (Nantes)

Série Service des Oeuvres françaises à l'étranger

01   Constitution du service: Personnel
02   Dossiers généraux (1925–1931)
39–40   Etats-Unis, 1923–1931. Section oeuvres diverses
41–42   Projet d'un "Palais de France" à New York, 1925–1931
43   Dossier général, Section littéraires et artistiques
59   Comité catholique des amitiés françaises . . . 1920–1927
            Comité protestant de propagande, 1921–1930
69   Oeuvres. Section diverse, 1923–1931
84   Oeuvres. Section tourisme, sports et cinéma, 1915–1930
91   Etats-Unis. Section tourisme, sports et cinéma, 1921–1935
92   Oeuvres. Section tourisme, sports et cinéma, 1922–1926
477   Associations Section oeuvres diverses
478   Maison de France de New York, 1932–1935
481–482   Dossiers généraux, Section 1: littéraire et artistique, 1932–1940
485   Association d'expansion artistique, and comité, 1932–1936
490   Décorations, 1936–1940. Section littéraire
491   Société des gens de lettres, 1937. Section littéraire
569   Etats-Unis. Diverses. Section littéraire
570   Dossier général. Congrès . . . 1936–1940. Section litt.
571   Conférences, 1936–1939. Section litt.
576–577   Musique et théâtre, 1932–1940

Published Documents

Documents diplomatiques français. First and Second Series (1932–1938). Paris: Imprimerie Nationale, 1963–1986.
Foreign Relations of the United States: Diplomatic Papers. Washington, D.C.: Government Printing Office, 1946–1953.

Newspaper Press

Le Temps, 1900–1940, for materials relating to American policy and culture.
Chicago Tribune, Christian Science Monitor, New York Times, San Francisco Examiner, Washington Post, an extensive selection of materials relating to French policy and culture between 1900 and 1940.

Secondary Sources

Memoirs and Contemporary Perspectives

Allard, Paul. *Le Quai d'Orsay*. Paris: Editions de France, 1938.
"American Institute of Public Opinion Surveys, 1938–1939." *Political Science Quarterly* 3, no. 4 (1939): 581–607.
Amory, Cleveland. *The Proper Bostonians*. New York: Harper, 1932.
Aron, René, and Arnaud Dandieu. *Le cancer américain*. Paris: Rieder, 1931.
Baldwin, H. W., and S. Stone. *We Saw It Happen: The News behind the News That's Fit to Print*. New York: Simon and Schuster, 1938.
Barney, J. Stewart. "The Ecole des Beaux-Arts: Its Influence on Our Architecture." *Architectural Record* 22 (1907): 333–342.
Baudrillart, Alfred. *Les carnets du Cardinal Alfred Baudrillart, 1914–1918*. Ed. Paul Christophe. Paris: Les Editions du Cerf, 1994.
———. "Notre propagande." *Revue Hebdomadaire* 25 (8 April 1916): 141–184.
Bernays, Edward L. *Crystallizing Public Opinion*. 1923. Reprint, New York: Horace Liveright, 1961.
———. "Moulding Public Opinion." In *Pressure Groups and Propaganda*. Annals of the American Academy of Political and Social Science 179, ed. Harwood L. Childs, 82–87. Philadelphia, 1935.
———. *Propaganda*. New York: Horace Liveright, 1928.
Beucler, André. *Les instants de Giraudoux*. Paris: Milieu du Monde, 1948.
Boutroux, E. "L'Allemagne et la guerre." *Revue des Deux Mondes,* 15 October 1914, 385–401.
Bréal, Auguste. *Philippe Berthelot*. Paris: Gallimard, 1937.
Bret, Paul Louis *Au feu des événements*. Paris: Plon, 1959.
Bullitt, Orville H., ed. *For the President, Personal and Secret: Correspondence between Franklin D. Roosevelt and William C. Bullitt*. London: Andre Deutsch, 1973.
Cardinne-Petit, R. *Les soirées du Continental: Ce que j'ai vu à la censure 1939–1940*. Paris: Editions Jean-Renard, 1942.
Cherrington, Ben M. "The Division of Cultural Relations." *Political Science Quarterly* 3, no. 1 (1939): 136–138.

Childs, Harwood L., ed. *Pressure Groups and Propaganda*. Annals of the American Academy of Political and Social Science 179. Philadelpia, 1935.

Claudel, Paul. *Claudel diplomate*. Cahiers Paul Claudel 4. Paris: Gallimard, 1962.

———. *Claudel aux Etats-Unis, 1927–1933*. Cahiers Paul Claudel 11. Paris: Gallimard, 1982.

———. *Journal*. Vol. 1, 1904–1932. Ed. F. Varillon and J. Petit. Paris: Gallimard, 1968.

———. *Oeuvres diplomatiques: Ambassadeur aux Etats-Unis, 1927–1933*. Vol. 1, *1927–1929*. Lausanne: Age d'Homme, 1995.

———. *Oeuvres en prose*. Paris: Gallimard, 1965.

Creel, George. *How We Advertised America*. New York: Harper and Row, 1920.

———. *Rebel at Large: Recollections of Fifty Crowded Years*. New York: Putnam, 1947.

Croiset, Alfred, et al. "Lettres à M. Scott Mowrer." *L'Opinion* 9 (19 August 1916): 153–157.

Daniélou, Charles. *Les affaires étrangères*. Paris: Figuière, 1927.

Doob, Leonard. W., and Edward S. Robinson. "Psychology and Propaganda." In *Pressure Groups and Propaganda*. Annals of the American Academy of Political and Social Science 179, ed. Harwood L. Childs, 88–95. Philadelphia, 1935.

Doumic, René. "Le retour à la culture classique." *Revue des Deux Mondes* 15 (November 1914): 317–328.

Duhamel, Georges. *In Defence of Letters*. New York: Greystone Press, 1939.

———. *Scenès de la vie future*. Paris, 1930. Translated as *America the Menace: Scenes from the Life of the Future*. Boston: Houghton Mifflin, 1931.

Duranty, Walter. *I Write as I Please*. New York: Simon and Schuster, 1935.

Egbert, Donald Drew. "Foreign Influences in American Art." In *Foreign Influences in American Life*, ed. David F. Bowers, 99–125. Princeton: Princeton University Press, 1944.

Feuillerat, Albert. *French Life and Ideals*. New Haven: Yale University Press, 1925.

Gallup, George, and Claude Robinson. "American Institute of Public Opinion, 1935–1938." *Political Science Quarterly* 2, no. 3 (1938): 373–397.

———. "Gallup and Fortune Polls." *Political Science Quarterly* 4, no. 1 (1940): 83–115.

———. "Gallup and Fortune Polls." *Political Science Quarterly* 4, no. 3 (1940): 533–553.

The German Reich and Americans of German Origin. New York: Oxford University Press, 1938.

Giraudoux, Jean. *Amica America*. 1918. Reprint, Paris: Grasset, 1938.

———. "A propos de la rentrée des classes." In Cahiers Jean Giraudoux 13:175–179. Paris: Grasset, 1984.

———. *De pleins pouvoirs à sans pouvoirs*. Paris: Gallimard, 1950.

———. *La Française et la France*. Paris: Gallimard, 1951.

———. *La Guerre de Troie n'aura pas lieu*. Paris: Librairie Générale Française, 1991.

———. *Messages du Continental: Allocutions radiodiffusées du Commissaire général à l'information, 1939–1940*. Cahiers Jean Giraudoux 16. Paris: Grasset, 1987.

———. *Pleins pouvoirs*. Paris: Gallimard, 1939.

———. "Pour attirer le touriste . . . " In Cahiers Jean Giraudoux 13:162–167. Paris: Grasset, 1984.

————. "Propagande." In Cahiers Jean Giraudoux 13:158–161. Paris: Grasset, 1984.

Hanotaux, Gabriel. *Le Comité "France-Amérique": Son activité de 1909 à 1920*. Paris: Comité "France-Amérique," 1920.

Hastings, Thomas. "The Influence of the Ecole des Beaux-Arts upon American Architecture." *Architectural Record* 10 (1901): 65–90.

Heinberg, J. Gilbert. "The Personnel of French Cabinets, 1871–1930." *American Political Science Review* 25 (1931): 389–396.

Holt, Arthur E. "Organized Religion as a Pressure Group." In *Pressure Groups and Propaganda*. Annals of the American Academy of Political and Social Science 179, ed. Harwood L. Childs, 42–49. Philadelphia, 1935.

Ickes, Harold L. *The Autobiography of a Curmudgeon*, 1943. Reprint, Chicago: Quadrangle Paperbacks, 1969.

Jones, Howard M. *America and French Culture, 1750–1848*. Chapel Hill: University of North Carolina Press, 1927.

Jusserand, Jules. *What Me Befell*. London: Constable, 1933.

————. *With Americans of Past and Present Days*. New York: Charles Scribner's, 1916.

Krock, Arthur. *Memoirs: Sixty Years on the Firing Line*. New York: Funk and Wagnalls, 1968.

Krock, Arthur, et al. *We Saw It Happen: The News behind the News That's Fit to Print, by Thirteen Correspondents of the "New York Times."* New York: Simon and Schuster, 1939.

Lamont, Thomas W. *Across World Frontiers*. New York: Harcourt, Brace, 1951.

Lanux, Pierre de. *Young France and New America*. New York: Macmillan, 1917.

Lasswell, Harold. "Propaganda." *Encyclopedia of the Social Sciences*. Vol. 12, 521–528. New York: Macmillan, 1934.

Lauvrière, Emile. "La France dans le développement des Etats-Unis." *La Grande Revue* 148 (August 1935): 268–294.

Lavine, Harold, and James Wechsler. *War Propaganda and the United States*. New Haven: Yale University Press, 1940.

Lee, James Melvin. *History of American Journalism*. New York: Garden City Publishing, 1923.

Leeper, Rex A. "British Culture Abroad." *Contemporary Review* 148 (August 1935): 201–207.

Lippmann, Walter. "The Press and Public Opinion." *Political Science Quarterly* 46, no. 2 (1931): 161–170.

————. *Public Opinion*. 1922. Reprint, New York: Macmillan, 1938.

Lundberg, Ferdinand. *America's Sixty Families*. New York: Halcyon House, 1937.

McCormick, Anne O'Hare. "Ourselves and Europe." Helen Kenyon Lecture, Vassar College, 1941.

Maurois, André. *En Amérique*. New York: American Book Company, 1936.

————. *Memoirs, 1885–1967*. New York: Harper and Row, 1970.

Mirepoix, Emmanuel de Lévis. *Le Ministère des Affaires Etrangères*. Angers: Société Anonyme des Editions de l'Ouest, 1934.

Mock, James B., and Cedric Lawson. *Words That Won the War: The Story of the Committee on Public Information, 1917–1919*. Princeton: Princeton University Press, 1939.

Morand, Paul. *Giraudoux: Souvenirs de notre jeunesse.* Geneva: La Palatine, 1948.
———. *Journal d'un attaché d'ambassade.* Paris: Gallimard, 1963.
———. *New York.* Paris: Flammarion, 1930.
Niessel, General A. "La propagande par radio." *Revue des Deux Mondes,* 15 October 1938, 829–843.
Norton, Henry Kittredge. *Foreign Office Organization: A Comparison of the Organization of the British, French, German, and Italian Foreign Office with That of the Department of State of the U.S.A.* Annals of the American Academy of Political and Social Science 143: 1–81, supplement (Philadelphia, 1929).
Pezet, Ernest. *Défense et illustration de la France: Sous les yeux du monde.* Paris: Spès, 1935.
Riegel, Oscar W. *Mobilizing for Chaos: The Story of the New Propaganda.* 1934. Reprint, New York: Arno Press, 1972.
Romier, Lucien. *Qui sera le maître: Europe ou Amérique?* Paris: Hachette, 1927.
Root, Waverley. *The Paris Edition: The Autobiography of Waverley Root, 1927–1934.* San Francisco: North Point Press, 1987.
Saunders, D. A. "The Dies Committee: First Phase." *Political Science Quarterly* 3, no. 2 (1939): 223–238.
Schuman, F. L. *War and Diplomacy in the French Republic.* 1931. Reprint, New York: AMS Press, 1970.
Shirer, William L. *Twentieth Century Journey.* 3 vols. Vol. 1 (1904–1930) and Vol. 2 (1930–1940). Boston: Little, Brown, 1976–1984.
Siegfried, André. *Les Etats-Unis d'aujourd'hui.* Paris: Colin, 1928.
Spring Rice, Sir Cecil. *The Letters and Friendships of Sir Cecil Spring Rice.* Ed. Stephen Gwynn. 2 vols. 1929. Westport, Conn.: Greenwood Press, 1971.
Squires, James Duane. *British Propaganda at Home and in the United States from 1914 to 1917.* Cambridge: Harvard University Press, 1935.
Stein, Gertrude. *Paris France: Personal Recollections.* 1940. Reprint, London: Peter Owen, 1971.
Tardieu, André. *France and America: Some Experiences in Cooperation.* Boston: Houghton Mifflin, 1927.
Taylor, Edmond. "Democracy Demoralized: The French Collapse." *Political Science Quarterly* 4, no. 4 (1940): 630–650.
Thomas, Ivor. *Warfare by Words.* London: Penguin, 1942.
Trenholm, Lee. "Press Agents Irritate the Press." *Political Science Quarterly* 2, no. 4 (1938): 671–677.
Watson, Elmo Scott. *A History of Newspaper Syndicates in the United States, 1863–1935.* Chicago: Publisher's Authority, 1936.
White, Amber Blanco. *The New Propaganda.* London: Gollancz, 1939.

Biographical Studies

Reference Works

American Authors and Books. New York: Crown, 1962.
Contemporary Authors. Detroit: Gale Research, 1981–.
Current Biography Yearbook. New York: H. W. Wilson, 1940–.

Dictionary of Literary Biography. Detroit: Gale Research, 1982–.
Dictionary of North American Authors. Detroit: Gale Research, 1968.
Dictionnaire de biographie française. Paris: Letouzey & Ané, 1933–.
Dictionnaire des parlementaires français. 8 vols. Paris: Presses Universitaires de France, 1960–1977.
International Who's Who. London: Europea, 1935–.
New York Times Obituaries. New York: New York Times, 1900–.
Who Was Who among North American Authors, 1921–1939. Detroit: Gale Research, 1976.
Who Was Who in America. Chicago: Marquuis, 1960.
Who's Who in France. Paris: Editions Jacques Lafitte, 1953–.

Other Works

Baillou, Jean. "Giraudoux et la diplomatie: De l'école normale au Quai d'Orsay." In Cahiers Jean Giraudoux 13:9–14. Paris: Grasset, 1984.
Barthélemy, Maurice. "Giraudoux et la diplomatie: La 'Carrière' de Jean Giraudoux." In Cahiers Jean Giraudoux 13:15–41. Paris: Grasset, 1984.
Bibesco, Marthe. "Paul Claudel et Philippe Berthelot." *Revue de Paris* 72 (1965): 12–25.
Body, Jacques. *Giraudoux et l'Allemagne*. Paris: Didier, 1975.
———. *Jean Giraudoux: The Legend and the Secret*. Trans. James Norwood. Rutherford: Fairleigh Dickinson University Press, 1991.
Burton, David H. *Cecil Spring Rice: A Diplomat's Life*. Rutherford: Farleigh Dickinson University Press, 1990.
Carlisle, Rodney. "The Foreign Policy Views of an Isolationist Press Lord: W. R. Hearst and the International Crisis, 1936–1941." *Journal of Contemporary History* 9, no. 3 (1974): 217–227.
Dawson, Brett. "De Harvard au Quai d'Orsay: Les débuts de Jean Giraudoux." In *Jean Giraudoux*, special issue of *Revue d'Histoire Littéraire de la France*, 1983, 711–724.
———. "Giraudoux et la diplomatie: Jean Giraudoux et Philippe Berthelot." In Cahiers Jean Giraudoux 13:67–91. Paris: Grasset, 1984.
Doerries, Reinhard. *Imperial Challenge: Ambassador Count Bernstorff and German-American Relations, 1908–1917*. Chapel Hill: University of North Carolina Press, 1989.
Enjalran, Paulette. "Paul Claudel: Son intinéraire de consul et d'ambassadeur, 1890–1934." *Claudel Studies* 11 (1984): 4–23.
Gilbert, Roger P. "Paul Claudel diplomate." *Claudel Studies* 11 (1984): 67–94.
Hodgson, Godfrey. *The Colonel: The Life and Wars of Henry L. Stimson, 1867–1950*. Boston: Northeastern University Press, 1990.
Joire, Jean. "Giraudoux et la diplomatie: Jean Giraudoux et le Service des Oeuvres françaises à l'étranger." In Cahiers Jean Giraudoux 13:42–52, Paris: Grasset, 1984.
Lacouture, Jean. *André Malraux*. London: Deutsch, 1975
Lamont, Edward M. *The Ambassador from Wall Street: The Story of Thomas W. Lamont, J. P. Morgan's Chief Executive*. Lanham, Md.: Madison Books, 1994.

Langlois-Berthelot, Daniel. "Philippe Berthelot (1886–1934)." *Nouvelle Revue des Deux Mondes* 6 (1976): 574–582.

Monick, Emmanuel. "Paul Claudel, diplomate et économiste." In Cahiers Paul Claudel 4:347–349. Paris: Gallimard, 1962.

Monnet, F. *Refaire la République: André Tardieu, une dérive réactionnaire, 1876–1945.* Paris: Fayard, 1993.

Mott, Col. Thomas B. *Myron T. Herrick: Friend of France.* New York: Doubleday, Doran, 1929.

Mugridge, Ian. *The View from Xanadu: William Randolph Hearst and United States Foreign Policy.* Montreal: McGill-Queens University Press, 1995.

Ormesson, Wladimir d. "Deux grandes figures de la diplomatie française: Paul et Jules Cambon." *Revue d'Histoire Diplomatique* 57–59 (1943–1945): 33–71.

Price, Alan. *The End of the Age of Innocence: Edith Wharton and the First World War.* New York: St. Martin's Griffin, 1996.

Racine, Daniel. "Saint-John Perse aux Etats-Unis face à la Deuxième Guerre mondiale." *Mondes et Cultures* 46, no. 2 (1986): 320–330.

Wall, Joseph Frazier. *Andrew Carnegie.* New York: Oxford University Press, 1970.

Young, Robert J. *Power and Pleasure: Louis Barthou and the Third French Republic.* Montreal: McGill-Queen's University Press, 1991.

France and America

Abel, Richard. *The Red Rooster Scare: Making Cinema American, 1900–1910.* Berkeley and Los Angeles: University of California Press, 1998.

Albert, Pierre. *La France, les Etats-Unis et leurs presses.* Paris: Centre Pompidou, 1977.

Aldrich, Nelson W. *Old Money: The Mythology of America's Upper Class.* New York: Knopf, 1988.

Agulhon, Maurice. *Les métamophoses de Marianne: L'imagerie et la symbolique républicaines de 1914 à nos jours.* Paris: Flammarion, 2001.

Agulhon, Maurice, André Nouschi, and Ralph Schor. *La France de 1914 à 1940.* Paris: Nathan, 1993.

Almond, Gabriel A. *The American People and Foreign Policy.* New York: Praeger, 1960.

Anquetin, A. "Symboles, mythes et stéréotypes nationaux dans les cinémas français et allemand, 1933–1939." *Relations Internationales*, no. 23 (winter 1980): 465–484.

Ariès, Philippe, and Georges Duby. *Histoire de la vie privée.* Vols 4 and 5. Paris: Seuil, 1987.

Bachrach, Peter, ed. *Political Elites in a Democracy.* New York: Atherton Press, 1971.

Bakker, Gerben. "America's Master: The Decline and Fall of the European Film Industry (1907–1920)." In *Across the Atlantic: Cultural Exchanges between Europe and the United States*, ed. Luisa Passerini, 213–240. Brussels: Peter Lang, 2000.

Baltzell, E. Digby. "Who's Who in America." In *Class, Status, and Power*, ed. R. Bendix and S. M. Lipset, 266–275. New York: Free Press, 1966.

Barrot, Olivier, and Pascal Ory, eds. *Entre deux guerres: La création française, 1919–1939.* Paris: François Bourin, 1990.

Beale, Marjorie A. *The Modernist Enterprise: French Elites and the Threat of Modernity, 1900–1940*. Stanford: Stanford University Press, 1999.

Becker, Jean Jacques. *1914: Comment les Français sont entrés dans la guerre*. Paris: FNSP Editions, 1977.

Becker, Jean Jacques, and Stéphane Audoin-Rouzeau. *Les sociétés européennes et la guerre de 1914–1918*. Paris: Université de Paris X–Nanterre, 1990.

Bell, David, et al., eds. *Biographical Dictionary of French Political Leaders since 1870*. New York: Simon and Schuster, 1990.

Bellow, Saul. "Writers and Literature in American Society." In *Culture and Its Creators*, ed. Joseph Ben-David and Terry Nichols Clark, 173–196. Chicago: University of Chicago Press, 1977.

Bernstein, Martha E. "The French Dilemma: Reaction to U.S. Cultural Policy, 1950–1954." *Proceedings of the Western Society for French History (1999)* 27 (2001):182–189.

Berstein, Serge. *La France des années 30*. Paris: Colin, 1988.

———. "Le ministre sous la IIIè République." *Pouvoirs* 36 (1986): 15–27.

Berstein, Giselle, and Serge Berstein. *La Troisième République*. Paris: MA Editions, 1987.

Bloch, Marc. *Strange Defeat: A Statement of Evidence Written in 1940*. New York: Norton, 1968.

Blumenthal, Henry. *American and French Culture, 1800–1900: Interchange in Art, Science, Literature, and Society*. Baton Rouge: Louisiana State University Press, 1975.

———. *France and the United States: Their Diplomatic Relations, 1789–1914*. Chapel Hill: University of North Carolina Press, 1970.

———. *Illusion and Reality in Franco-American Diplomacy, 1914–1945*. Baton Rouge: Louisiana State University Press, 1986.

Brinnin, John Malcolm, and Kenneth Gaulin. *Grand Luxe: The Transatlantic Style*. New York: Henry Holt, 1988.

Brinton, Crane. *The Americans and the French*. Cambridge: Harvard University Press, 1968.

Brooks, Charles W. *America in France's Hopes and Fears, 1890–1920*. 2 vols. New York: Garland, 1987.

Burch, Philip. *Elites in American History*. 3 vols. New York: Holmes and Meier, 1980–1981.

Butts, R. Freeman, and Lawrence A. Cremin. *A History of Education in American Culture*. New York: Holt, Rinehart and Winston, 1953.

Cable, Mary. *Top Drawer: American High Society from the Gilded Age to the Roaring Twenties*. New York: Atheneum, 1984.

Charle, Christophe. *Les élites de la République, 1880–1890*. Paris: Fayard, 1987.

———. *Naissance des "Intellectuels," 1880–1900*. Paris: Editions de Minuit, 1990.

Chaussinand-Nogaret, G., J. M. Constant, C. Durandin, and A. Jouanna. *Histoire des élites en France du xvie au xxe siècle*. Paris: Tallandier, 1991.

Clark, Priscilla P. *Literary France: The Making of a Culture*. Berkeley and Los Angeles: University of California Press, 1987.

Clark, Priscilla P., and Terry Nichols Clark. "Patrons, Publishers, and Prizes: The

Writer's Estate in France." In *Culture and Its Creators: Essays in Honor of Edward Shils*, ed. Joseph Ben-David and Terry Nichols Clark, 197–225. Chicago: University of Chicago Press, 1977.

Clark, Terry Nichols. *Prophets and Patrons: The French Universities and the Emergence of the Social Sciences*. Cambridge: Harvard University Press, 1973.

Cohen, William B., ed. *The Transformation of Modern France*. Boston: Houghton Mifflin, 1997.

Colin, G., and Jean Jacques Becker. "Les écrivains, la guerre de 1914 et l'opinion publique." *Relations Internationales*, no. 24 (winter 1980): 425–442.

Coston, Henry. ed. *Dictionnaire de la politique française*. 2 vols. Paris: Publications Henry Coston, 1972.

Crémieux-Brilhac, Jean-Louis. *Ouvriers et soldats*. Vol. 1 of *Les Français de l'an 40*. Paris: Gallimard, 1990.

Crubellier, Maurice. *L'école républicaine, 1870–1940*. Paris: Editions Christian, 1993.

———. *Histoire culturelle de la France, 19è -20è siècles*. Paris: Colin, 1974. Digeon, Claude. *La crise allemande de la pensée française (1870–1914)*. 1959. Paris: Presses Universitaires de France, 1992.

Dogan, Mattei. "Filières pour devenir ministre de Thiers à Mitterand." *Pouvoirs* 36 (1986): 43–60.

Domhoff, G. William. *The Higher Circles: The Governing Class in America*. New York: Random House, 1970.

Duroselle, Jean Baptiste. *La France et les Etats-Unis des origines à nos jours*. Paris: Seuil, 1976.

Estèbe, Jean. *Les ministres de la République, 1871–1914*. Paris: Presses de la Fondation Nationale des Sciences Politiques, 1982.

Farwell, Byron. *Over There: The United States in the Great War, 1917–1918*. New York: Norton, 1999.

Ferro, Marc. "Cultural Life in France, 1914–1918." In *European Culture in the Great War*, ed. Aviel Roshwald, and Richard Stites, 295–307. Cambridge: Cambridge University Press, 1999.

Fischer, Diane P. *Paris 1900: The "American School" at the Universal Exposition*. New Brunswick: Rutgers University Press, 1999.

Fordham, Elizabeth. "From Whitman to Wilson: French Attitudes toward America around the Time of the Great War." In *Across the Atlantic: Cultural Exchanges between Europe and the United States*, ed. Luisa Passerini, 117–139. Brussels: Peter Lang, 2000.

Galloux-Fournier, Bernadette. "Un regard sur l'Amérique: Voyageurs français aux Etats-Unis (1919–1939)." *Revue d'Histoire Moderne et Contemporaine* 37 (April–June 1990): 308–323.

Genet-Delacroix, Marie-Claude. *Art et Etat sous la IIIe République*. Paris: Publications de la Sorbonne, 1992.

Gerbod, Paul. "L'enseignement de la langue française aux Etats-Unis au xxe siècle." *Revue Historique* 576 (October–December 1990): 387–406.

Gildea, Robert. *The Past in French History*. New Haven: Yale, 1994.

Gillot, Catherine. "La France au miroir de l'Amérique dans les années 1920: Morand, Duhamel." Ph.D. diss., New York University, 1998.

Goetschel, Pascale, and E. Loyer. *Histoire culturelle et intellectuelle de la France au XXe siècle.* Paris: Colin, 1994.

Gordon, Bertram M. "The Decline of a Cultural Icon: France in American Perspective." *French Historical Studies* 22, no. 4 (1999): 625–651.

Gruber, Carol S. *Mars and Minerva: World War I and the Uses of Higher Learning in America.* Baton Rouge: Louisiana State University Press, 1975.

Gunn, J.A.W. "Who Are the French, and Why Might It Matter?" *Queen's Quarterly* 107, no. 4 (2000): 503–513.

Horn, Martin A. *Britain, France, and the Financing of the First World War.* Montreal: McGill-Queen's, 2002

———. "A Private Bank at War: J. P. Morgan and Co. and France, 1914–1918." *Business History Review* 74 (spring 2000): 85–112.

Horn, Pierre L., ed. *Handbook of French Popular Culture.* Westport, Conn.: Greenwood Press, 1991.

Howard, John E. *Parliament and Foreign Policy in France.* London: Cresset Press, 1948.

Hutton, Patrick J., ed. *Historical Dictionary of the Third French Republic, 1870–1940.* 2 vols. Westport, Conn.: Greenwood Press, 1986.

Jackson, Julian. *The Popular Front in France Defending Democracy, 1934–1938.* Cambridge: Cambridge University Press, 1988.

Kaspi, André. *La vie quotidienne aux Etats-Unis au temps de la prospérité, 1919–1929.* Paris: Hachette, 1980.

Keylor, William R. "France and the Illusion of American Support, 1919–1940." In *The French Defeat of 1940*, ed. Joel Blatt, 204–244. Providence: Berghahn Books, 1998.

———. France's Futile Quest for American Military Protection, 1919–1922." In *Une occasion manquée? 1922: La reconstruction de l'Europe*, ed. Marta Petricioli, 61–80. Bern: Peter Lang, 1995.

Kuisel, Richard. *Seducing the French: The Dilemma of Americanization.* Berkeley and Los Angeles: University of California Press, 1993.

Lacorne, Denis, J. Rupnik, and M. F. Toinet, eds. *The Rise and Fall of Anti-Americanism: A Century of French Perception.* New York: St. Martin's Press, 1990.

Lasswell, Harold, et al. "The Elite Concept." In *Political Elites in a Democracy*, ed. Peter Bachrach, 13–26. New York: Atherton, 1971.

Lebovics, Herman. *True France: The Wars over Cultural Identity, 1900–1945.* Ithaca: Cornell University Press, 1992.

Leffler, Melvyn P. *The Elusive Quest: The American Pursuit of European Stability and French Security, 1919–1933.* Chapel Hill: University of North Carolina Press, 1979.

Lerner, Robert, Althea K. Nagai, and Stanley Rothman. *American Elites.* New Haven: Yale University Press, 1996.

Levenstein, Harvey. *Seductive Journey: American Tourists in France from Jefferson to the Jazz Age.* Berkeley and Los Angeles: University of California Press, 1998.

Levine, Lawrence W. *Highbrow/Lowbrow: The Emergence of Cultural Hierarchy in America.* Cambridge: Harvard University Press, 1988.

McKay, Donald C. *The United States and France.* Cambridge: Harvard University Press, 1951.

McLachlan, James. *American Boarding Schools: A Historical Study.* New York: Scribner's, 1970.

Magraw, Roger. *France, 1815–1914: The Bourgeois Century.* Oxford: Oxford University Press, 1986.

Mandell, Richard D. *Paris 1900: The Great World's Fair.* Toronto: University of Toronto Press, 1967.

Martin, Benjamin F. *France and the Après Guerre, 1918–1924.* Baton Rouge: Louisiana State University Press, 1999.

Martin, Bernd. "Les relations entre les Etats-Unis et les démocraties occidentales de 1938 à 1941: La prétention américaine au 'leadership' mondiale." *Guerres mondiales* 163 (July 1991): 33–50.

Martin, Marc. *Médias et journalistes de la République.* Paris: Editions Odile Jacob, 1997.

Mathy, Jean-Philippe. *Extrême Occident: French Intellectuals and America.* Chicago: University of Chicago Press, 1993.

Matthews, Donald. *The Social Background of Political Decision-Makers.* New York: Doubleday, 1954.

Mechoulan, Eric. "L'incompréhension diplomatique franco-américaine, 1932–33." *Revue d'Histoire Moderne et Contemporaine* 42–44 (October–December 1995): 577–592.

Mills, C. Wright. *The Power Elite.* New York: Oxford University Press, 1956.

Miquel, Pierre. *La paix de Versailles et l'opinion publique française.* Paris: Flammarion, 1972.

Mitchell, Allan. *The German Influence in France after 1870.* Chapel Hill: University of North Carolina Press, 1979.

Monaco, Paul. *Cinema and Society: France and Germany during the Twenties.* New York: Elsevier, 1976.

Montgomery, Maureen E. *Displaying Women: Spectacles of Leisure in Edith Wharton's New York.* New York: Routledge, 1998.

Mouré, Kenneth. "The Gold Standard Illusion: France and the Gold Standard in the Era of Currency Instability, 1914–1939." In *Crisis and Renewal in France, 1918–1962*, ed. Kenneth Mouré and Martin S. Alexander, 66–85. New York: Berghahn Books, 2002.

Nixon, Edgar B., ed. *Franklin D. Roosevelt and Foreign Affairs.* 3 vols. Cambridge: Belknap Press, 1969.

Nouailhat, Yves-Henri. *France et Etats-Unis: Août 1914–Avril 1917.* Paris: Publications de la Sorbonne, 1979.

Ory, Pascal. "Plus dure sera la chute: Les pavillons français aux Expositions internationales de 1939." *Relations Internationales*, no. 33 (spring 1983): 81–90.

Ory, Pascal, and Jean-François Sirinelli. *Les intellectuels en France de l'affaire Dreyfus à nos jours.* Paris: Colin, 1992.

Perrot, Marguerite. *Le mode de vie des familles bourgeoises.* Paris: FNSP Editions, 1982.

Popkin, Jeremy "'Made in U.S.A.': Les historiens français d'outre-Atlantique et leur histoire." *Revue d'Histoire Moderne et Contemporaine* 40, no. 2 (1993): 303–320.

Portes, Jacques. *Une fascination réticente: Les Etats-Unis dans l'opinion française 1870–1914*. Nancy: Presses Universitaires de Nancy, 1990.

Prochasson, Christophe, and Anne Rasmussen. *Au nom de la patrie: Les intellectuels et la Première Guerre mondiale (1910–1919)*. Paris: Editions la Découverte, 1996.

Prost, Antoine. *Histoire de l'enseignement en France, 1800–1967*. Paris: Colin, 1968.

―――. "The Impact of War on French and German Political Cultures." *Historical Journal* 37 (1994): 209–217.

Pyenson, Lewis. *Civilizing Mission: Exact Sciences and French Overseas Expansion, 1830–1940*. Baltimore: Johns Hopkins University Press, 1993.

Rearick, Charles. *The French in Love and War: Popular Culture in the Era of the World Wars*. New Haven: Yale University Press, 1997.

Reszler, A., and A. Browning. "Identité culturelle et relations internationales: Libres propos sur un grand thème." *Relations Internationales*, no. 24 (winter 1980): 381–399.

Rioux, Jean-Pierre, and Jean-François Sirinelli. *Le temps des masses*. Vol. 4 of *Histoire culturelle de la France*. Paris: Seuil, 1998.

Robitaille, Louis-Bernard. *Et Dieu créa les Français*. Montreal: Editions Robert Davies, 1995.

Rolland, Denis. *Vichy et la France libre au Mexique: Guerre, cultures et propagandes pendant la Deuxième Guerre mondiale*. Paris: L'Harmattan, 1990.

Rossi, Mario. *Roosevelt and the French*. Westport, Conn.: Praeger, 1993.

Rossi-Landi, Guy. *La drôle de guerre: La vie politique en France, 2 septembre 1929– 10 mai 1940*. Paris: Colin, 1971.

Schor, Ralph. "Les Etats-Unis vus de droite: La crise américaine de 1929 à travers la presse française de droite." *Revue d'Histoire Moderne et Contemporaine*, 42– 44 (October–December 1995): 568–576.

―――. *L'opinion française et les étrangers: 1919–1939*. Paris: Publications de la Sorbonne, 1985.

Sellin, Christine. "L'image de la puissance française à travers les manuels scolaires." *Relations Internationales*, no. 33 (spring 1983): 103–111.

Silver, Kenneth E. *Esprit de Corps: The Art of the Parisian Avant-Garde and the First World War, 1914–1925*. Princeton: Princeton University Press, 1989.

Singer, Barnett. "From Patriots to Pacifists: The French Primary School Teachers, 1880–1940." *Journal of Contemporary History* 12, no. 3 (1977): 413–434.

―――. *Modern France: Mind, Politics, Society*. Montreal: Harvest House, 1980.

Sirinelli, Jean-François. "Les intellectuels français et la guerre." In *Les sociétés européennes et la guerre de 1914–1918*, ed. Jean Jacques Becker and Stéphane Audoin-Rouzeau, 145–161. Nanterre: Université de Nanterre, 1990.

―――. *Intellectuels et passions françaises: Manifestes et pétitions au xxe siècle*. Paris: Fayard, 1990.

Sirinelli, Jean-François, and Pascal Ory. *Les intellectuels en France de l'affaire Dreyfus à nos jours*. Paris: Colin, 1992.

Skard, Sigmund. *The American Myth and the European Mind: American Studies in Europe, 1776–1960*. New York: Perpetua, 1964.

Slater, Catherine. *Defeatists and Their Enemies: Political Invective in France, 1914– 1918*. Oxford: Oxford University Press, 1981.

Strauss, David. *Menace in the West: The Rise of French Anti-Americanism in Modern Times*. Westport, Conn.: Greenwood Press, 1978.

Suleiman, Ezra N. *Elites in French Society: The Politics of Survival*. Princeton: Princeton University Press, 1978.

Thuillier, Guy. *La bureaucratie en France aux XIX–XX siècles*. Paris: Economica, 1987.

Tiersten, Lisa. *Marianne in the Market: Envisioning Consumer Society in Fin-de-Siècle France*. Berkeley and Los Angeles: University of California Press, 2001.

Wall, Irwin M. "From Anti-Americanism to Francophobia: The Saga of French and American Intellectuals." *French Historical Studies* 18, no. 4 (1994): 1083–1100.

Weber, Eugen. *France: Fin de Siècle*. Cambridge: Harvard University Press, 1986.

———. *The Hollow Years: France in the 1930s*. New York: Norton, 1994.

———. *Peasants into Frenchmen: The Modernization of Rural France, 1870–1914*. Stanford: Stanford University Press, 1976.

Weir, Kathy Calhoun. "Franco-American Relations, 1931–1933: The War Debts." Ph.D. diss., Washington State University, 1987.

Wickes, Georges. *Americans in Paris*. New York: Doubleday, 1969.

Wiser, William. *The Crazy Years: Paris in the Twenties*. New York: Atheneum, 1983.

Young, Robert J., ed. *Under Siege: Portraits of Civilian Life in France during World War 1*. New York: Berghahn Books, 2000.

———. "The Use and Abuse of Fear: France and the Air Menace in the 1930s." *Intelligence and National Security* 2, no. 4 (1987): 88–109.

Zeldin, Theodore. *France, 1848–1945*. Vol. 1, *Ambition, Love, and Politics*. Vol. 2, *Intellect, Taste, and Anxiety*. Oxford: Clarendon Press, 1973–1977.

International Politics

Adamthwaite, Anthony P. *France and the Coming of the Second World War*. London: Cass, 1977.

Alexander, Martin S., ed. *Knowing Your Friends: Intelligence inside Alliances and Coalitions from 1914 to the Cold War*. London: Frank Cass, 1998.

Allain, Jean-Claude, and Marc Auffret. "Le Ministère français des affaires étrangères: Crédits et effectifs pendant la IIIe République." *Relations Internationales*, no. 32 (winter 1982): 405–446.

Baillou, Jean. *Les affaires étrangères et le corps diplomatique français*. Vol. 1, *De l'Ancien Régime au Second Empire*. Vol. 2, *1870–1980*. Paris: CNRS Editions, 1984.

Blatt, Joel. "France and the Washington Conference." In *The Washington Conference, 1921–22: Naval Rivalry, East Asian Stability, and the Road to Pearl Harbor*, ed. Erik Goldstein and John Maurer, 192–219. London: Cass, 1994.

———, ed. *The French Defeat of 1940: Reassessments*. Providence: Berghahn Books, 1998.

Bock, Hans Manfred, Reinhart Meyer-Kalkus, and Michael Trebitsch. *Entre Locarno et Vichy: Les relations culturelles franco-allemandes dans les années 1930*. 2 vols. Paris: CNRS Editions, 1993.

Boemeke, Manfred F., Gerald D. Feldman, and Elizabeth Glaser, eds. *The Treaty of*

Versailles: A Reassessment after 75 Years. New York: Cambridge University Press, 1998.

Boyce, Robert, ed. *French Foreign and Defence Policy, 1918–1940: The Decline and Fall of a Great Power*. London: LSE/Routledge, 1998.

Carley, Michael J. *1939: The Alliance That Never Was and the Coming of World War II*. Chicago: Ivan R. Dee, 1999.

Carroll, John M. "Owen D. Young and German Reparations: The Diplomacy of an Enlightened Businessman." In *U.S. Diplomats in Europe, 1919–1941*, ed. Kenneth Paul Jones, 43–60. Santa Barbara: ABC-Clio, 1983.

Dallek, Robert. *Franklin D. Roosevelt and American Foreign Policy, 1932–1945*. New York: Oxford University Press, 1979.

Dethan, Georges. "The Ministry of Foreign Affairs since the Nineteenth Century." In *The Times Survey of Foreign Ministries of the World*, ed. Zara Steiner, 203–233. London: Times Books, 1982.

Diamond, Sander. *The Nazi Movement and the United States, 1924–1941*. Ithaca: Cornell University Press, 1974.

Ferrell, Robert W. *American Diplomacy in the Great Depression: Hoover-Stimson Foreign Policy, 1929–1932*. New York: Norton, 1970.

Finkelman, Paul. "The War on German Language and Culture, 1917–1925." In *Confrontation and Cooperation: Germany and the United States in the Era of World War I, 1900–1924*, ed. Hans-Jurgen Schroder, 177–205. Providence: Berg, 1993.

Finney, Patrick, ed. *The Origins of the Second World War*. London: Arnold, 1997.

Goldstein, Erik, and Maurer, John, eds. *The Washington Conference, 1921–22*. London: Cass, 1994.

Hanks, Robert K. "Culture versus Diplomacy: Clemenceau and Anglo-American Relations during the First World War." Ph.D. diss., University of Toronto, 2001.

Hodeir, Catherine, and Michel Pierre. *L'Exposition Coloniale*. Paris: Editions Complexe, 1991.

Hogan, Michael J. "Thomas W. Lamont and European Recovery: The Diplomacy of Privatism in a Corporatist Age." In *U.S. Diplomats in Europe, 1919–1941*, ed. K. P. Jones, 5–22. Santa Barbara: ABC-Clio, 1983.

Jones, Kenneth Paul, ed. *U.S. Diplomats in Europe, 1919–1941*. Santa Barbara: ABC-Clio, 1983.

Keylor, William R. *The Legacy of the Great War: Peacemaking 1919*. Boston: Houghton Mifflin, 1998.

Knock, Thomas J. *To End All Wars: Woodrow Wilson and the Quest for a New World Order*. Princeton: Princeton University Press, 1992.

Lauren, Paul Gordon. *Diplomats and Bureaucrats: The First Institutional Responses to Twentieth-Century Diplomacy in France and Germany*. Stanford: Hoover Institution Press, 1976.

Lebel, Claude. "L'organisation et les services du Ministère des affaires étrangères." In *Les affaires étrangères*. Paris: Presses Universitaires de France, 1959.

Marks, Frederick W. III. *Wind over Sand: The Diplomacy of Franklin Roosevelt*. Athens: University of Georgia Press, 1988.

Marks, Sally. "Black Watch on the Rhine: A Study in Propaganda, Prejudice, and Prurience." *European Studies Review* 13 (1983): 297–334.

————. *The Ebbing of European Ascendancy: An International History of the World 1914–1945.* London: Arnold, 2002.

————. *The Illusion of Peace. International Relations in Europe, 1918–1933.* London: Macmillan, 1976.

May, Ernest R. *Strange Victory: Hitler's Conquest of France.* New York: Hill and Wang, 2000.

Milza, P. "Culture et relations internationales." *Relations Internationales,* no. 24 (winter 1980): 361–379.

Ministère des relations extérieures. *Les archives du Ministère des relations extérieures depuis les origines.* 2 vols. Paris: Imprimerie Nationale, 1984–1985.

Offner, Arnold A. "The United States and Nationalist Socialist Germany." In *The Origins of the Second World War,* ed. Patrick Finney, 245–261. London: Arnold, 1997.

Outry, Amédée. "Histoire et principes de l'Administration française des affaires etrangères." *Revue Française de Science Politique* 3, nos. 2, 3, 4 (1953): 298–318, 491–510, 414–438.

Parker, Geoffrey. "French Geopolitical Thought in the Interwar Years and the Emergence of the European Idea." *Political Geography Quarterly* 6 (1987): 145–150.

Passerini, Luisa, ed. *Across the Atlantic: Cultural Exchanges between Europe and the United States.* Brussels: Peter Lang, 2000.

Reszler, A., and A. Browning. "Identité culturelle et relations internationales," *Relations Internationales* no. 24 (winter 1980): 381–399.

Richard, Lionel. "Aspects des relations intellectuelles et universitaires entre la France et l'Allemagne dans les années vingt." In *La France et l'Allemagne entre les deux guerres mondiales: Colloque 1987,* ed. Jacques Bariéty, Alfred Guth, and Jean-Marie Valentin, 111–124. Nancy: Presses Universitaires de Nancy, 1987.

Rosenau, James N., Kenneth W. Thompson, and Gavin Boyd, eds. *World Politics: An Introduction.* New York: Free Press, 1976.

Schroder, Hans-Jurgen, ed. *Confrontation and Cooperation: Germany and the United States in the Era of World War 1, 1900–1924.* Providence: Berg, 1993.

Smith, Arthur L. *The Deutschtum of Nazi Germany and the United States.* The Hague, Martinus Nijhoff, 1965.

Stevenson, David. "France at the Paris Peace Conference: Addressing the Dilemmas of Security." In *French Foreign and Defence Policy 1918–1940,* ed. Robert Boyce, 10–29. London: Routledge, 1998.

————. *French War Aims against Germany, 1914–1919.* Oxford: Clarendon Press, 1982.

————. "French War Aims and the American Challenge, 1914–1918." *Historical Journal* 22, no. 4 (1979): 877–894.

Thomas, Martin. *Britain, France, and Appeasement: Anglo-French Relations in the Popular Front Era.* New York: Berg, 1997.

Thompson, Kenneth W., and Soedjatmoko Thompson. "Cultural Diplomacy." In *World Politics: An Introduction,* ed. J. N. Rosenau, et al, 404–412. New York: Free Press, 1976.

Trommler, Frank. "Inventing the Enemy: German-American Cultural Relations, 1900–1917." In *Confrontation and Cooperation,* ed. Hans-Jurgen Schroder, 99–126. Providence, R.I.: Berg, 1993.

Vaisse, Maurice. "L'adaptation du Quai d'Orsay aux nouvelles conditions diplo-matiques (1919–1939)." *R.H.M.C.* 32 (1985): 145–162.

Young, Robert J. *France and the Origins of the Second World War.* London: Macmillan, 1996.

———. *In Command of France: French Foreign Policy and Military Planning, 1933–1940.* Cambridge: Harvard University Press, 1978.

———, ed. *French Foreign Policy 1918–1945: A Guide to Research and Research Materials.* Wilmington: Scholarly Resources, 1992.

Press, Propaganda, and Opinion

Albert, Pierre. "La presse française de 1871 à 1940." In *Histoire générale de la presse française,* ed. Claude Bellanger et al., 135–622. Paris: Presses Universitaires de France, 1972.

Amaury, Francine. *Histoire du plus grand quotidien de la IIIe République: Le Petit Parisien, 1874–1944.* Paris: Presses Universitaires de France, 1972.

Amaury, Philippe. *De l'information et de la propagande d'Etat: Les deux premières expériences d'un "Ministère de l'information" en France . . . juillet 1939–juin 1940, juillet 1940–août 1944.* Paris: Librairie Générale de Droit et de Jurispru-dence, 1969.

Arnold, W. Vincent. *The Illusion of Victory: Fascist Propaganda and the Second World War.* New York: Peter Lang, 1998.

Atherton, Louise. "Lord Lloyd at the British Council and the Balkan Front, 1937–1940." *International History Review* 16, no. 1 (1994): 25–48.

Audoin-Rouzeau, Stéphane. "'Bourrage de Crâne' et information en France en 1914–1918." In *Les sociétées européennes,* ed. Jean Jacques Becker and Stéphane Audoin-Rouzeau, 163–174. Nanterre: Université de Nanterre, 1990.

August, Thomas G. *The Selling of the Empire: British and French Imperialist Propa-ganda, 1890–1940.* Westport, Conn.: Greenwood Press, 1985.

Bennett, Todd. "The Celluloid War: State and Studio in Anglo-American Propaganda Film-Making, 1939–1941." *International History Review* 24, no. 1 (2002): 64–102.

Berger, Meyer. *The Story of the "New York Times" 1851–1951.* New York: Simon and Schuster, 1951.

Black, John B. *Organising the Propaganda Instrument: The British Experience.* The Hague: Martinus Nijhoff, 1975.

Bray, Howard. *The Pillars of the Post: The Making of a News Empire in Washington.* New York: Norton, 1980.

Brown, J.A.C. *Techniques of Persuasion: From Propaganda to Brainwashing.* Lon-don: Penguin, 1963.

Brownstein, Ronald. "The *New York Times* on Naziism, 1933–1939." *Midstream* 26, no. 4 (1980): 14–19.

Buitenhuis, Peter. *The Great War of Words: British, American, and Canadian Propaganda and Fiction, 1914–1933.* Vancouver: University of British Columbia Press, 1987.

Canham, Erwin D. *Commitment to Freedom: The Story of the "Christian Science Moni-tor."* Boston: Houghton Mifflin, 1958.

Carse, Alice Felicitas. "The Reception of German Literature in America as Exemplified by the *New York Times*, 1919–1944." Ph.D. diss., New York University, 1973.

Cazals, Rémy. "La propagande en 14–18." *Histoire*, no. 6 (November 1978): 87–88.

Chabord, M. T. "Les Services français de l'Information de 1936 à 1947." *Revue d'Histoire de la Deuxième Guerre mondiale* 16, no. 64 (1966): 81–87.

Chafer, Tony, and Amanda Sackur, eds. *Promoting the Colonial Idea: Propaganda and Visions of Empire in France*. New York: Palgrave, 2002.

Chittick, William O. *State Department, Press, and Pressure Groups: A Role Analysis*. New York: Wiley-Interscience, 1970.

Cohen, Bernard C. *The Press and Foreign Policy*. Princeton: Princeton University Press, 1963.

————. "The Relationship between Public Opinion and Foreign Policy Maker." In *Public Opinion and Historians*, ed. Melvin Small, 65–80. Detroit: Wayne State University Press, 1970.

Collins, Ross F. "The Development of Censorship in World War I France." *Journalism Monographs*, no. 131 (1992): 1–25.

Crémieux-Brilhac, Jean Louis. "Les propagandes radiophoniques et l'opinion publique en France de 1940 à 1944." *Revue d'Histoire de la Deuxième Guerre Mondiale* no. 101 (1976): 1–18.

Davis, Elmer H. *History of the "New York Times," 1851–1921*. 1969. Reprint, New York: Scholarly Press, 1971.

Davison, W. Phillips. "Voices of America." In *Public Opinion and Foreign Policy*, ed. Lester Markel, 156–179. New York: Harper and Brothers, 1949.

Demm, Eberhard. "Propaganda and Caricatures in the First World War." *Journal of Contemporary History* 28, no. 1 (1993): 163–192.

Doerries, Reinhard R. "Promoting *Kaiser* and *Reich*:Imperial German Propaganda in the United States during World War I." In *Confrontation and Cooperation*, ed. Hans-Jurgen Schroder, 135–165. Providence: Berg, 1993.

Domenach, Jean-Marie. *La propagande politique*. Paris: Presses Universitaires de France, 1969.

Douglas, Kenneth. "The French Intellectuals: Situation and Outlook." In *Modern France: Problems of the Third and Fourth Republics*, ed. E. M. Earle, 61–80. Princeton: Princeton University Press, 1951.

Duroselle, Jean Baptiste. "Opinion, attitude, mentalité, mythe idéologie: Essai de clarification." *Relations Internationales,* no. 3 (November 1974): 3–23.

Duval, René. "Radio-Paris." In *Entre deux guerres*, ed. Olivier Barrot, and Pascal Ory, 129–146. Paris: Bourin, 1990.

Edwards, Jerome E. *The Foreign Policy of Col. McCormick's "Tribune," 1929–1941*. Reno: University of Nevada Press, 1971.

Ellul, Jacques. *Propaganda: The Formation of Men's Attitudes*. New York: Knopf, 1965.

Fielding, Raymond. *The March of Time, 1935–1951*. New York: Oxford University Press, 1978.

Fischer, E. J., and H. D. Fischer, eds. *The "New York Times" Facing World War II*. New York: Peter Lang, 1990.

Flood, P. J. *France, 1914–1918: Public Opinion and the War Effort*. London: Macmillan, 1990.

Foulkes, A. Peter. *Literature and Propaganda*. London: Methuen, 1983.

Frédérix, Pierre. *Un siècle de chasse aux nouvelles: De l'Agence d'Information Havas à l'Agence France-Presse, 1835–1957*. Paris: Flammarion, 1959.

Gary, Brett. *The Nervous Liberals: Propaganda Anxieties from World War I to the Cold War*. New York: Columbia University Press, 1999.

Hanna, Martha. "French Women and American Men: 'Foreign' Students at the University of Paris, 1915–1925." *French Historical Studies* 22, no. 1 (1999): 87–112.

———. *The Mobilization of Intellect: French Scholars and Writers during the Great War*. Cambridge: Harvard University Press, 1996.

Harp, Stephen L. *Marketing Michelin: Advertising and Cultural Identity in Twentieth-Century France*. Baltimore: Johns Hopkins University Press, 2001.

Herbst, Susan. "Assessing Public Opinion in the 1930s–1940s: Retrospective Views of Journalists." *Journalism Quarterly* 64 (winter 1990): 943–949.

Hilderbrand, Robert C. *Power and the People: Executive Management of Public Opinion in Foreign Affairs, 1897–1921*. Chapel Hill: University of North Carolina Press, 1981.

Holman, Valerie, and Debra Kelly, eds. *France at War in the Twentieth Century: Propaganda, Myth, and Metaphor*. Oxford: Berghahn, 2000.

Horne, John, and Alan Kramer. "German 'Atrocities' and Franco-German Opinion, 1914: The Evidence of German Soldiers' Diaries." *Journal of Modern History* 66 (March 1994): 1–33.

———. *German Atrocities, 1914*. New York: Yale University Press, 2000.

Issacs, Harold R. "Sources for Images of Foreign Countries." In *Public Opinion and Historians*, ed. Melvin Small, 91–105. Detroit: Wayne State University Press, 1970.

Jowett, Garth S., and Victoria O'Donnell. *Propaganda and Persuasion*. London: Sage, 1986.

Kelley, Tom. *The Imperial Post: The Meyers, the Grahams, and the Paper That Rules Washington*. New York: William Morrow, 1983.

Keylor, William R. "'How They Advertised France': The French Propaganda Campaign in the United States during the Breakup of the Franco-American Entente, 1918–1923." *Diplomatic History* 17, no. 3 (1993): 351–373.

King, Erika G. "Exposing the 'Age of Lies': The Propaganda Menace as Portrayed in American Magazines in the Aftermath of World War I." *Journal of American Culture* 12, no. 1 (1989): 35–40.

Knightley, Phillip. *The First Casualty. From the Crimea to Vietnam: The War Correspondent as Hero, Propagandist, and Myth Maker*. New York: Harcourt Brace Jovanovich, 1975.

Kriesberg, Martin. "Dark Areas of Ignorance." In *Public Opinion and Foreign Policy*, ed. Lester Markel, 49–61. New York: Harper and Brothers, 1949.

Laurie, Clayton D. *The Propaganda Warriors: America's Crusade against Nazi Germany*. Lawrence: University Press of Kansas, 1996.

Levering, Ralph B. *The Public and American Foreign Policy, 1918–1978*. New York: William Morrow, 1978.

Lipstadt, Deborah E. *Beyond Belief: The American Press and the Coming of the Holocaust, 1933–1945*. New York: Free Press, 1986.

Lumsden, Linda. "'You're a Tough Guy, Mary—and a First-Rate Newspaperman': Gender and Women Journalists in the 1920s and 1930s." *Journalism and Mass Communication Quarterly* 72, no. 4 (1995): 913–921.

Marès, Antoine. "Puissance et présence culturelle de la France: L'exemple du Service des Oeuvres françaises à l'étranger dans les années 30." *Relations Internationales*, no. 33 (spring 1983): 65–80.

Markel, Lester. "Opinion: A Neglected Instrument." In *Public Opinion and Foreign Policy*, ed. Lester Markel, 1–48. New York: Harper and Row, 1949.

———, ed. *Public Opinion and Foreign Policy*. New York: Harper and Row, 1949.

Martin, Marc. *Médias et journalistes de la République*. Paris; Editions Odile Jacob, 1997.

Maurin, Jean-Louis. "Les missions de presse près l'armée française pendant la Première Guerre mondiale." *Guerres Mondiales et Conflits Contemporains* 164 (October 1991): 27–48.

Mégret, Maurice. "Les origines de la propagande de guerre française: Du Service général de l'information au Commissariat général à l'information." *Revue d'Histoire de la Deuxième Guerre mondiale*, no. 41 (January 1961): 3–27.

Montant, Jean-Claude. "L'organisation centrale des Services d'informations et de propagande du Quai d'Orsay pendant la Grande Guerre." In *Les sociétés européennes et la guerre de 1914–1918*, ed. Jean Jacques Becker and Stéphane Audoin-Rouzeau, 135–143. Paris: Université de Paris X, Nanterre, 1990.

———. "Propagande et guerre psychologique: La Maison de la Presse." In *Les affaires étrangères et le corps diplomatique français*, ed. Jean Baillou, vol. 2, 334–345. Paris: Presses Universitaires de France, 1984.

———. *La propagande extérieure de la France pendant la Première Guerre mondiale: L'exemple de quelques neutres européens*. 9 vols. Doctorat d'Etat, Paris I, June 1988.

Nigro, Louis John. *The New Diplomacy in Italy: American Propaganda and U.S.-Italian Relations, 1917–1919*. New York: Peter Lang, 1999.

Palmer, Michael B. "L'Office français d'information, 1940–1944." *Revue d'Histoire de la Deuxième Guerre mondiale*, no. 101 (January 1976): 19–40.

Perkins, Dexter. "The Department of State and American Public Opinion." In *The Diplomats, 1919–1939*, ed. Gordon Craig and Felix Gilbert, vol. 1, 282–308. New York: Atheneum, 1963.

Peschanski, Denis, and Gervais de Laurent, eds. *La propagande sous Vichy, 1940–1944*. Paris: Bibliothèque de Documentation Internationale Contemporaine, 1990.

Pithon, Rémy. "Cinéma français et cinema allemand des années trente." In *Entre Locarno et Vichy*, ed. Hans Manfred Bock et al., 587–596. Paris: CNRS Editions, 1993.

———. "Opinions publiques et représentations culturelles face aux problèmes de la puissance: Le témoignage du cinéma français (1938–39)." *Relations Internationales*, no. 33 (spring 1983): 91–102.

Planchais, Jean. "Paris-Soir." In *Entre deux guerres*, ed. Olivier Barrot and Pascal Ory, 95–110. Paris: Bourin, 1990.

Rheims, Maurice "Le Normandie." In *Entre deux guerres,* eds. Olivier Barrot and Pascal Ory, 475–486. Paris: Bourin, 1990.

Roberts, Chalmers M. *The "Washington Post": The First 100 Years*. Boston: Houghton Mifflin, 1977.

Rolland, Denis. *Vichy et la France libre au Mexique: Guerre, cultures et propagandes pendant la Deuxième Guerre mondiale*. Paris: Publications de la Sorbonne, 1990.

Roshwald, Aviel, and Richard Stites, eds. *European Culture in the Great War: The Arts, Entertainment, and Propaganda, 1914–1918*. New York: Cambridge University Press, 1999.

Rossignol, Dominique. *Histoire de la propagande en France de 1940 à 1944: L'utopie Pétain*. Paris: Presses universitaires de France, 1991.

Rudy, Willis. *Total War and Twentieth-Century Higher Learning: Universities of the Western World in the First and Second World Wars*. Rutherford, N.J.: Fairleigh Dickinson University, 1991.

Rutherford, Paul. *Endless Propaganda: The Advertising of Public Goods*. Toronto: University of Toronto Press, 2000.

Salisbury, Harrison E. *Without Fear or Favor: The "New York Times" and Its Times*. New York: Times Books, 1980.

Schneider, James C. "The Battle of the Two Colonels." *Chicago History* 18, no. 3 (1989): 4–33.

Schneider, William H. *An Empire for the Masses: The French Popular Image of Africa, 1870–1900*. Westport, Conn.: Greenwood Press, 1982.

Schudson, Michael. *Discovering the News: A Social History of the American Newspaper*. New York: Basic Books, 1978.

Small, Melvin. "Historians Look at Public Opinion." In *Public Opinion and Historians: Interdisciplinary Perspectives*, ed. Melvin Small, 13–32. Detroit: Wayne State University Press, 1970.

———, ed. *Public Opinion and Historians: Interdisciplinary Perspectives*. Detroit: Wayne State University Press, 1970.

Steele, Richard W. "The Pulse of the People: Franklin D. Roosevelt and the Gauging of American Public Opinion." *Journal of Contemporary History* 9, no. 4 (1974): 195–216.

Storey, Graham. *Reuters: The Story of a Century of News Gathering*. New York: Greenwood Press, 1969.

Stromberg, Roland N. *Redemption by War: The Intellectuals and 1914*. Lawrence: Regents Press of Kansas, 1982.

Sussman, Leila A. "FDR and the White House Mail." *Public Opinion Quarterly* 9, no. 1 (1956): 5–16.

Talese, Gay. *The Kingdom and the Power*. New York: World, 1969.

Taylor, Philip. M. *The Projection of Britain: British Overseas Publicity and Propaganda, 1919–1939*. Cambridge: Cambridge University Press, 1981.

———. "Propaganda in International Politics, 1919–1939." In *The Origins of the Second World War*, ed. Patrick Finney, 351–371. London: Arnold, 1997.

Tovell, Freeman M. "A Comparison of Canadian, French, British, and German International Cultural Policies." In *Canadian Culture: International Dimensions*, ed. Andrew F. Cooper, 69–82. Waterloo: Wilfrid Laurier University, 1985.

Tudesq, André-Jean. "L'utilisation gouvernmentale de la radio." In *Edouard Daladier Chef du Gouvernement*, 255–264. Paris: Fondation Nationale des Sciences Politiques, 1977.

Vaughn, Stephen. *Holding Fast the Inner Lines: Democracy, Nationalism, and the*

Committee on Public Information. Chapel Hill: University of North Carolina Press, 1980.

Weigle, Clifford F. "The Rise and Fall of the Havas News Agency." *Journalism Quarterly* 19 (September 1942): 277–286.

Welch, David. *Germany, Propaganda, and Total War, 1914–1918*. London: Athlone, 2000.

Wendt, Lloyd. *"Chicago Tribune": The Rise of a Great American Newspaper*. Chicago: Rand McNally, 1979.

White, Graham J. *FDR and the Press*. Chicago: University of Chicago Press, 1979.

Young, Robert J. "A Douce and Dextrous Persuasion: French Propaganda and Franco-American Relations in the 1930s." In *French Foreign and Defence Policy, 1918–1940*, ed. Robert Boyce, 195–214. London: LSE/Routledge, 1998.

———. "Forgotten Words and Faded Images: American Journalists before the Fall of France, 1940." *Historical Reflections* 24, no. 2 (1998): 205–229.

———. "In the Eye of the Beholder: The Cultural Representation of France and Germany by the *New York Times*, 1939–1940." In *The French Defeat of 1940*, ed. Joel Blatt, 245–268. Providence: Berghahn Books, 1998.

INDEX

Robert J. Young is a professor of history at the University of Winnipeg. His most recent books include *Power and Pleasure: Louis Barthou and the Third French Republic* (1992) and *France and the Origins of the Second World War* (1996). In 1996 he was named Canadian Professor of the Year by the Council for the Advancement and Support of Education.